T0229574

# Unit and Ubiquitous
# Internet of Things

# Unit and Ubiquitous Internet of Things

## Huansheng Ning

CRC Press
Taylor & Francis Group
Boca Raton   London   New York

CRC Press is an imprint of the
Taylor & Francis Group, an **informa** business

CRC Press
Taylor & Francis Group
6000 Broken Sound Parkway NW, Suite 300
Boca Raton, FL 33487-2742

© 2013 by Taylor & Francis Group, LLC
CRC Press is an imprint of Taylor & Francis Group, an Informa business

No claim to original U.S. Government works

Printed on acid-free paper
Version Date: 20130304

International Standard Book Number-13: 978-1-4665-6166-3 (Hardback)

### Library of Congress Cataloging-in-Publication Data

Ning, Huansheng.
  Unit and ubiquitous Internet of things / author, Huansheng Ning.
  pages cm
  Includes bibliographical references and index.
  ISBN 978-1-4665-6166-3 (hardback)
  1. Embedded Internet devices. 2. Internet of things. 3. Ubiquitous computing. I. Title.

  TK7895.E43N46 2013
  004--dc23                                                                    2013002112

**Visit the Taylor & Francis Web site at**
**http://www.taylorandfrancis.com**

**and the CRC Press Web site at**
**http://www.crcpress.com**

# Contents

# Preface

Internet of Things (IoT) attracts great attention, and brings promising opportunities and challenges. Research on IoT has important economic and social values for developing the next generation of information, network, and communication technologies. However, it is still confusing for most people to understand IoT well, including definitions, content, and differences from other similar concepts.

IoT connects and fuses the physical world and cyber world by ubiquitous sensing, connection, and control with definite social attributes. It is hopeful that IoT can emancipate humans from onerous human-machine interface work and information exploration.

This book attempts to provide a future IoT vision, and answer some fundamental questions from various aspects, including concepts, architectures, models, and key technologies. It aims to help readers discover the fundamental issues in IoT, and to be a valuable IoT literature for college students, practicing engineers, researchers, business operators, and policy makers.

The book accomplishes three main objectives:

- Introduces IoT essential concepts and content from the perspectives of mapping and interaction between the physical world and cyber world. Meanwhile, social attributes are emphatically discussed in IoT.

- Builds a fundamental architecture for future IoT, based on the IoT layered model, topological structure, various existence forms, and corresponding logical relationships are described. Specific case studies are also presented in different application scenarios.
- Establishes an IoT technology system based on the knowledge of IoT scientific problems, and gives an overview for core technologies, including basic connotation, development status, and open challenges.

Accordingly, this book is organized in three main parts.

Chapter 1 introduces the basic IoT concept, the intrinsic characteristics of IoT, IoT development and applications, and future IoT vision, which helps readers get an overall understanding on IoT.

The next section includes Chapters 2 to 4. Chapter 2 discusses IoT architecture and fundamentals, including the main aspects of architecture, layered models, IoT development phases, the science category, and supporting technologies. Here, unit and ubiquitous IoT (U2IoT) architecture and a six-layer model are designed for future IoT. Unit IoT and ubiquitous IoT are respectively introduced in Chapters 3 and 4. Concretely, Chapter 3 introduces ubiquitous sensing, networking and communications, and information management involved in unit IoT, and presents several typical application scenarios. Chapter 4 illustrates ubiquitous IoT, including local IoT, industrial IoT, national IoT, transnational IoT, and global application IoT by analyzing their concepts, characteristics, and some typical cases.

Chapters 5 to 14 compose the last section, in which 10 main supporting technologies are respectively discussed: resource management, loop control in actuation, session management, space-time consistency, security and privacy, energy management, spectrum management, nanotechnology, quantum technology, and big data.

# About the Author

**Huansheng Ning, Ph.D.,** is an associate professor in the School of Electronic and Information Engineering, Beihang University. He was born in Anhui, China, and received a B.S. from Anhui University, China, and a Ph.D. from Beihang University, China. From 2002 to 2003, Dr. Ning worked at Aisino Corporation, Beijing, China. From 2004 to 2005, he was a post-Ph.D. at Beihang University. He has presided over several research projects supported by the National Natural Science Foundation of China (NSFC), the National High Technology Research and Development Program of China (863 Program), and other organizations. He has published many papers and books on radio frequency identification (RFID) and Internet of Things (IoT). Dr. Ning serves as an editor on *Advances in Internet of Things* (2012–Present), is a guest editor for the *Journal of Universal Computer Science Special Issue on Internet of Things* (*JUCS*), and coeditor for *The Internet of Things: From RFID to the Next-Generation Pervasive Networked Systems* (Taylor & Francis Group). He also serves as a chair or program committee member for international conferences/workshops, for example, program chair (IEEE iThings 2012), program committee member (AMT 2012),

Internet of Things and CPS track chair (IEEE CIT'12), workshop chair (IEEE iThings 2011), and general chair (UMES 2011). Dr. Ning's current research focuses on Internet of Things, electromagnetic sensing, and aviation security.

# Acknowledgments

I thank my graduate students, Hong Liu, Sha Hu, Yang Fu, Wei He, Wei Du, and Jun Wang, for their help in preparing this book.

I am also grateful to all the quoted authors and the corresponding publications, and thank IEEE, John Wiley & Sons, and Scientific Research Publishing for permission to reuse the related materials.

Finally, I am very thankful to editor Ruijun He for his guidance and suggestions, and Stephanie Morkert and Linda Leggio for their help in the production of this book.

# 1

# INTRODUCTION

Internet of Things (IoT) attracts great attention, and brings with it promising opportunities and challenges. Research on IoT has important economic and social value for the development of the next generation of information, network, and communication technologies. To introduce IoT, four aspects are discussed: the concept of IoT, the intrinsic characteristics of IoT, IoT development and application, and the vision for the future of IoT.

## 1.1 IoT Concept

The phrase "Internet of Things" was proposed by MIT Auto-ID Center in 1999 [1]. Such an embryonic definition of IoT refers to constructing an Internet-based network covering all the things in the world by using related technologies (e.g., radio frequency identification [RFID]) to realize things' automatic identification and information sharing. In 2005, *ITU Internet Reports 2005: The Internet of Things*, published by the International Telecommunications Union [2], pointed out the IoT concept and expanded its meaning, and indicated that RFID technology, sensor technology, nanotechnology, and intelligent embedded technology are the four core technologies to realize IoT. After IBM announced the SmartPlanet concept in 2009, IoT became a hot topic and has been incorporated into many nations' development strategies. Along with the changes of application requirements and technology development, the IoT concept has been rapidly extended and new technologies have been involved in it.

In recent years, IoT has been redefined depending on different perspectives and application scenarios. The Cluster of European Research Projects on the Internet of Things *Strategic Research Roadmap*, announced by the European Union in 2009 [3], stated that "IoT is an integrated part of Future Internet and could be defined as a dynamic global network infrastructure with self-configuring capabilities based on standard and interoperable communication protocol." This IoT explanation is relatively comprehensive based on the network development. There are several other IoT definitions. For example, some researchers think that IoT is for addressing physical objects, and some think that IoT is ubiquitous with the feature of "everything connected, intelligently controlled, and anywhere covered." In this book, we think that mapping and interconnecting "things" between the physical world and cyber world are foundational features of IoT. In IoT, things refer to the ubiquitous things in the physical world and cyber world. They are classified into two types: physical things and cyber things. This classification is shown in Figure 1.1.

The physical things mainly include objects, behaviors, tendencies, and physical events. Objects (e.g., a person, vehicle, table, and bird) indicate concrete things with tangible bodies. Behaviors (e.g., running, monitoring, eating, shouting, catching, and driving) indicate movements with certain motivations of certain objects. Tendency (e.g., weather is becoming clear, the traffic is becoming crowded, and communication is going to finish) indicates trends in the things of themselves or under a certain external environment. Physical events (e.g., a tornado happens in a certain place) generally consist of objects, behaviors, and certain causation, indicating things happening, which are triggered by certain conditions in the physical world.

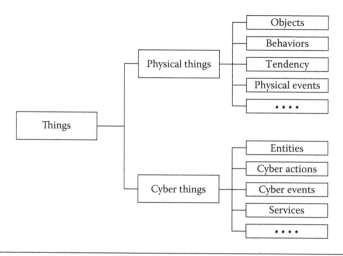

**Figure 1.1**   Things classification in IoT.

The cyber things include entities, cyber actions, cyber events, and services. Entities (e.g., Web page, software, codes, and data) indicate the abstract things in the cyber world. Cyber actions (e.g., things, coding, and data transmission) indicate the processing of virtual things. Cyber events (e.g., online payment is conducted) indicate the things consisting of entities, cyber actions, and certain causation in the cyber world. Service (e.g., the Domain Name System [DNS] query service) indicates the functions that a thing can offer or be offered for certain goals.

## 1.2 Related Concepts to IoT

As the concept of IoT is usually confused with other related concepts, such as radio frequency identification (RFID), wireless sensor network (WSN), electronic product code (EPC), machine to machine (M2M), cloud computing, and cyber-physical systems (CPS), they are briefly introduced as follows:

- RFID is a wireless automatic identification technology, relying on the RF communication technology to identify objects attached with RFID tags by an RFID reader. The identification can be performed to determine presence, location, consistency, authentication, and other identity-related applications. Currently, RFID has been widely applied in fields including transportation, logistics, and anticounterfeiting. It is an important sensing method for IoT, and will be described further in Chapter 3.
- EPC is a typical early IoT solution based on RFID technology for the global logistics applications proposed by EPCglobal. EPC standards are regarded as a special kind of RFID application standard, as the front-end sensing is RFID, while only two RFID frequency bands in ISO/IEC 18000 are involved. In addition, it also includes EPC coding, Object Naming Service (ONS), and EPC Information Services (EPCIS), and is a global and systematic specification. Similarly, ubiquitous ID (UID) proposed by Japan is another typical early IoT solution based on RFID technology, which is composed of ubiquitous code (Ucode), ubiquitous communication, a Ucode resolution

server, and an information system server. Ucode is used to identify objects and help index object-related information.

- WSN is a highlighted information technology, integrating sensing, computation, and communication. It is a wireless network consisting of enormous distributed autonomous sensors to monitor an environment or object's information, and has low-power, low-cost, distributed, and self-organization characteristics. WSN belongs to a kind of access network for IoT. Thus far, main technologies used to realize WSN include Zigbee, Bluetooth, Wi-Fi, and so on.

- M2M is machine-to-machine communication mode, to realize the connection of systems and remote devices. With the expansion of the M2M concept, it also refers to the communication that transmits data to applications. IoT involves various kinds of communication modes, such as thing-to-human, human-to-thing, and thing-to-thing communications. For the relation between IoT and M2M, there are different opinions. M2M is thought to be a promising technology for IoT [4]. Meanwhile, M2M is also regarded as an application form of IoT [5]. Moreover, M2M is also known as IoT [6].

- Cloud computing is a network application mode, providing services in a demand assignment and scalable way by the network. It includes three fundamental types of models: infrastructure as a service (IaaS), platform as a service (PaaS), and software as a service (SaaS). Services are provided according to one type. The end users just need to focus on the required resources and access approaches. Cloud computing aims to solve the huge data storage and processing problems brought on by the Internet. Currently, companies such as Google, Amazon, IBM, and SUN have increased investment and research efforts in cloud computing. With IoT development, the huge data storage and computing need the support of cloud computing technology. In turn, cloud computing technology advancement will drive IoT development.

- CPS is the system that combines computing, network, and physical environment. It provides services such as real-time sensing, dynamic control, and information feedback to realize the interaction of the physical world and cyber world by integration and collaboration of computation, communication, and control (3C) technologies. CPS and IoT have many similarities, and both need sensing, computing, information transmitting, and interaction technologies to enhance the combination of the cyber world and physical world. Meanwhile, they also have some differences. IoT emphasizes the connection of things with networks, while CPS emphasizes the integration of computational and physical elements information [7]. Additionally, IoT involves the physical world, cyber world, and social world. CPS has also recently been extended to cyber-physical-social systems. In this perspective, the concepts of IoT and CPS are almost the same, as both highlight the social attributes.

## 1.3 The Intrinsic Characteristics of IoT

Future IoT is highly unified with ubiquitous networks, services, and things, and it establishes the Internet of services, Internet of networks, and Internet of everything. The mentioned "things" covers things in both the physical world and cyber world. IoT has three main features:

- *Ubiquitous sensing.* Beyond the sensing ability of humans to the physical world (e.g., vision, hearing, smell, and touch) and the specific sensing function of sensor networks, ideal sensing in IoT includes all the sensing technologies that realize things identification, named ubiquitous sensing. The sensing information can include a thing's identifier (i.e., ID), static attributes (e.g., size, color, and shape), dynamic attributes (e.g., behavior tendency and interactions), and environmental information (e.g., temperature, pressure, and humidity). One important goal of future IoT is to unify the physical world and cyber world, and solve human-machine interface bottlenecks by using ubiquitous sensing technologies. In addition, along with more and more things mapping from the physical world to the cyber world, there is also increasing feedback from the cyber world to the physical world, and thus control of the physical world is also becoming wider.

- *Network of networks.* IoT involves various kinds of networks. On the one hand, there are many heterogeneous access networks in the sensor-actuator layer. On the other hand, heterogeneous communication networks, such as the Global System for Mobile Communications (GSM), code division multiple access (CDMA), and wideband code division multiple access (WCDMA), coexist in the network layer. Future IoT should construct the network of networks, which is a crucial part of IoT development to connect things in both the physical world and cyber world.
- *Intelligent processing.* Intelligent processing is similar to human wisdom, but also beyond human wisdom in many aspects, such as it overcomes the shortcomings of the long amount of time needed for learning and the limited ability for parallel information processing. In IoT, processing should be realized intelligently. An ideal scene is that things can be sensed and controlled automatically with high intelligence. Real-time information management, flexible production scheduling, and accurate tracking can be achieved. Intelligent processing capabilities is another goal of future IoT: freeing humans from the information explosion is another qualitative leap after the two industrial revolutions in history.

Based on the intrinsic characteristics, IoT should be developed from the three aspects mentioned above to realize the connection of everything and integration of the physical world and cyber world.

## 1.4 IoT Development and Application

IoT is regarded as an emerging industry by some people and even the governments of some nations, while it is also thought to be a new stage in information technology (IT) development. In our opinion, taking IoT as a new stage of IT development is more appropriate, no matter whether it is from IoT-related technologies or the involved industries.

IoT has attracted great attention in many nations. The United States puts significant emphasis on IoT-related technologies, especially standards, architectures, security, and management, trying to possess dominance in the IoT field. In 2008, the U.S. National Intelligence Council announced IoT as one of the six technologies in *Disruptive Civil Technologies—Six Technologies with Potential Impacts on U.S. Interests out to 2025*. Meanwhile, many enterprises facilitate IoT development through technology, product, and application innovation.

In the European Union, IoT research and development (R&D) has been supported by the European Commission (EC) and established as the strategic development plan of European information and communication technologies. In 2008, the EC developed a policy road map for European IoT, and four authoritative documents were announced in 2009, in which *Internet of Things—An Action Plan for Europe* [8] indicates that the development of IoT has been upgraded to a higher level. In addition to the technology and standard aspects, relevant organizations, such as the European Telecommunications Standards Institute (ETSI) and IoT European Research Cluster (IERC), are committed to IoT research projects. Some enterprises are also gradually taking action to deploy applications. For example, Vodafone has cooperated with Alcart-lucent to develop solutions for the smart grid [9]. T-Mobile has cooperated with Sierra Wireless to focus on the automobile, shipbuilding, and navigation industries [10].

In China, the government has created a favorable policy environment for IoT development. Many national-level projects, such as those supported by the National Natural Science Foundation of China (NSFC), the National High Technology Research and Development Program of China (863 Program), and the Major State Basic Research Development Program of China (973 Program), give powerful support to the development of IoT. In addition, government ministries cooperate from different aspects to promote IoT development.

In Japan, the Ministry of Internal Affairs and Communications (MIC) proposed the u-Japan strategy to realize a 4U (i.e., ubiquitous, universal, user-oriented, unit) connection, which is supported by many companies, such as Sony, Mitsubishi, and Hitachi. Thereafter, i-Japan was further proposed, which mainly focused on three aspects: electronic government management, education and talent training, and medical health information service. The information and communications technology (ICT) Hatoyama Plan launched by Japan also guides and facilitates the rapid development of IoT [11].

Australia, Singapore, Korea, France, Germany, and some other nations are also accelerating the pace of next-generation network infrastructure construction and facilitating IoT development.

Applications in IoT are rapidly increasing. The United States, European Union, China, Japan, Korea, and some other nations place great emphasis on IoT research and applications. From the initial applications in commercial retail and logistics fields, applications are extended to other fields, such as environmental and biomedical monitoring. Recently in China, nine key supporting fields of IoT application are pointed out in *The Twelfth Five-Year-Plan Outline for Internet of Things* [12], covering intelligent industry, intelligent agriculture, intelligent circulation, intelligent transportation, smart grid, intelligent environmental protection, intelligent public safety, intelligent health care, and smart home. However, at the present stage, some central enterprises have more abilities to launch some large-scale or ultra-large-scale industrial applications, and IoT promotion needs support from the government.

## 1.5 Future IoT Vision

The ideal IoT vision in the future may be an era of harmony of humans with nature, which means harmony, coordination, and coexistence of the physical world, cyber world, and social world. In future IoT, human development will witness emancipation not only from onerous labor works brought by the machine-human interface, but also from the brainwork from information exploration, achieving a substantial leap to share the benefits brought on by IT technologies. For instance, for IoT in the logistics industry, the flow of goods can be instantly monitored and automatically reported, instead of manual searching; for IoT in the power industry, generation, transmission, storage, and distribution of electricity can be arranged efficiently and dynamically; for IoT in the public security field, intelligence monitoring can be achieved for significant security regions and action can be taken intelligently. Future IoT will bring changes in most fields, and make things more intelligent to promote the revolution of production capability and modes.

In the future, communications between humans and things, and among things, will be intelligent and provide huge conveniences and effects for daily life. Future IoT will create a brand new world with high intelligence and automatics.

## References

1. Cluster of European Research Projects on the Internet of Things, CERP-IoT. 2010. *Vision and challenges for realising the Internet of Things.*
2. ITU. 2005. *The Internet of Things.* ITU International Reports.
3. Cluster of European Research Projects on the Internet of Things, CERP-IoT. 2009. *Internet of Things: Strategic research roadmap.*
4. Foschini, L., T. Taleb, A. Corradi, and D. Bottazzi. 2011. M2M-based metropolitan platform for IMS-enabled road traffic management in IoT. *IEEE Communications Magazine* 49: 50–57.
5. Du, J., and S. Chao. 2010. A study of information security for M2M of IOT. In *2010 3rd International Conference on Advanced Computer Theory and Engineering (ICACTE)*, 3: 20–22.
6. Wang, H. 2011. M2M communications. Presented at *IET International Conference on Communication Technology and Application (ICCTA 2011)*.
7. Li, W., P. Jagtap, L. Zavala, A. Joshi, and T. Finin. 2011. CARE-CPS: Context-aware trust evaluation for wireless networks in cyber-physical system using policies. In *2011 IEEE International Symposium on Policies for Distributed Systems and Networks (POLICY)*, 171–172.
8. Internet of Things—An action plan for Europe. http://ec.europa.eu/information_society/policy-/rfid/documents/commiot2009.pdf (accessed August 2, 2012).
9. Vodafone and Alcart-lucent jointly launch Internet of Things services. 2009. http://ww-w.c114.net/-news/133/a467344.html (accessed August 2, 2012).
10. Internet of Things new development trends in Europe. 2010. http://www.wat888.com/news-info.asp?id=216 (accessed August 2, 2012).
11. MIC Communications News. http://www.soumu.go.jp/main_sosiki/joho_tsusin/eng/Releases/NewsLetter/Vol20/Vol20_01/Vol20_01.pdf (accessed August 2, 2012).
12. The twelfth five-year-plan outline for Internet of Things. 2012. http://www.gov.cn/zwgk-/2012-02-/14/content_2065999.htm (accessed August 15, 2012).

# 2

# ARCHITECTURE AND FUNDAMENTALS

Internet of Things (IoT) architecture is the cornerstone for future IoT. It is a fundamental issue that provides a supporting platform for addressing other issues in IoT. The rapid development of IoT around the world has triggered a wave of unprecedented expectation. Several governments have launched massive projects despite the fact that the key technologies, including the fundamental architecture of IoT, are still open issues. It has become urgent to study future IoT architecture. Thus far, there are various kinds of IoT architectures proposed by researchers. Especially, different from other architectures, unit and ubiquitous IoT (U2IoT) proposed for future IoT incorporates social attributes.

IoT layered models have also been studied and proposed for building IoT. After considering more about the social attributes, a corresponding layered model is also built based on the U2IoT architecture in this chapter.

IoT development phases are summarized to give an overview of IoT. To facilitate IoT development, the study of the science category and supporting technologies is necessary for IoT talent education and industrial guidelines. Both are significant aspects to help build IoT.

It should be noticed that architecture is different than model. Architecture describes IoT from the network topology and IoT logical organization view, while model describes IoT from different functional aspects. Below, Section 2.1 introduces several IoT architectures, and Section 2.2 introduces the proposed U2IoT architecture. Section 2.3 discusses layered models, and the six-layer model based on U2IoT architecture is proposed in Section 2.4. In Section 2.5, IoT development phases are presented. Section 2.6 introduces the science category and supporting technologies. Finally, a conclusion is drawn in Section 2.7.

## 2.1 Some Research on IoT Architecture

There has been much research on IoT architecture. The electronic product code (EPC) [1] can be regarded as a representative earlier scheme for global logistics application. It is a vision that all physical objects can be connected by a radio frequency identification (RFID) transponder through a global unique EPC attached to RFID tags. Japan also proposed a global application prototype—ubiquitous ID (UID). Afterward, architectures were studied in projects that were subsequently launched. Table 2.1 lists several typical architectures in related projects.

**Table 2.1**   IoT Architectures and Related Projects

| PROJECTS | ARCHITECTURE DESCRIPTION | PRINCIPLES/ CONTRIBUTIONS | DESIGN GOALS |
|---|---|---|---|
| SENSEI | Build system model, resource model, and information model, and provide services for users and applications providers in the physical world | Bridge the physical and cyber worlds | Develop essential elements for future IoT |
| PECES | Provide a general software layer for the application devices | Help communities construct easier and facilitate cooperation in smart spaces | Enable the devices' cooperation among different intelligent applications |
| SemSorGrid4Env | Provide a software platform and include a set of Web services as service-oriented architecture | Gain benefits through applying semantic technology into resource discovery and integration | Back up the applications involving various data sources |
| FIA | Four different levels of network architecture design | Name and change data to ensure secure content; take mobility as normality; take cloud computing data center as storing place; address diverse patterns and demand for reliable communications | Encourage full consideration of the social, economic, and legal issues |
| U2IoT | Provide U2IoT (unit and ubiquitous IoT) for future IoT architecture | Provide IoT architecture by building unit and ubiquitous IoT with social attributes | Try to build ubiquitous IoT architectures |

SENSEI is a project in the European Union's Seventh Framework Program to integrate the physical world with the cyber world [2]. The architecture includes the system model, resource model, and information model, and provides services for users and applications for providers in the physical world via wireless sensor and actuator network (WSAN) systems. The PECES [3] architecture provides a general software layer for global application devices. SemSorGrid4Env architecture also provides a software platform, and it includes a set of Web services as a service-oriented architecture [4]. As part of Future Internet Architectures (FIA) [5], there are four supported projects that study different levels of network architecture design. The projects encourage research groups to fully consider social, economic, and legal issues brought from interaction between the Internet and society, and to design and experiment with brand new Internet architecture and networking ideas. U2IoT architecture includes unit IoT and ubiquitous IoT, in which unit IoT refers to a single application and ubiquitous refers to the collection of multiple unit IoTs. It tries to provide the direction for future IoT development and adapts to the development trend.

## 2.2 Ubiquitous IoT (U2IoT) Architecture

Future IoT is the fusion of the physical world, cyber world, and social world. Things are sensed via ubiquitous sensors. Future IoT architecture should be ubiquitous. Meanwhile, the architecture shall help existing intelligent applications immigrate to IoT, and satisfy the requirements for the insufficiently developing infrastructure in the underdeveloped regions around the world [6]. The nervous system structure in the human body and social organization consisting of individuals are good examples for designing IoT architecture. In the human body, the nervous system is a kind of complicated intelligent system that can see, taste, feel, and control things, or even make decisions. Though different individuals' nervous systems have common physical components and operating rules, an individual body possesses its own sophisticated and unique consciousness and behaviors. Individuals constitute a family, group, industry, nation, or other organization according to some certain rules in a harmonious manner. For example, each nation has sovereignty and its own operating system, but it can cooperate, compete, and communicate with others. Inspired by the human nervous system and the social organization framework, future IoT architecture will be introduced from two aspects: unit IoT and ubiquitous IoT (U2IoT) architecture.

### 2.2.1 Unit IoT Definition and Its Architecture Design

Unit IoT is the basic IoT unit with a focus on providing solutions for a special application. Unit IoT architecture is a man-like nervous system (MLN), which is a kind of complicated intelligent system that can sense and control things or make decisions. It can be classified into two types, as shown in Figure 2.1.

One type works like the human nervous system with a centralized data center (Figure 2.1a). It has three main components: the brain (management and data center [M&DC]), the spinal cord (distributed control nodes), and a network of nerves (IoT network, sensors, and actuators). In general, the IoT network transmits the data from sensors to the corresponding control nodes and M&DC, which receives, translates, and transmits messages to actuators to control the things. In unit IoT, M&DC is a centralized data center for processing and storing data and managing the whole networks. Although the working flow is similar to humankind's nervous system, there still remains an important difference: the distributed control nodes are more capable

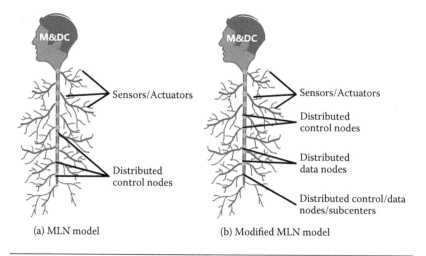

(a) MLN model      (b) Modified MLN model

**Figure 2.1**   Two models for unit IoT architecture.

of controlling or responding to external or internal stimulation in some cases.

The other type of unit IoT is a modified MLN model. Its distributed data center lies not only in the M&DC but also in some distributed cord nodes. In this model, whether a distributed control node works as a distributed data node or not is determined by the requirements (Figure 2.1b).

One important issue is how the existing intelligent system prototypes can be integrated or immigrated into future IoT. In general, these intelligent systems can retain their own structures while adding proper M&DCs as unit IoTs to access future IoT. In some cases, revising or reorganizing is required. This point is similar to how a relatively separated tribe goes out of its dwelling and gets along with modern society.

### 2.2.2 Ubiquitous IoT Definition and Its Architecture Design

Ubiquitous IoT refers to the collection of multiple IoT applications, including local IoT, industrial IoT, national IoT, and global application IoT, which are composed of multiple unit IoTs and management platforms with certain service goals. *Ubiquitous* means coverage of different services in unit IoTs and provides the higher-level service by integration of various unit IoTs.

Local IoT includes the unit IoTs within a certain region and management platforms. The management platform is the local management and data center (lM&DC), which manages the covered local unit IoTs in the corresponding region.

Industrial IoT includes the unit IoTs that belong to a specific industry as well as management platforms. The industry management and data center (iM&DC) for industry IoT is responsible for the management of covered unit IoTs in a particular industry (e.g., logistic, agriculture, and smart grid) and is managed by a specific industrial authority.

National IoT includes all unit IoTs that belong to one specific nation and management platform. A national management and data center (nM&DC) is responsible for the management of national IoT. It manages the corresponding nationwide unit IoTs, and controls iM&DC and lM&DC around the nation.

Global application IoT refers to the specific application on a global scale. The global coordinator establishes the coordination mechanism when developing and applying IoT among nations, such as coordination and cooperation in terms of policy, standards, technology, and application. It includes the current international organization, such as the International Telecommunications Union (ITU), as well as other possible future global coordination institutions.

Ubiquitous IoT architecture is shown in Figure 2.2 [7]. nM&DC directly or indirectly manages iM&DCs and lM&DCs, which are also coordinated by the global coordinator. Solid dots denote unit IoT. iM&DC manages unit IoTs in the corresponding industry (solid dots in the rectangle connected to the iM&DC). lM&DC manages unit IoTs in its corresponding region (solid dots on the line connected to the lM&DC). It can be seen that industry IoT and local IoT overlap. Nationwide unit IoTs in different regions and industries construct

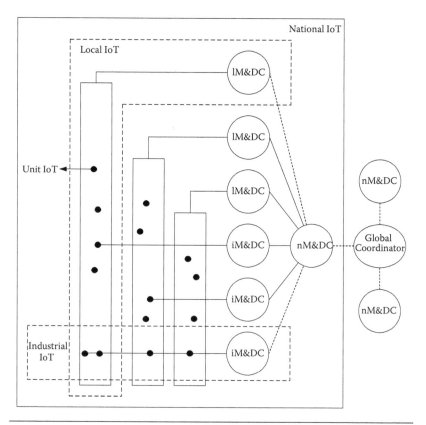

**Figure 2.2**   Ubiquitous IoT architecture.

national IoT. The global coordinator manages the cooperation for different nations.

## 2.3 Some Layered Models for IoT

IoT can be layered according to different functional aspects. Thus far, various kinds of layered models have been raised. Here, three models are mainly introduced, including the three-layer model, four-layer model, and IBM eight-layer model.

### 2.3.1 Three-Layer Model

IoT is generally divided into three layers from the aspect of technologies, which are the perception layer (also called the sensing layer), the network layer, and the application layer, as shown in Figure 2.3. The perception layer consists of various sensors, sensor gateways, and actuators. It is responsible for identifying things, collecting information, and controlling things. The network layer includes a variety of private networks, the Internet, mobile networks, the local area network, and the wide area network. The application layer is the interface of the IoT service and users. Combining IoT technologies with actual requirements, the intelligent application of IoT can be realized.

### 2.3.2 Four-Layer Model

The four-layer model is similar to the three-layer model, as shown in Figure 2.4. The difference is an additional supporting layer split from the application layer. The network layer utilizes networks to ensure secure and reliable data transmission. The supporting layer adopts unified coding, data fusion, data management, cloud computing, cloud storage technology, and so forth.

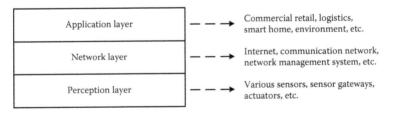

**Figure 2.3**  The three-layer IoT model.

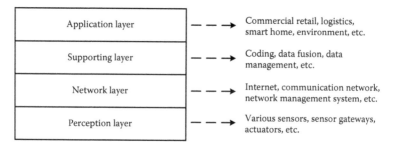

**Figure 2.4**  The four-layer IoT model.

### 2.3.3 Eight-Layer Model

The eight-layer model is proposed by IBM [8], which includes the sensor-actuator layer, sensor network layer, sensing gateway layer, wide area network layer, application gateway layer, service platform layer, application layer, and analysis and optimization layer, as shown in Figure 2.5. Compared to the three-layer and four-layer models, more aspects about ubiquitous IoT are considered in the IBM eight-layer model.

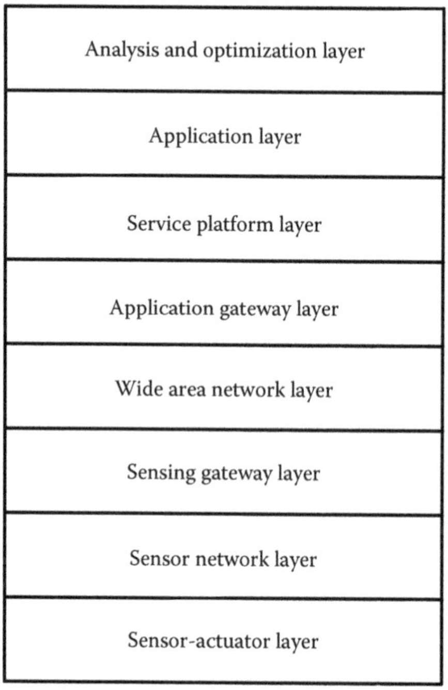

| |
|---|
| Analysis and optimization layer |
| Application layer |
| Service platform layer |
| Application gateway layer |
| Wide area network layer |
| Sensing gateway layer |
| Sensor network layer |
| Sensor-actuator layer |

**Figure 2.5**  IBM eight-layer IoT model.

*2.3.4 Discussion on the above Layered Models*

In the above three IoT layered models, the three-layer and four-layer models are more suitable to describe unit IoT. Compared to them, the eight-layer model adds more content for multiple applications, and it considers characteristics in heterogeneous sensing, communications, and applications. However, for ubiquitous IoT, there are still some limitations in the eight-layer model. In Section 2.4, based on U2IoT architecture, a new layered model and the social attributes involved in IoT are discussed.

## 2.4 Layered Model Proposed and Social Attributes Discussion for U2IoT

*2.4.1 Layered Model Designed for U2IoT*

Based on U2IoT architecture, a six-layer model is proposed as shown in Figure 2.6, including the sensor-actuator layer, network layer, application layer, service integration layer, national management layer, and international coordinator layer. The sensor-actuator layer, network layer, and application layer are similar to those in the three-layer model. The upper three layers are designed for ubiquitous IoT. Concretely, the purpose of the service integration layer is

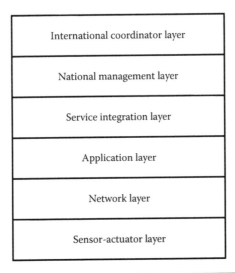

**Figure 2.6**  The six-layer model based on U2IoT. (The sensor-actuator layer is the same as the perception layer in the three-layer model. Here it is renamed for a better description of its contents.)

to manage the set of different applications for service providing, such as iM&DC. The national management layer is responsible for the regulation of local IoT and industrial IoT, which is guided by the nation. The international coordinator layer is mainly responsible for the coordination of IoT applications and development and standards in different nations; it coordinates IoT development, regulations, and applications on a global scale.

### 2.4.2 Layer Description and Social Attributes for Unit IoT

As shown in Figure 2.7, unit IoT has three layers with social attributes, including the sensor-actuator layer, network layer, and application layer. Note that the sensor-actuator layer and network layer in the figure only refer to those in a single application.

- *Sensor-actuator layer.* The sensor-actuator layer comprises sensors and actuators to perform things' identification, resource/service discovery, and execution control. It senses things to extract information and realize semantic resource discovery, and performs actions to realize control. Sensing techniques in this layer include RFID, camera, Wi-Fi, Bluetooth, global positioning system (GPS), radar, and so on.
- *Network layer.* The network layer includes the network interfaces, gateways, communication channels, and information management. A heterogeneous network existing in IoT mainly refers to communication networks such as the Internet and mobile networks, and access networks such as wireless sensor networks (WSNs), in which the hybrid network topologies are involved to assist in monitoring real-time network configuration. The network layer ensures reliable data transmission by applying the data coding, extraction, fusion, restructuring, mining, and aggregation algorithms.
- *Application layer.* The application layer supports embedded interfaces to provide diverse functionalities, realizing information aggregation and distribution and providing users with certain services. It includes different application processing systems. The systems process, analyze, and execute different functionalities and make decisions. This layer should fully

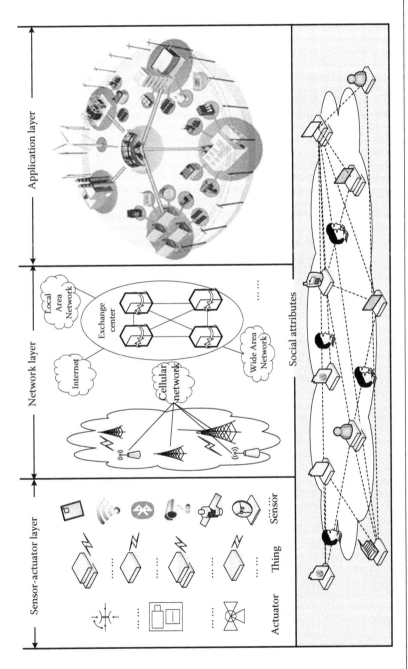

**Figure 2.7**  Layers and social attributes in unit IoT.

consider the specific requirements for the application and provide a user-friendly interface for operation.

- *Social attributes.* The social attributes consider those throughout the three layers, and are devoted to digging out social relationships among other things. The social attributes influence unit IoT from many different aspects. The heterogeneous networks to which unit IoT applies, security and privacy, things involved in unit IoT, concrete local IoT, industrial IoT, or national IoT to which it belongs are all affecting factors. Here, the discussion focuses on physical things involved in unit IoT. Table 2.2 lists the social affecting factors to the physical things in unit IoT and the corresponding attributes.

1. Objects are affected by various social factors, including space-time, adscription, and relation. For example, when a car is parked in the static state, little attention is paid to it, but if it moves with dynamic space-time parameters, the possibilities of driving danger it may bring should be considered. Attributions of objects in society determine the legal owner of the corresponding object, and the relation determines whether the object can be used by others or perform any interaction with others.
2. An object's behavior can affect the object itself and other objects. For instance, when we drive a car, the "driving" behavior affects the car's attributes/status.
3. Tendency is affected by the developing rule. If the tendency is regular, the situation can be predicted and under

**Table 2.2**    Social Affecting Factors and Attributes Brought to the Physical Things

| THINGS | SOCIAL AFFECTING FACTORS | ATTRIBUTES BROUGHT TO THE PHYSICAL THINGS |
|---|---|---|
| | Space-time | Static/dynamic |
| Objects | Attribution | Legal/illegal |
| | Relation | Interactive or not |
| Behaviors | Affecting object itself or others | Influence |
| Tendency | Developing rule | Regular or not |
| Physical events | Influence group | Involving range |

control. Otherwise, contingency measures should be prepared for the possible change of tendency. For instance, a traffic jam is regular at most times, so when the number of increasing cars on the road tends to be stable, it can be regarded as a normal situation. However, when the increasing number becomes unexpectedly large, serious attention should be paid to keeping the normal operation of transportation.

4. Physical events are affected by the influence group. For example, if a local policy is established by the government and acts on one particular region, the unit IoTs in the region will be affected, while the effects on other unit IoTs may be small.

In addition, the environment should be considered for physical things. The effects of the event also depend on different environments. Otherwise, the event may largely affect and influence the local life. Unit IoT should consider more specific attributes of concrete things and the environment and then make adjustments to the different situations.

### 2.4.3 Layer Description and Social Attributes for Ubiquitous IoT

Ubiquitous IoT includes the service integration layer, national management layer, international coordinator layer, and social attributes as well, as shown in Figure 2.8.

- *Service integration layer.* The service integration layer is responsible for the coordination of various unit IoTs in the corresponding local IoT or industrial IoT. In many cases, unit IoTs need to be integrated to provide better and more comprehensive services. M&DCs in these unit IoTs are often managed by the lM&DC or iM&DC in this layer. An interface to integrate the services provided by different unit IoTs should be built in this layer, as well as local regulations or industrial standards. This layer provides approaches and platforms for various unit IoTs' integration.
- *National management layer.* The national management layer is the regulation of local and industrial IoT, providing the

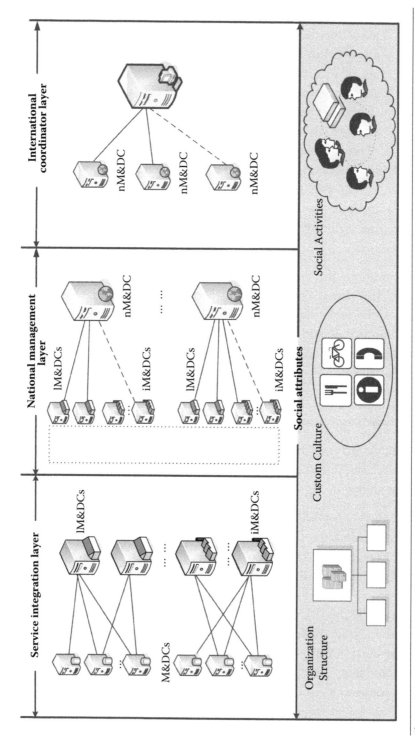

**Figure 2.8**   Layers and social attributes in ubiquitous IoT.

industry planning and guidance functions. In each nation, the industry and local development situation is dissimilar, so corresponding national management is needed for better construction of IoT, satisfying different cases and requirements. nM&DC manages lM&DC or iM&DC in this layer, and related regulations, laws, and platforms should be provided for coordination and supervision. It should be noted that national information security is especially important in this layer.

- *International coordinator layer.* The international coordinator layer manages transnational IoTs, builds international standards, and coordinates interaction among IoTs in different nations. It is similar to the United Nations Organization (UNO), in which different nations participate, establishing standards and protocols, or the International Organization for Standardization (ISO), building international standards. In this layer, nM&DC in nations all over the world may not be coordinated by one centralized global coordinator only. Several international organizations can coordinate jointly.

- *Social attributes.* Social attributes of ubiquitous IoT should also be mapped from the social world to the cyber world. For ubiquitous IoT, as a collection of unit IoTs, its social attributes include organization function and structure, geographical terrain and custom culture, security and privacy, and competition and cooperation among nations, industries, and regions, instead of the specific things involved in unit IoT.

  1. The organization function and structure considers more about the organization form. How it is formalized should also be reflected in the cyber world. For instance, if the ubiquitous IoT is formalized by the region division, the corresponding characteristics, such as physiognomy of the region, will affect it as well.

  2. The geographical terrain and custom culture influence ubiquitous IoT, and should be mapped to the cyber world, as it reflects regional characteristics and common human habits. Effects that the terrain and custom culture bring in their located place are significant for the operation of ubiquitous IoT and need full consideration.

3. Security and privacy affect ubiquitous IoT by the difference of required degree that different IoTs may involve. Generally, the highest degree should be taken as the overall security level, and privacy should be protected by setting a different access level.

4. The competition and cooperation among nations, industries, and regions influence ubiquitous IoT as well. In a certain IoT, there are features or requirements according to the corresponding requirements. So when the competition and cooperation relationship emerges, compatible and interactive issues should be considered.

### 2.5 IoT Development Phases Summary and Discussion

The ideal future IoT vision may be an era of harmony of humans with nature, which means harmony, coordination, and coexistence of the physical world, cyber world, and social world. Thus far, IoT development can be summarized as three stages before achieving the ideal IoT vision era: the early stage, unit IoT stage, and industrial/local IoT stage, as shown in Figure 2.9.

#### 2.5.1 Early Stage

The early stage is the beginning of the IoT early development stage. In this stage, two typical schemes are the EPC system and UID. The EPC system realizes that all physical objects can be identified

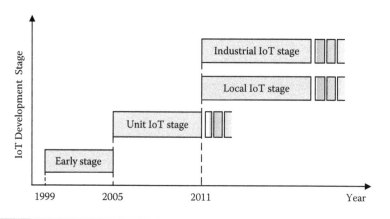

**Figure 2.9**  The overview of IoT development phases.

uniquely by assigning an EPC code carried by RFID tags. The UID solution was proposed by Japan and identifies objects through ubiquitous code (Ucode). The main feature at this stage is using RFID technology to identify objects uniquely and trace them globally.

### 2.5.2 Unit IoT Stage

The unit IoT stage focuses on a specific IoT application. It can be dated back to 2005 with its milestone—publishing of the IoT report by ITU [9], followed by some important events: the U.S. government made a positive statement to develop IoT in 2008, the European Union launched cluster research on IoT and announced some reports [10, 11], and China announced that a sensor network would be developed as an important industry in 2009. One of the stage characteristics is the sensing method in IoT, which not only includes RFID identification, but also involves a variety of ubiquitous sensing methods (including sound, light, and electricity-based contact, contactless, and remote sensing methods). Another characteristic is the application of intelligence to IoT. For example, Smarter Planet [12] proposed by IBM has already gained increasing popularity. Despite IoT's development, IoT is still a blurred concept for the public. This is the result of disconnection of the academe and industries. Some industrialists have already taken hasty moves to informationize their applications to the IoT concept, while a distinct scientific and technological framework for future IoT has still not been established. Therefore, it is difficult to establish IoT standards in the real sense at this stage. Compared to the early stage, one of the significant differences is that involved sensing and networking technologies include RFID, WSN, ZigBee, Wi-Fi, and so on. Thus far, IoT development has experienced two stages: the early development stage and the unit IoT stage.

### 2.5.3 Industrial/Local IoT Stage

From 2011, industrial IoT and local IoT have simultaneously developed. They can be formalized gradually and in parallel.

- *Industrial IoT.* The beginning of 2011 saw a milestone when China announced a push in IoT development in 10 important application fields, namely, industrial IoT. Though IBM had developed solutions such as Smart Bank in 2008, it is, after all, a corporation aiming at unit IoT other than establishing and operating an industrial IoT led by a nation. Speaking of policy making, China strides ahead of other countries and has become one of the leads of IoT development. As a pioneer, China will not be daunted by the obstacles at this stage but will probe the way steadily. Meanwhile, scientific problems concerning IoT will be solved at this stage. Some national standards for industrial IoT will be formulated, and cross-field cooperation mechanisms will be established. Some global industrial standards concerning transnational communication, such as global logistics, will emerge at this stage. At this stage, the standards will be a significant issue. The regulation of industrial IoT should be seriously taken into consideration by the government. The compatibility and data interaction also bring privacy and security challenges. This should negotiate the willingness of users as well as concrete applications.

- *Local IoT.* Local IoT is generated at this stage to coordinate and manage unit IoTs at the local place. Security and privacy are also significant for local IoT, and local customs and culture should be fully considered. For local IoT, permission rights among different local IoT may conflict, and coordination should be taken into consideration by the local government. Resource usage among different IoT applications in the same region may also be considered a priority. An agreement or coordinator is needed for negotiation in local IoT.

### 2.5.4 National IoT

When industrial IoT and local IoT maturely develop, national IoT that manages all IoT applications in the nation will be formed with relatively mature technologies, user consciousness and cultivation, laws, regulations, and security. Nations can independently control their information network and resources. Cross-disciplinary subjects such as science, technology, and engineering associated with IoT will be introduced, and IoT-relevant subjects and humanities and social science, such as economics, managing, sociology, the law, and philosophy, will also be considered in IoT. The standards for national IoT will be established. Finally, when national IoT connects and develops maturely, IoT covering different countries will be connective and the international cooperation mechanism will also be basically founded. Under the new information network, changes will occur in people's lifestyles, ideals, social organization structures, and government functions.

## 2.6 Science Category and Supporting Technologies for IoT

### 2.6.1 Science Category Based on Cyber-Physical-Social Aspects

IoT combines three worlds—the physical world, cyber world, and social world—and links all the things to achieve an ideal IoT. Correspondingly, we classify social science, physical science, and cyber science for IoT. Basically, from the aspect of study and IoT required knowledge, fundamental science is also involved, including geography science, system science, mathematics science, and philosophy, as shown in Figure 2.10.

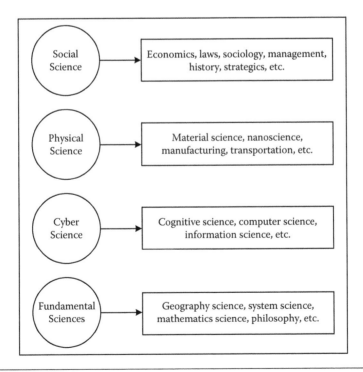

**Figure 2.10**   The science category in IoT.

- *Social science* is the study of society development, which covers economics, law, sociology, management, history, and strategies. It services humans and society, studying issues of social attributes, property rights transfer, markets, investments, organization, coordination, operation, management, supervision, law enforcement, privacy protection inter- and intra-applications, industries, regions, and nations. By studying the entire behavior of society, rules can be found and used to establish new regulations for future IoT development. Social science addresses the issues of IoT management and operation regulation.

- *Physical science* studies things in the physical world, for example, material science, nanoscience, manufacturing, and transportation. This science is different from the current physics as a concrete subject. It means the study of things that exist objectively in the physical world, not only humans, but also other things. This science discusses aspects of materials, devices, equipment, networks, and their production, construction, operation, maintenance, energy consumption, and so forth.

- *Cyber science* focuses on things in the cyber world, including cognitive science, computer science, and information science, excluding the building of the physical devices that realize the cyber things' interaction. The range of this science covers electronic information, computers, networks, control, intelligence, systems management, information security, and collecting, processing, transmitting, storing, and utilizing procedures of information.

- *Fundamental sciences* include geography science, system science, mathematics science, and philosophy. Geographical science studies the earth and society, and the mutual relationship and reciprocity of space objects. System science studies IoT from aspects of the whole and part, local and global, and the hierarchical relation, including the overall IoT-relevant system optimization, the relationship between system structure and function, the system stability, and so on. Mathematics science studies quantitative relations of quantity and quality, not considering the nature difference. Philosophy is the most abstract and basic level of all and guides IoT development. In addition, physics, chemistry, and spatial orientation are also basic parts of science.

### 2.6.2 Supporting Technologies

IoT involves various kinds of supporting technologies, covering resource management, security and privacy, energy management, loop control, session management, space-time consistency, spectrum management, nanotechnology, and quantum technologies. There are different classification methods for these technologies. One is to classify them according to sensing, network, application, and intelligent processing, which will be introduced in detail in Chapter 3. The other is to classify them according to the IoT definition and meaning of mapping between the physical world and cyber world, as shown in Figure 2.11.

These technologies are divided into two kinds. One is the supporting technologies based on the interaction between the physical world

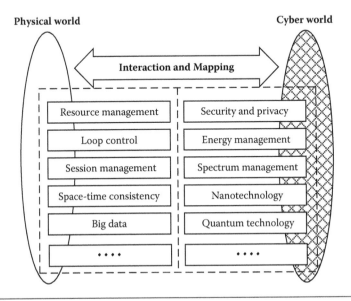

**Figure 2.11**  The main supporting technologies in IoT.

and cyber world, including resource management, loop control, session management, space-time consistency, and big data. Resources exist in both the physical world and cyber world, and are required to be managed to achieve resource-optimized utilization. Loop control is needed for the decision of the actuation loop's logic/components/ process, and the maintenance of loop executing. Session management is also involved in IoT, as it is required to manage interactions between the ubiquitous resources and resource users. Time and space are basic dimensions in the physical world, so when mapping things to the cyber world, space-time consistency should be taken as a supporting technology and researched with great attention. Big data is a data set that is beyond the common tool's ability to capture, manage, and process. It has become a contact bond of the physical world, cyber world, and social world.

The other is the common supporting technologies, including security and privacy, energy management, spectrum management, nanotechnology, and quantum technology. As IoT involves a large amount of information about humans and human life, threats to security and privacy issues will become unprecedentedly serious. Therefore, security and privacy have to be considered when mapping information between the physical world and cyber world. Energy consumption should be considered in concrete applications, which is a serious global problem because of energy limitation. Frequency management manages the procedures of planning, coordinating, and managing the spectrum utilization in IoT. Nanotechnology is a new emerging technology of controlling matter on the scale of 1 ~ 100 nm and affects many disciplines and technologies. Quantum technology brings us new materials, devices, communications, and computing mechanisms. These technologies are basically needed for IoT as common supporting technologies.

The above 10 technologies will be introduced in Chapters 5 to 14 in accordance with the objectives.

## 2.7 Conclusion

This chapter discusses IoT architecture and fundamentals, including the main aspects of architecture, layered models, the summary of IoT development phases, the science category, and supporting technologies. U2IoT architecture and the six-layer model are designed for future IoT, in which social attributes are highlighted during constructing IoT.

For more descriptions of U2IoT, unit IoT and ubiquitous IoT are explained in detail in the next two chapters. Afterward, the supporting technologies are presented.

# References

1. EPCglobal. 2009. The EPCglobal architecture framework. http://www.gs1hk.org-/files/documen t/epc_standards/architecture_1_3-fra mework-20090319.pdf (accessed August 2, 2012).
2. SENSEI: Integrating the physical with the digital world of the network of the future. FP7. http://www.ict-sensei.org (accessed August 2, 2012).
3. Pervasive computing in embedded systems. FP7. http://www.ict-peces.eu (accessed November 14, 2011).
4. Semantic sensor grids for rapid application development for environmental management. FP7. http://www.sem sorgrid4env.eu/ (accessed September 26, 2012).
5. Future Internet assembly: European future Internet portal—The information hub for European R&D activities on the Internet of the future. http://www.future-internet.eu/home-/future-internet-assembly.html (accessed August 2, 2012).
6. Ning, H., and Z. Wang. 2011. Future Internet of Things architecture: Like mankind neural system or social organization framework? *IEEE Communications Letters* 15: 461–463.
7. Ning, H., and S. Hu. 2012. Technology classification, industry, and education for future Internet of Things. *International Journal of Communication Systems* 25: 1230–1241.
8. Perspective of Internet of Things eight-layer structure. http://cloud.51cto.c om/art/201010-/230208.htm (accessed August 2, 2012).
9. ITU. 2005. *The Internet of Things*. ITU International Reports.
10. Cluster of European Research Projects on the Internet of Things, CERP-IoT. 2009. *Internet of Things: Strategic research roadmap*.
11. Cluster of European Research Projects on the Internet of Things, CERP-IoT. 2010. *Vision and challenges for realising the Internet of things*.
12. IBM. Smarter Planet—United States. http://www.ibm.co m/smarterpl anet/us/en/?ca=v_smart-erplanet (accessed August 2, 2012).

# 3

# UNIT INTERNET OF THINGS

## 3.1 Introduction

Unit Internet of Things (unit IoT) refers to a specific application, including multiple sensors, actuators, a management and data center (M&DC), and heterogeneous networks. Multiple unit IoTs could jointly constitute ubiquitous IoT.

Unit IoT can also be regarded as an interactive system referring to sensing, controlling, and networking, and it realizes the interconnections among ubiquitous things. In unit and ubiquitous IoT (U2IoT), objects and entities are respectively associated with the corresponding identifiers and attributes (e.g., size, color, location, and attribution) in the physical world and cyber world. Such identifiers and attributes are the things' important elements, which bring new challenges for data sensing, actuation implementation, networking and communications, and information management throughout both the cyber world and physical world.

- *Toward data sensing.* Sensors perform persistent or intermittent data collection, and sensing technologies are applied to achieve an object being mapped as an entity from the physical world into the cyber world.
- *Toward actuation implementation.* Actuators execute actions as responses to the collected data, for which the centralized mode and distributed mode can be launched for implementation. The actuators may be managed by sensors or M&DCs, and perform actuations in the physical world and cyber world.
- *Toward networking and communications.* Heterogeneous wireless networking technologies can be combined to realize efficient and reliable data transmission. The next-generation mobile communication network, telecommunication network,

and Internet technologies can also be connected in IoT, and bring noteworthy prospects for the interconnection between the physical world and cyber world.

- *Toward information management.* M&DC acts as a management platform to provide functions such as intelligent decisions, data processing, and systemic management. Raw data are addressed to extract advanced knowledge to provide smart services, based on which entity mapping from the cyber world into the physical world is achieved.

Accordingly, the mentioned aspects are respectively introduced in the following sections. Section 3.2 focuses on sensors and actuators. Section 3.3 introduces the ubiquitous sensing technologies, and Section 3.4 presents the networking and communications. Section 3.5 further discusses M&DC according to its information service-related functions. Thereafter, some typical application scenarios are further discussed in Section 3.6.

### 3.2 Sensors and Actuators

In unit IoT, sensors and actuators are mainly linked via wired or wireless networks in the sensor-actuator layer [1]. The sensors and actuators are used to collect data for identifying things, gathering information, and executing tasks without direct human intervention, which realizes the interaction and coupling between the physical world and cyber world [2]. In unit IoT, sensors and actuators have the following features:

- *Sensing.* Sensors have the ability to perform sensing on things, and the collected data are usually used by actuators to perform appointed actions.
- *Communication.* Sensors and actuators can establish wired or wireless communications, and can be connected into heterogeneous networks among the interconnected things.
- *Identification.* Things can be identified by sensors via identifiers or attributes (e.g., size, location, and temperature). Therefore, physical objects' physical identities and attributes, and their corresponding cyber identities and attributes, can be correlated with the mutually mapped relationships.

- *Interaction.* Things can interact with the surrounding environment and the back-end systems through the sensing and controlling capabilities.


### 3.2.1 Sensors

Sensors act as detectors and converters to capture the data of physical things, and sensors are usually low-cost and low-power devices that are equipped with limited energy, computation, and communication capabilities. There are different sensors to detect and measure physical things and the surrounding environment, including acceleration, vibration, electromagnetic properties, temperature, humidity, machine vision, velocity, and positions of physical things. According to the sensed data, sensors can be classified into two types: identifier (ID)-based sensors, and attribute (non-ID, short for nID)-based sensors.

- *ID-based sensors* mainly refer to the sensors that detect physical things with identifiers. Such things can be organized into networks to achieve interconnection.
- *nID-based sensors* mainly include sensors that detect physical things' attributes. Such sensors can detect inherent attributes and other relevant attributes.

Generally, ID-based sensors are applied to detect an object with identifiers (e.g., radio frequency identification [RFID] tag identifier and quick-response [QR] code) in unit IoT. Note that a sensor may be assigned with a unique identifier along with other associated attributes. For ID-based sensors, multiple identifiers may be assigned to an object according to different IoT scenarios, and different identifier fields may be authorized to multiple users with different authority. It turns out that:

- An object may have multiple identifiers in different applications.
- An identifier may have multiple identifier fields for different users.
- A user may access multiple identifiers of different objects, or may access multiple identifier fields of an object.

The relationships of the object, identifier, and user reflect the interconnection between the physical world and cyber world. In unit IoT, an object may have the corresponding identity information (i.e., identifier), in which the sensors are applied to transfer the attached data to point to an object by electromagnetic signals.

Beyond the sensors used to detect an object's ID, there are also nID-based sensors applied to detect an object's attributes (e.g., temperature and location). There are several examples of nID-based sensors. For instance, image detection devices can identify the objects and their activities, and can be used to monitor and evaluate the scene; radar applies electromagnetic waves to detect the object, and obtain an object's information by radar cross section, doppler, glint, and so forth.

In unit IoT, both ID- and nID-based sensors are usually organized in the hybrid detection and identification mode, in which complementary and cooperative relationships are established among heterogeneous sensors.

### 3.2.2 Actuators

Actuators are defined with the functions of automation and control, which convert the collected data into action commands to enhance efficiency in self-adaptive applications [1]. Concretely, actuators are usually mechanical or electronic devices (e.g., valves and switches) that execute commands and instructions, and perform appropriate actions on physical things and the surrounding environments. In some cases, sensors and actuators are pairwise devices to perform actions on the physical world. For example, a gas transducer detects that a gas concentration of carbon dioxide exceeds the standard limitation, and the switch of an air conditioner will be launched to address the abnormal situation.

In wireless sensor-actuator networks (WSANs), actuators can be organized in different modes according to whether there is an integrated or an independent controller attached in an actuator [3]. Similarly, actuators can be organized in a centralized actuation mode and distributed actuation mode in unit IoT.

- *Centralized actuation mode.* In the centralized mode, there are one or multiple controllers to perform management on sensors and actuators within the given jurisdiction, and the controller

is an independent functional module with sufficient computation and communication capacities. The sensors transmit
the collected data to a controller. Thereafter, the controller
executes the corresponding control algorithms, and assigns
executive commands to actuators. Upon receiving the control
commands, the actuators perform the appointed actuations.

- *Distributed actuation mode.* In the distributed mode, an actuator acts as both an actuator and a controller. The controller
has the assigned control algorithms, and is applied to provide an actuation strategic decision for the detailed actuation
execution in the physical world. The sensors collect physical
things–related data, which are transmitted to the corresponding actuators. Thereafter, the actuators invoke the predefined
control algorithm to perform data processing, and to execute
appropriate actions. Generally, the controller and actuators
are logically integrated into a whole entity, and the sensed
data are used by actuators with executive commands to react
upon the physical world.

## 3.3 Ubiquitous Sensing

Ubiquitous sensing refers to a great variety of sensor-based technologies,
and mainly serves for the sensor-actuator layer to achieve ubiquitous
sensing and controlling. There are wired sensing technologies and wireless sensing technologies according to the communication channels.

Wired sensing technologies belong to the traditional monitoring
modes, and usually have more reliable communication channels. The
wired sensing technologies have obvious limitations (e.g., mobility and
expandability), and therefore wireless sensing technologies appear to
be an emerging technology. It is noteworthy that the wireless sensor network (WSN) is a suitable access network platform consisting
of a huge number of distributed autonomous sensors for monitoring
and detecting objects. Multiple wireless sensing technologies can be
integrated into WSNs, based on which sensors cooperatively transmit
the collected data into heterogeneous networks. During data transmission, multihop and self-organizing wireless routes are established
with bidirectional communications. The sensors may actively collect
data by constantly performing omnidirectional scanning, and may

passively gather data by unobtrusively waiting for an object's appearance. Both active sensors and passive sensors can be called motes, which are components of the network of sensor nodes.

The wireless sensing technologies also bring several open issues, including network structure (e.g., heterogeneous network and hierarchical network), network deployment (e.g., one time, incremental, and random), communication modality (e.g., single hop and multihop), network topology (e.g., single hop, star, multihop, mesh, and multitier), and coverage (e.g., sparse, dense, and redundant) [4]. In the following sections, the typical wireless sensing technologies are introduced, including RFID, Bluetooth, Wi-Fi, ultra-wideband (UWB), ZigBee, and infrared data transmission (IrDA).

### 3.3.1 Radio Frequency Identification (RFID)

RFID is a wireless automatic identification technology to achieve data acquisition from tagged objects by electromagnetic fields or electrostatic coupling. In the open wireless air interface, there are two main components: tag and reader.

- A tag is embedded with a unique identifier, and is attached to objects. In RFID systems, the identified objects may include goods, materials, products, assembly machinery, assets, and even persons/animals. The object is tagged with a tag, and the sensed data can be collected by an identifier for identification via wireless channels.
- The reader emits radio signals within the electromagnetic range, which is determined upon the power output and working frequency. When a tag passes through its range, it detects the reader's activation challenge signal, which is transmitted to the back-end system for data processing and management. Note that the reader may have a built-in database for offline identification and authentication in distributed systems.

According to NIST Special Publication 800-98, *Guidelines for Securing Radio Frequency Identification (RFID) Systems*, there are several types of RFID tags with different cost, size, power, performance, and security mechanisms [5]. Even though the tags design are based on a particular standard, they may be further customized for specific application requirements.

In RFID applications, near-field communication (NFC) as 13.56 MHz frequency-based RFID technology becomes noteworthy for smart phones and other mobile devices to establish radio communication, and provides services such as mobile payment, ticketing, information collection/exchange, and access control. NFC standards are based on the ISO/IEC 14443 international standard to specify the communications protocols and data exchange formats. The main features of NFC include physical noncontact identification, multiple applicability, open standards, inherent security, and interoperation [6].

### 3.3.2 Bluetooth

Bluetooth is a wireless technology based on short-range radio transmissions in the 2.4 GHz frequency, and it establishes personal area networks (PANs) with high security requirements. Bluetooth is a specification for low-power radio communications to establish wireless intercommunications of devices and their peripherals, including mobile phones, personal digital assistants (PDAs), wireless headsets, computers, and other network devices.

Based on Bluetooth technology, graph, voice, and data can be transmitted within the effective range (e.g., less than 10 m) at a low data rate. A Bluetooth special interest group has developed wireless communications standard IEEE 802.15.1 for mobile devices. In a basic Bluetooth network, there is a dynamic topology piconet, which includes a minimum of two and a maximum of eight peer devices for communication. There are several features and requirements that should be considered [7–9].

- The same standard should be regulated around different regions in the world.
- The radio transceiver must be small and operate at low power and globally.
- The system supports peer-to-peer connectivity and separates the frequency band into hops. The spread spectrum is used to hop from one channel to another with security consideration.

- The system should support data in multimedia applications. Meanwhile, signals can be transmitted without needing a line of sight, and devices can be identified by omnidirectional signals. Both synchronous and asynchronous applications are supported, which makes it easy to implement on different device-based services.

### 3.3.3  Wireless Fidelity (Wi-Fi)

Wi-Fi is a wireless technology that allows an electronic device to exchange data over a high-speed computer network (e.g., Internet), and it is a typical communication of wireless local area networks (WLANs) based on IEEE 802.11 family standards. The Wi-Fi standard covers a relatively large area with high transmission speed. The Wi-Fi alliance defines that Wi-Fi is used based on IEEE 802.11b, which supports the 2.4 GHz frequency of wireless access points. Additionally, Wi-Fi alliance has expanded the generic standard to other related standards, including IEEE 802.11a, 802.11g, and 802.11n. A Wi-Fi device can connect and access network resources via a wireless network access point or hotspot. The network range of an access point is about 250 m outdoors and 70 m indoors. Hotspot coverage comprises a small network area by applying multiple overlapping access points. During Wi-Fi-based communications, the interactive objects use a frequency within the electromagnetic spectrum associated with radio wave propagation to achieve a nonphysical connection. Therefore, the access point is an important component to broadcast an available wireless signal, and wireless network adapters are used to realize connections among Wi-Fi devices and computer networks via the access points. Additionally, Wired Equivalent Privacy (WEP) is presented to provide confidentiality in point-to-point links, in which a shared key is involved for data encryption. Meanwhile, Wi-Fi Protected Access (WPA) and Wi-Fi Protected Access II (WPA2) are proposed for security protection on Wi-Fi communications.

### 3.3.4  Ultra-Wideband (UWB)

Ultra-wideband (UWB) applies wireless signals for data collection and transmission, and is based on a low energy level for short-range, high-bandwidth communications with a large portion of the electromagnetic spectrum. The main applications of UWB include noncooperative radar imaging, target sensor data collection, and precision locating and tracking. UWB offers both high-data-rate communication and high-accuracy positioning capabilities, and can use a low transmitted signal power level with an extremely wide bandwidth. Due to the spread spectrum characteristics, UWB communications can coexist with the other radio networks, such as traditional narrowband and the same-frequency band-based carrier wave. UWB uses a pulse-based approach or a multiband orthogonal frequency division multiplexing-based approach for transmission, to achieve high-rate, short-range or low-rate, moderate-range communications [10].

There are several UWB applications, such as voice conversations and streaming, automation and control, medical monitoring, vehicular radar systems, and other high-rate data transfer applications. Moreover, UWB can enable a variety of wireless personal area network (WPAN) applications, such as wireless PC peripheral connectivity, wireless multimedia connectivity for devices, cable replacement and network access for mobile computing devices, and *ad hoc* connections between UWB-enabled devices [11,12].

The main features of UWB are as follows:

1. Low transmission energy and high bandwidth within a short range
2. Low energy density minimizes the interference on other services, and the communication is hard to intercept along with multipath immunity
3. Universal signal generation and processing architectures with low cost, and frequency diversity with minimal hardware modifications

### 3.3.5 ZigBee

ZigBee is characterized by low-rate, low-power, and short-range data transmission for personal area networks. The IEEE 802.15.4 physical radio specification is the ZigBee standard to operate in unlicensed bands, including 2.4 GHz, 900 MHz, and 868 MHz. The specification defines the network layer, application layer, and correlative security strategies, which are based on the physical layer and medium access control layer. Therefore, the application layer refers to the application specification for different scenarios and contexts [13], and the network layer mainly includes network topology, network establishment, network maintenance, and routing. ZigBee is mainly organized into three network topologies: star topology, tree topology, and mesh topology.

- Star topology is mainly designed for point-to-multipoint-based communication.
- Tree topology uses a hierarchical routing mechanism.
- Mesh topology uses the mixed routing method combined with *ad hoc* on-demand distance vector routing and hierarchical routing.

During the deployment of ZigBee-enabled devices in home area networks (HANs) or building area networks (BANs), the devices are usually organized in mesh networks to achieve long-distance transmission via intermediate devices. The defined specification is used to address packet-based communication according to self-organized network topologies, in which multiple devices form *ad hoc* networks without any centralized management center or high-power transceiver [14]. The main features of ZigBee are as follows:

- Support for multiple network topologies (e.g., point-to-point, point-to-multipoint, and mesh networks)
- Low duty cycle, low rate, low power, and low latency
- A large number of sensor nodes per network
- Support security mechanism for data transmission, such as 128-bit AES encryption
- Collision avoidance, retries, and acknowledgments

*3.3.6 Infrared Data Transmission*

The Infrared Data Association (IrDA) is an organization that defines physical specifications communications protocol standards for wireless infrared communications between devices. Infrared data transmission is a short-range infrared wireless technology to achieve point-to-point connections. Infrared signals require line of sight (LOS) with a short range, and provide low-cost, small-size, low-power-consumption, low-bit-error-rate (BER), cross-platform, and point-to-point communications. Infrared signals support the dynamic *ad hoc* connectivity but has restrictions: two devices must be in short distance and line of sight. Such a short-range optical communication technique is mainly used to wirelessly transfer data with point-and-shoot principles between devices, including computers, PDAs, mobile phones, laptops, and cameras. The applications of infrared data transmission mainly include end-to-end digital payment systems, in which the IrDA Financial Messaging (IrFM) standard has been used for financial services infrastructures (e.g., credit cards) to realize efficient payment transactions [15].

## 3.4 Networking and Communications

Networking and communications technologies are pivotal for interconnection among remote things, in which mobile communication and the Internet are the mainstream technologies.

### 3.4.1 Mobile Communication Technology

Mobile communication has developed through first-generation (1G) analog cellular networks (e.g., Advanced Mobile Phone System [AMPS]), 2G digital cellular networks (e.g., Global System for Mobile Communications [GSM]), and 2.5G (e.g., general packet radio service [GPRS]), and is evolving toward 3G and 4G standards.

*3.4.1.1 Third-Generation Technology (3G)*   3G technology is a generation of standards for mobile phones and mobile telecommunication services fulfilling the International Mobile Telecommunications 2000 (IMT-2000) specifications proposed by the International Telecommunication Union. Application services include wide-area wireless voice telephone, mobile Internet access, video calls, and mobile TV, all in a mobile environment. The typical 3G standards include wideband code division multiple access (W-CDMA), CDMA2000, and time division-synchronous code division multiple access (TD-SCDMA).

Universal Mobile Telecommunications System (UMTS) architecture is specified by the 3G Partnership Project (3GPP), and evolved from the Global System for Mobile Communications (GSM) and general packet radio service (GPRS) of 2G/2.5G infrastructures. For UMTS, there are two types of standards: W-CDMA and TD-SCDMA. W-CDMA applies direct sequence–code division multiple access (DS-CDMA) and frequency division duplexing (FDD) to achieve higher speeds. W-CDMA supports an asynchronous operating mode and fast cell acquisition operation, which is a dominant 3G technology considering the dominance of existing 3G networks. TD-SCDMA is short for time division–synchronous code division multiple access, and is only used in China. CDMA2000 is standardized by a 3GPP2 sharing infrastructure that is compatible with the IS-95 standard. It applies the synchronous operating mode to achieve data transmission and reception timing that are synchronized for cell sites, in which all cell sites are based on a unified timing source (e.g., global positioning system [GPS]).

Additionally, worldwide interoperability for microwave access (WiMAX) aims to become a 4G mobile communication technology, and has become an evolved 3G technology. WiMAX refers to a broadband wireless data access standard to implement IEEE 802.16 family standards. WiMAX enables wireless data transmission based on IEEE 802.16d for the fixed or slowly moving users, and IEEE 802.16e adds mobility support to mobile WiMAX. Furthermore, WiMAX is integrated with an IP network to provide IP connectivity and connection-oriented wireless communications.

*3.4.1.2 Wireless Local Area Network (WLAN)*   WLAN applies wireless distribution technologies such as spread spectrum or orthogonal frequency division multiplexing (OFDM) to achieve multiple devices interconnection. It has the advantages of a high data transmission rate, and becomes ubiquitous in indoor scenarios (e.g., building environments). In WLAN, no additional installation costs are needed, and multiple mobile devices can seamlessly connect to positioning systems, in which the fingerprinting method is used for position estimation. Note that WLANs are mainly based on IEEE 802.11 standards, which define two basic operation modes: infrastructure mode and *ad hoc* mode. In infrastructure mode, wireless mobile units communicate via an access point to a wired network infrastructure. In *ad hoc* mode, the mobile units communicate in a peer-to-peer mode.

*3.4.1.3 Fourth-Generation Technology (4G)*   U.S. President Obama stressed that "the 4th generation (4G) mobile technology is becoming the emerging solution to drive the new growth of the industry, and help foster state-of-the-art technology, novel partnership arrangements or transformational business models" [16]. 4G technology is an integration of 3G and WLAN technologies, and is basically an extension of 3G technology, with more bandwidth and services.

In IoT, it is significant to merge fixed, mobile, and wireless communications to establish heterogeneous communications. It becomes an open issue to achieve both high data rate and seamless mobility; therefore, hybrid communication technologies should be optimized according to the contexts of mobile applications. For a 4G system, the all-IP-based secure mobile broadband communication scheme is provided for smart phones and other mobile devices. In addition, other application-oriented facilities (e.g., ultra-broadband Internet access, IP telephony, and streaming multimedia) may be provided to users [17]. International Mobile Telecommunications–Advanced (IMT-Advanced) are proposed to support 4G mobile phone and Internet access service. The official designation 4G standards include Long-Term Evolution (LTE)–Advanced and WirelessMAN–Advanced (IEEE 802.16m). There are also several forerunner versions, including Mobile WiMAX, 3GPP LTE, and TD-LTE, to support 4G standardization.

4G turns out to be a packet-based network, in which several issues should be considered, such as mobility management, congestion control, and quality of service (QoS). The main features of 4G are as follows:

- Supports interactive multimedia, wireless Internet, and other broadband services
- High data rate, high capacity, and low cost per bit
- Mobility, service portability, and scalable mobile networks
- Seamless switching and QoS-based services
- Enhanced scheduling and call admission control techniques
- *Ad hoc* networks and multihop networks

*3.4.2 Next-Generation Internet Technology*

The Internet is global computer networks used to achieve connection by the standard Internet protocol suite Transmission Control Protocol/Internet Protocol (TCP/IP), and it applies electronic, wireless, and optical networking technologies to establish a compositive network structure. The network structure mainly includes multiple private, public, local, industry, and national area networks. Due to the increasing address requirements, the next-generation Internet becomes attractive for IoT development, and brings new challenges for network interconnections.

IoT accelerates the development of the next-generation Internet technology. Due to the requirement of ubiquitous connectivity among a mass of things, it becomes necessary to assign more addresses to newly increasing things. Internet Protocol version 6 (IPv6), with its expanded address space, enables addressing, connecting, and tracking things, and is introduced to replace the traditional Internet [18]. It seems that it is possible to establish convergence of heterogeneous networks and applications based on the next-generation Internet-based network [19]. The main features of IPv6 are as follows:

- Large address space: Expanded addressing capacity ($2^{128}$ addresses in IPv6, compared with $2^{32}$ in IPv4)
- Built-in security support for authentication and privacy
- Built-in support for mobile communications
- A new protocol for neighboring node interactions defined, and a new packet format to minimize packet header processing by routers
- Better support for QoS with prioritization of communications
- Plug-and-play autoconfiguration of network settings to achieve stateless and stateful address configurations
- Support extensibility with hierarchical addressing and routing infrastructure

Along with the development of heterogeneous networks, 6LoWPAN (i.e., IPv6 over low-power wireless personal area networks) has been introduced to realize that low-power devices with limited processing capabilities can participate in future IoT. 6LoWPAN allows network interaction between IPv6-based Internet and IEEE 802.15.4-based wireless networks, for which connectivity, interoperability, and compatibility requirements should be considered. Things linked by IP and wireless communications, usually have limited power and lower data rates, and are suitable for automation and entertainment applications in home and building area networks. 6LoWPAN enables resource-limited things in wireless networks to be connected with the Internet, which will bring a bright perspective for the future Internet.

## 3.5  Management and Data Centers (M&DCs)

M&DCs mainly consider the aspects of pervasive management, and data fusion and data mining.

### 3.5.1  Pervasive Management

Pervasive management considers object/entity, networks, and services in unit IoT, to achieve intelligent and self-adaptive management [20].

*3.5.1.1 Object/Entity Management*   Object/entity management in unit IoT mainly refers to managing the system components, including sensors, actuators, gateways/base stations, user terminals, back-end databases, and other network elements. These components include objects distributed in geographical areas, and the corresponding entities with different function abstractions. In unit IoT, object/entity management mainly has the following functions:

- Monitors, controls, and supervises cyber entities, and network components in an individual network
- Controls and maintains the physical infrastructures
- Establishes things' interaction records and other statistical communication parameters
- Performs strong security protection and privacy preservation, energy maintenance, and spectrum management

*3.5.1.2 Network Management*   Network management focuses on networking-related actions in the cyber world. The main aspects refer to the network entities' activities, networking protocols, and accessing procedures, which work on the network operation, maintenance, and provision. Network management mainly has the following functions:

- Manages network topology and its network structural relations
- Maintains reliable interconnection in internetwork, intranetwork, and cross-network; maintains network availability to avoid channels jamming and blocking

- Designs secure communication protocols/algorithms, and adopts efficient mechanisms for safeguard
- Establishes heterogeneous network interfaces to improve network compatibility
- Optimizes network resource allocation, and coordinates resource distribution to achieve enhanced network performance

*3.5.1.3 Service Management*　Service management mainly serves individual or group users in unit IoT. Its aim is to improve the quality of services, and to provide appropriate services for users or potential users. Service-oriented computing (SOC) is an important aspect of service management [21]. A service-oriented architecture introduces loose coupling and flexibility into IoT, which allows seamless integrations of heterogeneous interfaces and platforms. For service management, different services are provided for applications with hybrid management structures, and shared information resources are used to support different service operations. To some degree, service management directly influences the user's experiences in IoT.

*3.5.2 Data Fusion and Data Mining*

The purpose of data fusion is to integrate multiple data and knowledge of objects with a consistent, accurate, and useful representation in unit IoT. It can be classified into three types: data-level fusion, feature-level fusion, and decision-level fusion. Data-level fusion is based on the sensors that combine several raw data sources to obtain refined data. Feature-level fusion expresses the data as a series of feature vectors, extracts the feature values, and represents things' attributes. Decision-level fusion provides advanced strategic decisions for different requirements. In data fusion, there are two main issues: data conflicts and data integration [22]. Data conflicts should be avoided from heterogeneous data sources, and data integration should be achieved with both data redundancy and correctness considerations [23]. The main features of data conflicts and data integration are as follows.

Data conflicts mainly include data uncertainty and data contradiction.

- Data uncertainty refers to an object's certain data (e.g., identifier and attribute) being represented by an expression value.

Meanwhile, data may also be described by another expression value. Such expression values may cause data uncertainty.

- Data contradiction refers to different expression values being applied to represent the same data, which may lead to inconsistent data representation for the object.

Data integration mainly considers the features of completeness, conciseness, and correctness.

- Data completeness ensures the integrity in terms of data elements (e.g., identifier and attributes) that cannot be modified (e.g., deleted, added, inserted, or recombined) without authorization.
- Data conciseness ensures the uniqueness of things' representations, which are described by the integrated data in terms of the objects and the corresponding identifiers/attributes.
- Data correctness ensures the validity of data sources, which should conform to the interaction relationships between the physical world and cyber world.

Data mining refers to knowledge discovery, which utilizes interleaving techniques of artificial intelligence, machine learning, statistics, and database technologies. It mainly addresses the aspects of database management, the data structure model, data preprocessing, data complexity analysis, interestingness metrics, visualization, and online interaction. The goal of data mining is to extract available knowledge from an existing data set. There are four basic data mining models [24–26], including multilayer data mining, distributed data mining, grid data mining, and heterogeneous data mining, that can be applied in unit IoT.

- *Hierarchical data mining.* In the hierarchical data mining model, there are four layers, including the data collection layer, data management layer, event processing layer, and data mining service layer. (1) The data collection layer refers to preliminary data management. (2) The data management layer mainly uses the centralized or distributed database to manage the collected data. (3) The event processing layer is applied to perform multiple events–based data analysis. (4) The data mining service layer is established by data management and event processing to support applications.

- *Distributed data mining.* The distributed data model is based on distributed storage, without needing a management and data center according to mass, distributed, space-time attributes. The data mining system includes a top data center and multiple data subcenters. The subcenter receives the raw sensed data for preprocessing, data abstraction, and data compression. Thereafter, the preprocessed data are transmitted to the local database. Here, the local database performs the corresponding event filtering and event detection, and it transmits the aggregated data to the top center for further processing. The top center acts as the whole manager and does not directly participate in the preliminary data mining on the sensed data, and mainly controls the subcenters. Based on such a model, data mining is mainly performed by the multiple local data agents–based collaborative mechanism.

- *Grid data mining.* A grid computing infrastructure can be introduced into data mining with the principle of breaking up the whole into parts. The grids are in the independent distributed system with noninteractive operations, and are suitable for loosely coupled, heterogeneous, and geographically dispersed networks. In a grid data mining model, a grid is a local data mining unit, and a multiagent-based collaborative management mechanism is applied for data aggregation to support different applications.

- *Heterogeneous data mining.* Heterogeneous data may be collected by different sensor and communication networks according to the context awareness of an environment, things, and individuals. The integrated data mining model should be established by combining the advantages of hierarchical, distributed, and grid models. Self-adaptive data mining algorithms can be support service-oriented applications (e.g., intelligent transportation and intelligent logistics).

## 3.6 Case Study for Unit IoT

Unit IoTs are developed with different practical functions and requirements. Libelium [27] has unveiled the top IoT applications grouped by 12 vertical markets, and Table 3.1 shows typical application scenarios

**Table 3.1**  Typical Application Scenarios

| CLASSIFICATION | TYPICAL APPLICATION SCENARIOS |
| --- | --- |
| Identification | Asset management, biometrics identification, e-passport, inventory management, logistics management, supply chain control, NFC payment, smart item management |
| Information aggregation | Smart home, smart building, smart community, satellite remote sensing system, photovoltaic installations, smart grid, smart parking, traffic congestion, waste management, intelligent transportation systems |
| Safety awareness | Bird strike avoidance radar system, river navigation safety system, perimeter access control, liquid presence, radiation levels, explosive and hazardous gases |
| Monitoring and control | Precision manufacturing system, environmental monitoring, smart health care monitoring, forest fire detection, air pollution, earthquake early detection, water quality, indoor air quality, temperature monitoring, indoor location, vehicle autodiagnosis |

*Note:*  For more information, please refer to Libelium, 50 Sensor Applications for a Smarter World, http://www.libelium.com/top_50_iot_sensor_applications_ranking/ (accessed May 10, 2012).

in which unit IoTs are classified into four aspects: identification, information aggregation, safety awareness, and monitoring and control.

### 3.6.1 Identification

Identification applications refer to an object's identifier (i.e., ID) or other attributes (i.e., nID) being identified by sensors to achieve efficient identity management, authentication, and access control. In the following, asset management considers the scenario that assets are identified based on ID, biometric identification is performed based on nID, and both ID and nID are introduced in the e-passport application.

*3.6.1.1 Asset Management*   Asset management refers to identifying, monitoring, and managing things that are of value to an individual or group user. Based on a unique identifier, asset management provides efficient asset identification, tracking, configuration, and management services to achieve intelligent maintenance throughout an asset's entire life cycle. The mentioned assets mainly refer to both tangible assets (e.g., goods, materials, and buildings) and intangible assets (e.g., software and intellectual property), which should be addressed with systematic management, including status supervision, financial accounting, preventive maintenance, and theft deterrence.

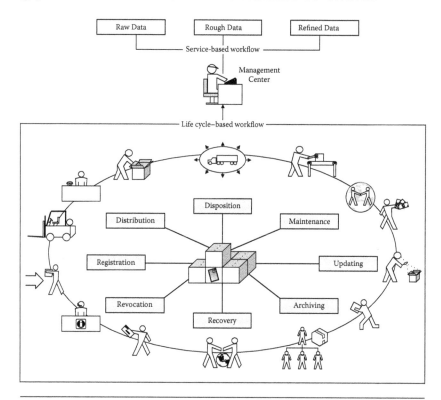

**Figure 3.1**    The asset management system model.

In IoT, sensing technologies (e.g., RFID) can provide enhanced identification with high efficiency, accuracy, and flexibility. The identification enables seamless interoperability during various phases of a fixed asset's life cycle. Figure 3.1 shows an asset management system model with two main workflows: life cycle–based workflow and service-based dataflow.

- *Life cycle–based workflow* addresses inventory management according to the involved operations during an asset's life cycle. Management mainly includes phases such as registration, distribution, disposition, maintenance, upgrading, archiving, recovery, and revocation. Note that the phases may be performed in parallel or sequential modes.
- *Service-based dataflow* considers asset data and interactive data during interoperation, and performs management to provide intelligent decision and support. The related data can

be classified into three types providing different services: raw data, rough data, and refined data. Raw data are persistently acquired by sensors, to provide the primal data source for a back-end management system. The rough data are periodically obtained according to dynamic conditions and behaviors, to provide further data fusion and mining, and to achieve dynamic supervision. The refined data are obtained by performing intelligent management algorithms considering multiple data factors, to support efficient allocation, scheduling, and assistant decisions.

*3.6.1.2 Biometrics Identification*    Biometrics identification belongs to nID-based identification technologies. Typical biometrics identification attributes include fingerprint, hand geometry, palm vein, retina/ iris, face, signature, and voice [28].

- *Fingerprint.* A fingerprint is congenitally formed and progressively grows with age. However, the relationship between the ridges in a fingerprint always remains the same, which can be used for identification.
- *Hand geometry.* Hand geometry is used to measure and compare the hands' physical features, including different shapes of points, lines, and combined shapes, with the feature value location and distribution. Note that hand geometry is gradually changing along with the external environment, and internal physical/health condition, but it is relatively invariable during a certain period.
- *Palm vein.* Palm vein identification applies palm vascular patterns as identification data, which indicate complicated biological information with distinguishable features for personal identification. Such identification applies an infrared beam to penetrate the hand, and the veins within the palm are returned as visualization information. Due to the complexity of internal vein patterns of the palm, it provides high authentication accuracy. The contactless identification consists of image sensing and data processing. The palm vein sensor is used to capture a palm infrared ray image for data analysis.

- *Retina/iris.* A retina scan provides data of the capillary blood vessels located in the back of the eye for identification, by using a low-intensity light to establish a pattern formed by the blood vessels. Although each retina pattern is unique, it has built-in limitations for being affected by disease, such as glaucoma, diabetes, and autoimmune deficiency syndrome. Iris identification refers to the combined technologies, including computer vision, pattern recognition, statistical interference, and optics. An iris scan provides an analysis of the rings, furrows, and freckles in the colored ring that surrounds the pupil. Both retina and iris identification are used to achieve near-instant, highly accurate recognition based on a digitally represented image of the scanned eye, and can be regarded as a lifelong password for an individual's identity.
- *Face.* Face recognition is based on facial characteristics (e.g., size, shape, and facial relationship) according to geometric/feature and photometric/view features. There are several predominant approaches for identification, including principal component analysis, linear discriminant analysis, and elastic bunch graph matching.
- *Signature.* Signature identification refers to handwriting style-based recognition. The offline and online modes are used for signature scanning, character extraction, and character recognition. Therefore, an offline signature is easier to be forged than an online signature. Signature identification is still an open issue due to the nonvision-based technology, in which an individual's handwriting is a dynamic representation.
- *Voice.* Voice analysis focuses on key parameters, including pitch, tone, cadence, and frequency.

*3.6.1.3 E-Passport*  An e-passport can be regarded as an identification application by using both identifier- and attribute-based technologies. Individual identity information and biometric information are contained in e-passports for identification. The ID-based information is stored in a microprocessor chip, and is embedded in the passport's front, center, or back cover. The communication protocol satisfies international standards such as ISO/IEC 14443. The nID-based information mainly includes biometrics identification (e.g., facial, fingerprint, and iris), and the digital format of each biometric feature is also stored. E-passports have the following main functions:

- *Identification.* An e-passport is often embedded with a low-frequency RFID tag (e.g., 13.56 MHz tags) to realize efficient, quick, and accurate identification. Meanwhile, a tag-based e-passport provides identity protection to reduce impersonation risk.
- *Anticounterfeiting.* E-passports store both identity and biometrics information in tag chips, including a unique identifier (or pseudonym), digital imaging, a fingerprint, and facial information. The combination of the biometrics provides enhanced security protection against malicious misuse and tampering.
- *Additional service.* E-passports can be correlated with the individual's other extended functions, such as convenient international payment and credit record information to support international services.

The e-passport brings security and privacy challenges to individual data protection—the main security mechanisms are as follows:

- *Pseudonym.* Pseudonyms are used to hide the real identifiers by being wrapped with pseudorandom numbers. The attackers cannot track the e-passport by the pseudonyms.
- *Authentication* (i.e., mandatory passive authentication and optional active authentication). Passive authentication is performed to prevent content modification to achieve data integrity. The private tag data are protected by the hash function and the corresponding digital signature, in which a signing key is applied to achieve data confidentiality. Additionally, active authentication focuses on the chip cloning attack, in which any private data cannot be physically duplicated.
- *Access control* (i.e., basic access control and extended access control). Access control considers different authorization-related issues. Basic access control is used to realize that a reader can only obtain the authorized data in an e-passport. The extended

access control adds additional functions to perform authentication and authorization on the e-passport and reader.

- *Electromagnetic shielding.* Shielding belongs to an optional physical mechanism to prevent unauthorized data accessing. The main principle is based on the Faraday cage, by which a thin metal mesh is integrated into the passport's cover to form a shield upon closing the passport cover.

### 3.6.2 Information Aggregation

Information aggregation is applied in applications in which multiple sensors collect data for compositive data processing, which assists the management system to perform intelligent decision support.

*3.6.2.1 Smart Home*    Smart home has been established to realize intelligent and convenient human-inhabited environments. In the application, sensors and actuators are distributed around the environment to automatically monitor environmental parameters and launch control actions (e.g., switch on/off lighting), and to proactively adapt to users' demands/expectations. Such a scenario involves information from multiple heterogeneous sensors, and requires high standardization to ensure interoperability. Smart home has received much attention from industry; for instance, Netropolus provides a series of smart home products and solutions [29]. Based on main functional modules in practical scenarios, the following four subsystems jointly establish a tiny smart home to achieve comfortable user experiences, as shown in Figure 3.2.

- *Smart environmental monitoring.* Environmental monitoring mainly considers the factors of temperature, humidity, and lighting to realize user comfort and energy conservation. (1) Users may locally and remotely manage temperature by controlling smart heating and cooling devices by mobile communications and the Internet. (2) Users may be notified in the case that an environmental emergency occurs (e.g., smoke, flood, or fire). (3) Users may be provided an energy-saving heating/cooling proposal to lessen energy wasting. (4) Users can control any light from any switch at home, and can also

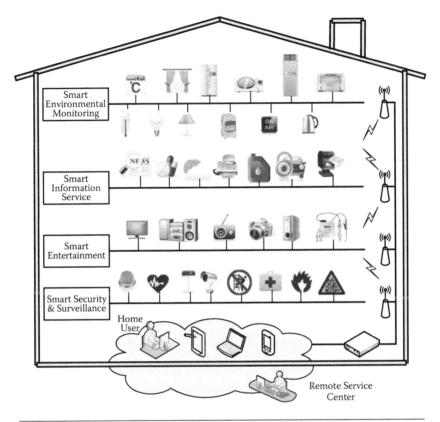

**Figure 3.2** The smart home system model.

remotely control a light via a smart phone or Internet. The lights can automatically adjust their brightness according to the surroundings.

- *Smart information service.* A smart information service aims to provide appropriate recommended information for users. One aspect includes custom-defined information can be subscribed by a user's active behaviors, and will be periodically transmitted to the user. The information covers the weather, newspaper, billing, and subscribe-and-save–related products. Another aspect includes providing information according to dynamic scenes. For example, when a user puts vegetables in the refrigerator, the sensors may detect the detailed nutrient content and provide health knowledge or recipes via the Internet and smart phone. The information service is provided in push mode and pull mode.

- *Smart entertainment.* Smart entertainment establishes an intelligent smart home theater based on smart multimedia, including multiple video and audio (V/A) devices (e.g., flat-screen TV and speakers). V/A systems refer to centralized networks to distribute music and video signals in the home. Users can enjoy multimedia entertainment by optical and coax wiring communications, and control V/A systems by wireless infrared or radio signals. Meanwhile, multimedia content can be loaded locally or remotely downloaded according to users' interests.

- *Smart security and surveillance.* A smart security system mainly uses sensors to detect conditions such as door/window contact, glass break, motion, smoke, and flood. A wireless controller is used for safety monitoring on various sensors and actuators. In the case that an abnormality occurs, a controller will launch the emergency response mechanisms, and notify users with an alarm. A smart surveillance system mainly provides on-site supervision with data acquisition devices (e.g., camera, recorder, and viewer) to assist in remote controlling.

*3.6.2.2 Satellite Remote Sensing System*    A remote sensing system refers to a remote detection technology that is mainly based on aeronautics- and astronautics-related aerial sensors (e.g., unmanned plane and satellite) to detect hydrology, meteorology, geology, and other environmental-related data. Therefore, satellite remote sensing is an important remote sensing technology, and can be applied for remote data acquisition. Different types of aerial sensors (e.g., meteorological satellite, Landsat, and ocean satellite) provide remote sensing by propagated electromagnetic radiation signals.

For satellite remote sensing, optical and infrared remote sensing and microwave remote sensing are the two main technologies. Concretely, the former sensing detects the reflected or scattered solar radiation or its own radiation to obtain thermal infrared images, and the latter sensing uses passive and active microwave sensors to detect scattered microwave energy [30]. Figure 3.3 shows a scenario of a satellite remote sensing system, including data acquisition, information extraction, and service distribution.

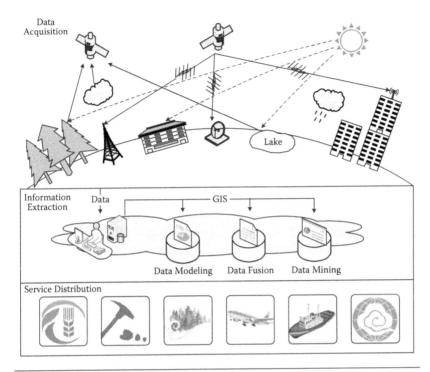

**Figure 3.3** The satellite remote sensing system model.

- *Data acquisition.* Infrared/microwave sensors are used to detect information from the earth, such as meteorology, hydrology, and geology. The sensing process is performed by reflecting visible infrared signals or emitting pulses of microwave radiation to draw an image with a mass of raw data.
- *Information extraction.* The collected data are addressed to realize data-to-information conversion, and information processing is performed referring to the visual and digital image processing. Therefore, the radiomimetic and geometric correction algorithms can be applied for data preprocessing. Additionally, cartography and geographic information systems (GIS) are used jointly for data modeling, fusion, and mining to extract the available information.
- *Service distribution.* The information is further distributed as a service presentation, which is provided to practical applications (e.g., agricultural, mining, forestry aviation, maritime, and meteorological). For instance, geology information serves

mining and agriculture industries, and can be used to explore minerals, monitor land usage, detect deforestation, and examine plants/crops.

### 3.6.3 Safety Awareness

Safety awareness–related applications address safety-related issues in applications, to guarantee system reliability and to provide enhanced safety protection and hazard prevention.

*3.6.3.1 Bird Strike Avoidance Radar System*   Bird strikes pose a threat to aviation safety, and bird strike avoidance is a typical approach to address aviation safety. Bird strikes usually happen during an airplane approaching process, and Figure 3.4a shows an airplane flight process, in which the phases (e.g., pushing back, taxiing, approaching, and landing) in airport terminal areas should be highlighted due to its severe risk of bird strikes. Traditional manual methods of artificial bird observation and driving are increasingly unable to meet the

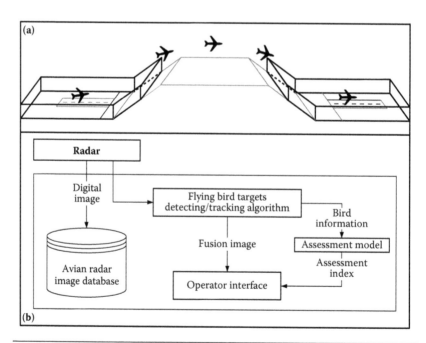

**Figure 3.4**   (a) The flight process with different phases. (b) The bird strike avoidance radar system.

airport requirements. A radar-based avian detection system becomes an important technical means for avian detection, which is unrestricted by factors such as invisibility and bad weather, so it can be operated automatically in all weather. Figure 3.4b shows a model of a bird strike avoidance radar system. The radar data are collected for the design of a flying bird target detecting/tracking algorithm. Thereafter, the extracted bird information is transmitted to the assessment model, and then a fusion image and assessment index are transmitted to the operator interface for further data processing.

In bird strike avoidance applications, flying bird target detecting and tracking are the core techniques in the avian radar system. The original radar image is processed by the target detecting and information extraction algorithm. The tracking scheme is selected by the group confirmation step, and the flying bird trajectory that is extracted from complex radar images is overlapped onto a satellite map, generating a fused image that improves the observation. Therefore, the target detecting and information extraction step (i.e., background subtraction, clutter suppression, and measurement information extraction) separates flying bird location information from original images. In order to improve the detection rate, a lower threshold is generally set in clutter suppression, introducing dozens of false alarms. Excellent tracking and detection algorithms can eliminate false alarms while tracking dim targets. The purpose is to track an unknown number of targets at the same time, making the system track targets with high safety protection in cluttered environments.

*3.6.3.2 River Navigation Safety System*   River navigation mainly refers to ship transport in rivers, lakes, and inland canals. Its purpose is to mainly ensure the safeguard of people, goods, and ships from the departing port to the arriving destination. In river navigation application, multiple sensing and networking technologies are introduced to monitor and keep track of ship status, movements, and to provide real-time secure navigation solutions. Due to the limitations of on-water and underwater environments, electromagnetic signals have exponential attenuation, which causes adverse conditions for water traffic safety. Therefore, the available underwater wireless sensing technologies mainly include GPS, laser radar, and sonar radar. Other sensing technologies such as RFID can also be used for data collection

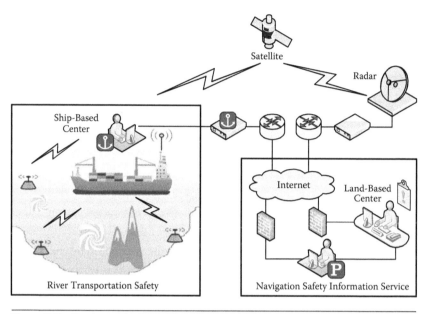

**Figure 3.5**   The river navigation safety system model.

aboard or onshore. The core function of marine traffic safety is to detect and alleviate navigational risk, achieve reliable ship operation, and provide integrated safety traffic service. Figure 3.5 shows the model of the marine traffic safety system, which mainly includes the following safety aspects:

- *River transportation safety.* Transportation safety addresses ship-related safety issues. During maritime transportation, a smart float rod can be used as a detection device to track the monitoring data, such as a river structure, submerged reef, dangerous shoal, and undercurrent. The main safety aspects include ship navigation and operation, dangerous/nondangerous goods freightage, and major traffic accident emergency response.
- *Navigation safety information service.* The navigation safety information service guarantees the safety of navigation. The safety aspects contain real-time safety satiation, a search-and-rescue service for people and ships in distress, wreck/sinker salvage information, and a ship towing service. The navigation safety information service is performed based on wireless detection devices (e.g., underwater radar and GPS) to

realize hydrologic detection and underwater positioning. The collected data support extracting the navigation information, which is exchanged between the back-end land-based and ship-based management and control centers to achieve safety information interaction.

### 3.6.4 Monitoring and Control

Monitoring- and control-related applications are mainly based on sensing technologies to detect and record an object's information of behavior, status, and performance to provide information and services.

*3.6.4.1 Precision Manufacturing System*   Precision manufacturing refers to industrial product manufacturing (e.g., linear and coordinate machine) with high-precision requirements. Traditional precision manufacturing is mainly based on mechanical equipment for product quality monitoring, which has limitations of information services or online support. In IoT, interconnections can be established between product line terminals and the back-end information system. A precision manufacturing system model mainly includes three functional modules referring to multiplex data collection, smart automatic monitoring and control, and remote expert support service.

- *Multiplex data collection.* Multiplex data collection is performed by heterogeneous sensors, and the collected data include product line processing (e.g., procedure and linkage), production equipment conditions, workplace environments (e.g., temperature, humidity, and noise), and other physical information. Sensors either have built-in actuators to directly perform operations or connect to external actuators to execute a response. The sensed data by different sensors may interact with each other, and standard data interaction protocols should be designed to be suitable for heterogeneous network interfaces.
- *Smart automatic monitoring and control.* The monitoring and control are performed by sensors and actuators. Advanced alarm processing and multiple notification mechanisms are applied to alert to abnormal and malicious conditions. In the

case where sensors detect an abnormality and transmit the information to the actuators, automatic and interactive error detection and correction mechanisms are launched to achieve error recovery.

- *Remote service support.* Service support is regarded as a remote intelligent decision support function provided by artificial intelligence systems, including engineering design, production planning, resource scheduling, organization arrangement, market forecasting, user experience feedback, and other intelligent functions. It applies wired or wireless networking technologies to achieve control and configure and monitor different system components. The aggregated service information is published for transparent accessing, and customizable production reports and services are transmitted back to production manufacturing.

### 3.7 Conclusion

Unit IoT involves multiple sensing, controlling, networking, and communication technologies to realize interconnections among sensors, actuators, and M&DC. Accordingly, ubiquitous sensing, networking and communications, and information management are introduced, and several typical application scenarios are presented to describe unit IoT.

# References

1. Chui, M., M. Löffler, and R. Roberts. 2010. The Internet of Things. *McKinsey Quarterly.* http://www.mckinsey.com/insights/mgi/research/technology_and_innovation/the_internet_of_things (accessed May 10, 2012).
2. Miorandi, D., S. Sicari, F. D. Pellegrini, and I. Chlamtac. 2012. Internet of Things: Vision, applications and research challenges. *Ad Hoc Networks* 10: 1497–1516.
3. Xia, F., Y. C. Tian, Y. Li, and Y. Sung. 2007. Wireless sensor/actuator network design for mobile control applications. *Sensors* 7: 2157–2173.
4. Cluster of European Research Projects on the Internet of Things, CERP-IoT. 2009. *Internet of Things: Strategic research roadmap.*
5. National Institute of Standards and Technology. 2007. *Guidelines for securing radio frequency identification (RFID) systems.* NIST Special Publication 800–98.

6. The NFC Forum: About NFC. http://www.nfc-forum.org/aboutnfc/ (accessed May 10, 2012).

7. Haartsen, J. C., and S. Mattisson. 2000. Bluetooth—A new low-power radio interface providing short-range connectivity. *Proceedings of the IEEE* 88: 1651–1661.

8. McDermott-Wells, P. 2005. What is Bluetooth? *IEEE Potentials* 23: 33–35.

9. Liu, Y., S. Li, and L. Cao. 2009. Application of Bluetooth communication in digital photo frame. *International Colloquium on Computing, Communication, Control, and Management* 370–373.

10. Zin, M. S. I. M., and M. Hope. 2010. A review of UWB MAC protocols. In *2010 6th Advanced International Conference on Telecommunications*, 526–534.

11. Intel: Ultra-wideband (UWB technology)—Enabling high-speed wireless personal area networks. http://www.intel.com/technology/comms/uwb/download/ultra-wideband.pdf (accessed May 10, 2012).

12. Young, M. K. 2003. Ultra wide band (UWB) technology and applications. http://www.comlab.hut.fi/opetus/333/2004_2005_slides/UWB.pdf (accessed May 10, 2012).

13. Peng, R., M. Sun, and Y. Zou. 2006. ZigBee routing selection strategy based on data services and energy-balanced ZigBee routing. In *IEEE Asia-Pacific Conference on Services Computing*, 400–404.

14. Zhang, Y., R. Yu, S. Xie, W. Yao, Y. Xiao, and M. Guizani. 2011. Home M2M networks: Architectures, standards, and QoS improvement. *IEEE Communications Magazine* 49: 44–52.

15. Vitsas, V., P. Barker, and A. C. Boucouvalas. 2003. IrDA infrared wireless communications: Protocol throughput optimization. *IEEE Wireless Communications* 10: 22–29.

16. Welcome to 4th Generation Open Mobile Initiative—The World's No.1 Events on 4G Technology Movement: About Global 4G Open Mobile Initiative. http://4gmobile.com/ (accessed May 10, 2012).

17. Future revolution. http://www.christiealwis.com/our_fut_myst/Future Revolution.pdf.

18. Bandyopadhyay, D., and J. Sen. 2011. Internet of Things: Applications and challenges in technology and standardization. *Wireless Personal Communications* 58: 49–69.

19. Domingo, M. C. 2012. An overview of the Internet of Things for people with disabilities. *Journal of Network and Computer Applications* 35: 584–596.

20. Miao, W., T. J. Lu, F. Y. Ling, J. Sun, and H. Y. Du. 2010. Research on the architecture of Internet of Things. In *2010 3rd International Conference on Advanced Computer Theory and Engineering*, 5: 484–487.

21. Gama, K., L. Touseau, and D. Donsez. 2012. Combining heterogeneous service technologies for building an Internet of Things middleware. *Computer Communications* 35: 405–417.

22. Qin, X., and Y. Gu. 2011. Data fusion in the Internet of Things, *Procedia Engineering* 15: 3023–3026.

23. Dong, X. L., and F. Naumann. 2009. Data fusion: Resolving data conflicts for integration. *Very Large Data Base (VLDB) Endowment* 2: 1654–1655.

24. Shen, B., Y. Liu, and X. Wang. 2010. Research on data mining models for the Internet of Things. In *2010 International Conference on Image Analysis and Signal Processing*, 127–132.

25. Chen, Y., M. Yang, and L. Zhang. 2009. General data mining model system based on sample data division. In *Second International Symposium on Knowledge Acquisition and Modeling*, 1.2: 182–185.

26. Huang, F., Z. Li, and X. Sun. 2008. A data mining model in knowledge grid. In *4th International Conference on Wireless Communications, Networking and Mobile Computing*, 1–4.

27. Libelium. 50 sensor applications for a smarter world. http://www.libelium.com/top_50_iot_sensor_applications_ranking/ (accessed May 10, 2012).

28. Biometric identification systems. http://www.technovelgy.com/ct/Technology-Article.asp?ArtNum=12 (accessed May 10, 2012).

29. Netropolus. Smart home online store & DIY solutions center. http://www.netropolus.com/.

30. CRISP. What is remote sensing? http://www.crisp.nus.edu.sg/~research/tutorial/intro.htm.

# 4

# UBIQUITOUS INTERNET OF THINGS

## 4.1 Introduction

Ubiquitous Internet of Things (ubiquitous IoT) is the collection of multiple unit IoTs. As an essential paradigm of future IoT with the meanings of network of services, network of networks, and even network of everything, ubiquitous IoT embodies the social attributes of future IoT [1]. Ubiquitous IoT makes it possible for the interaction and cooperation of multiple unit IoTs as well as pervasive management, access, and control of unit IoT resources. According to the architecture of ubiquitous IoT, which was described in Chapter 2 (as shown in Figure 4.1), local IoT, industrial IoT, national IoT, and global application IoT are introduced as typical kinds of ubiquitous IoT. Therefore, local IoT is the integration of multiple unit IoTs within a particular region under the management of a local management and data center (lM&DC). Similarly, industrial IoT is the integration of multiple unit IoTs that belong to a particular industry under the management of an industrial management and data center (iM&DC). Moreover, national IoT refers to all kinds of IoTs within a nation, and national management and data center (nM&DC) acts as the manager of national IoT. It is noteworthy that management politics and regulations play important roles in national IoT. Global application IoT is a specific IoT with a global scale. As a special kind of ubiquitous IoT, transnational IoT involves IoTs from multinations with some special services.

In the following, these typical ubiquitous IoTs are introduced separately. Local IoT and a case are presented in Section 4.2. Industrial IoT together with the corresponding cases are discussed in Section 4.3. Section 4.4 introduces national IoT from the aspects of concept, development plan, and management schemes. Transnational and

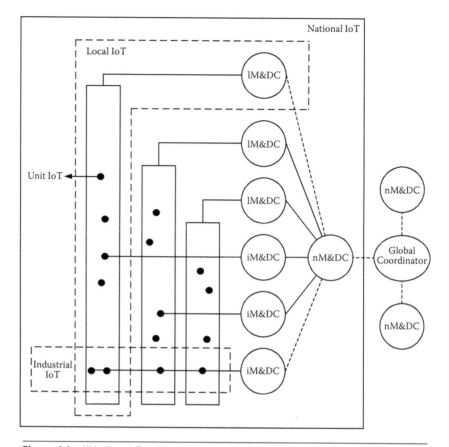

**Figure 4.1**  Ubiquitous IoT architecture.

global application IoT as well as typical cases are described in Sections 4.5 and 4.6. Finally, Section 4.7 draws a conclusion.

## 4.2  Local Internet of Things

### 4.2.1  Local IoT Concept

Local IoT is composed of lM&DC and the covered unit IoTs in the region. The unit IoTs within the range of local IoT provide the unit services for local IoT. As the head of local IoT, lM&DC acts as the management platform of local IoT and integrates unit IoTs' services to provide higher-level service.

Apart from the unit IoTs and lM&DC in a local IoT, the intra-/intersocial relationship among unit IoTs is also important. Local IoT is a regional-based relationship that holds the unit IoTs together.

Generally, regional-based relationships in local IoT can be classified into direct relationships and indirect relationships. Direct relationships are built when a unit IoT directly interacts with the other ones. Indirect relationships refer to the relationships that are built in the process of indirect interaction among unit IoTs. For example, an indirect relationship between two unit IoTs is built when both of them want to serve the same customer. Several typical kinds of direct and indirect relationships among unit IoTs in local IoT are introduced as follows.

- Some direct relationships:
  1. *Affiliation relationship.* Affiliation relationship indicates that one or more unit IoTs are only owned and controlled by another unit IoT. This kind of relationship is common in a dedicated situation where a unit IoT is designed only for accomplishing a special task.
  2. *Function calling.* Function calling means that one unit IoT provides services (e.g., command execution, status capturing, environment sensing, etc.) to multiple other unit IoTs. The difference between affiliation and function calling is that affiliation is a one-to-one relationship, while function calling is a one-to-many relationship, which denotes that a unit IoT can be called by more than one other unit IoT.
  3. *Data interchanging.* Data interchanging represents relationships that are built on the process of data exchanging in a peer-to-peer (P2P) mode between two unit IoTs.

- Some indirect relationships:
  1. *Coverage complementation.* Coverage complementation indicates that multiple unit IoTs with different coverage areas cooperate with each other to form a local IoT with larger coverage. Due to some reasons (e.g., the limitation of unit IoT coverage, operating cost, and industry pattern), coverage complementation is general in monitoring applications such as air quality monitoring, traffic monitoring, and battlefield surveillance.
  2. *Function complementation.* Since unit IoT is restricted by computing capability, communicating bandwidth, system complexity, energy supply, and other factors, it is better to adopt cooperation of multiple unit IoTs rather than

implementing all the functions into a single unit IoT in some cases.

3. *Service competition.* In local IoT, there may be several competitors (i.e., unit IoTs or a group of unit IoTs) that have the ability to provide the same service. In this situation, the relationship among these unit IoTs is service competition. Just like the competition in other fields (e.g., business environment), the competition among unit IoTs contributes to service improvement.

4. *Resource competition.* Competition exists in resources, such as energy, computing infrastructure, and communicating channel, which are needed by unit IoTs. A resource management strategy should be designed to supervise the resource competition, and to improve energy efficiency, system performance, and system robustness.

Due to the dynamic services and complex relationships in local IoT, appropriate management infrastructure and methods are needed to achieve optimized performance.

### 4.2.2 Main Characteristics of Local IoT

Based on the above discussion on local IoT, this section provides an insight into the main characteristics of local IoT as follows:

- *Diversity* denotes that one local IoT is generally different from the local IoTs located in other regions. Diversity is caused by many factors, such as geographical features (e.g., landscape and climate), cultural characteristics, economic characteristics, policy support, or some demands. Local IoT diversity is reflected in various aspects such as scale, function, and structure. The effect that diversity brings to local IoT is two-sided. On the one hand, local IoT diversity makes it possible to integrate regional characteristics into the implementation of local IoT and leads to better performance. On the other hand, as the planning and establishment of a local IoT are generally based on the local conditions and particular demands, the development mode is difficult to duplicate among different regions.

- *Regional fusion effect* refers to the covered unit IoTs being deeply fused by some core values to provide better services. For example, in a future smart city, the sustainable development concept will fusion the unit IoTs in the city to promote energy efficiency. The unit IoTs will cooperate as much as possible to provide optimized solutions to citizens. The regional fusion effect is the basis for achieving intelligent local IoT. Here, intelligent local IoT includes two aspects: (1) local IoT should obtain the ability to monitor and react to situations rationally, and (2) local IoT should be able to predict future trends and make early preparations for upcoming events in it. Intelligent local IoT cannot be accomplished without information sharing and mutual cooperation among unit IoTs, which are the preconditions of regional fusion.

In the following, two local IoT cases, smart city and the logistics network of Pearl River Delta (PRD), are discussed to illustrate local IoT.

### 4.2.3 Case Study: Smart City

With the development of urbanization around the world, the scale and population of urban cities have been a magnificent miracle in human history during a fast and increasing period. Currently, a large number of people live in urban cities, and this amount is climbing at a high speed [2]. The fast growth of city populations and scales has made cities overloaded, and has done great damage to the environment, making it uncomfortable to live in urban cities. Fortunately, the wide adoption of information and communication technology (ICT) has brought new solutions to these problems. More exciting, IoT is promising to bring attractive changes to current city status, making cities greener and better. Smart city focuses on the utilization of IoT technologies such as ubiquitous sensing, communication, and computing to realize the mapping between the cyber world and physical world (as shown in Figure 4.2). In the physical world, things are constrained by time and space, causing the limitation of functions/services. However, in the cyber world, many limitations can be overcome and services/functions with much better user experience can be implemented. The main purpose of

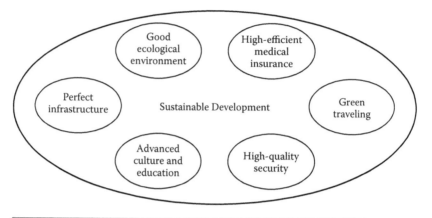

**Figure 4.2**   The conceptual diagram and function requirements in a smart city.

the smart city is to reduce city costs and improve efficiencies and quality of life by considering sustainable and environment-friendly development.

Smart city is a complex system that can be modeled as a system of services. The implementation of smart city is determined by the citizens' function requirements. Figure 4.2 shows a human-oriented services model of smart city, in which sustainable development is the foundation for smart city. Based on this, human-oriented function requirements, including a good ecological environment, robust infrastructure, high-efficiency medical insurance, green and low-carbon traveling, advanced culture and education, and a high-quality security system, should be satisfied in smart city. The function requirements and themes of the future smart city may vary prominently in different regions due to the regional diversity of local IoT.

Due to the bright future of smart city, many smart city projects have been launched to bring it into reality. Lee et al. [3] proposed an integrated service management platform for a ubiquitous city (ISMP-UC) that is equivalent to a smart city to overcome the limitations of stovepipe systems and enable synergistic service collaboration. The ISMP-UC has three aspects. The first aspect includes sensors, actuators, and other devices. The second aspect is service-oriented middleware in which context information data are stored and processed for service integration. The third aspect includes the services.

Based on the regional characteristics of smart city, it makes sense to model smart city as a local IoT that consists of lM&DC and multiple unit IoTs within the city. Unit IoTs in local IoT provide the services that satisfy the requirements of the smart city (e.g., intelligent transportation, energy management, and air quality monitoring). lM&DC manages unit IoTs within the city and provides interfaces for external IoTs.

### 4.2.4 Case Study: Logistics Network of China Pearl River Delta (PRD)

PRD refers to the region including Guangdong, Hong Kong, Macao, and the surrounding areas. As an important economic region in China, the strategy of the PRD is to explore a rational development model and build an advanced manufacturing and economic center in South China.

The strategy position and economic model of PRD have endowed the logistics in this region with the characteristics of high transportation capacity and trade frequency, which in turn cause great pressure on the logistics components (e.g., shipments, airlines, railway transportation, and warehouses). New logistics solutions are demanded for PRD development, and they should be capable of promoting logistics throughput and meeting other requirements, such as high efficiency and low-carbon emission. Many IoT projects have been launched to build efficient and robust logistics systems. In the future, the adoption of IoT technologies in the PRD transportation and logistics system will be promising to address the above challenges through systematic, real-time, and sea-land-air–based transportation networks.

## 4.3 Industrial Internet of Things

### 4.3.1 Industrial IoT Concept

Industrial IoT includes the unit IoTs that belong to a specific industry (e.g., logistic, agriculture, and smart grid), as well as management platforms to manage them (i.e., iM&DC). Unit IoTs also provide unit services. The industrial M&DC (iM&DC) is responsible for the management and integration of the involved unit IoTs and other functions, such as policy making, event monitoring, and security protecting. The function requirements and system components of industrial

IoT are based on the characteristics of the industry, which are significant factors for the development of industrial IoT.

### 4.3.2 Main Characteristics of Industrial IoT

Based on the above discussion on the industrial IoT concept and structure, in this section, the key characteristics of industrial IoT are discussed from two aspects.

#### 4.3.2.1 Geographical Dispersion
Different from local IoT, industrial IoT shows a strong geographic dispersion characteristic. The main reasons are as follows. For an industry, its functions are radiated to different areas. For example, in the manufacturing industry, two vital measures to achieve high profit are reducing cost and improving efficiency in each industrial link. The key approach to achieve low cost and high efficiency is making full use of the geographically dispersed resources (e.g., raw materials, labor resources, and information technologies). In addition, the market distribution may also disperse throughout the nation and even all over the world. Due to the integration of IoT and industry, industrial IoT definitely inherits such characteristics from the industry.

#### 4.3.2.2 Multiuser Orientation
Multiuser orientation denotes that industrial IoT has diverse orientations according to different users. For example, on the one hand, food industrial IoT tends to provide services that can lead to the promotion of productivity and efficiency for this industry. On the other hand, it is also responsible for providing security and qualified services to customers. A further discussion on the multioriented characteristics of industrial IoT is given from the government, industry, and customer perspectives.

- *Government orientation.* For government, the information used to make national industrial decisions and plans can be collected by industrial IoT. The government's policy and support are important for industry development, especially in an international trade environment. Currently, some national regulation and control policies from the government lag behind the industrial developing trends. Moreover, the response time and regulation efficiency are criteria are used to evaluate the government's performance. Industrial IoT endows the government with the capability to analyze information and make an optimized management strategy and plan. It is noteworthy that industrial IoT is able to strengthen the government's industrial emergency response capability due to its real-time monitoring and intelligence. Industrial IoT can also help governments revise local industrial policies.

- *Self-orientation.* It is obvious that industrial IoT can bring many advantages to the industry's operation and management, such as promoting production efficiency, reducing production cost, optimizing resource utilization, and standardizing production and management. For example, in the agriculture industry, great product promotion and cost reduction can be achieved by applying IoT technologies to a greenhouse environmental monitoring and controlling system.

- *Customer orientation.* Industrial IoT can provide diverse services for various customers. First, industrial IoT can provide high-quality services and promote the customer experience. For example, in pharmaceutical industrial IoT, radio frequency identification (RFID)-based commodity anticounterfeiting has been applied successfully to protect customers from counterfeit medications. Second, industrial IoT can provide an efficient platform for the user to supervise products on the market. For example, in the food industry, food safety is extremely vital to customers. However, extensive unsafe factors exist and have caused severe health and social problems. With food industrial IoT, these problems can be solved or at least mitigated. The customer-oriented functions of industrial IoT also include customization for products and sales services, and are not limited within the above range.

The main characteristics of industrial IoT have been discussed above. In order to obtain a specific view of industrial IoT, a further discussion about industrial IoT is given through an example: a smart grid.

### 4.3.3  An Example: A Smart Grid

A smart grid applies IoT technologies and other innovative technologies such as distributed generation into a traditional power grid. It can realize the optimized scheduling of electric power through bidirectional information and electric networks. The functions and scales of a smart grid depend on the specific situation in the nation. For example, in China, due to the vast territorial area, the smart grid is on great scale and complexity. Meanwhile, due to the unbalanced distribution of energy sources and energy demand (the distribution of energy sources is mainly scattered across the southwest, northwest, and north regions of China; however, the energy consumers are concentrated in eastern and southeastern China), the smart grid in China aims to increase the proportion of renewable energy access, improve transmission efficiency, reduce energy consumption, and maintain a good balance of energy demand and supply.

Due to common problems (e.g., resource depletion and environmental pollution), more and more renewable energy sources (e.g., wind and solar) need to be connected into the power grid. Another obvious trend of the smart grid is the adoption of smart meters that can be used to achieve optimized energy efficiency through real-time grid-user interaction.

A smart grid is an industrial IoT that aims at providing reliable and green energy flow to the customers. It is composed of multiple unit IoTs in different links from electricity generation to utilization with various functions (e.g., generation controlling, load sensing, transmission parameter monitoring, marketing, etc.). The iM&DC monitors and manages all the covered unit IoTs and provides interfaces to other external IoTs.

## 4.4  National Internet of Things

### 4.4.1  National IoT Concept

To achieve the ubiquitous characteristics of future IoT, local IoT and industrial IoT should be further integrated and extended to support more comprehensive applications. A larger scale of IoT is needed to realize more powerful services, including nationwide access and management of services. National IoT is the collection of unit IoTs in a specific nation, and provides the corresponding management/regulation/strategy mechanisms. nM&DC is the head of national IoT. It manages the corresponding nationwide unit IoTs, and controls iM&DC and lM&DC in the nation. The nM&DC also supports other functions, such as multinational cooperation, data backup, arbitration, and macroeconomic regulation and control. In a word, nM&DC's main functions are to manage local and industrial IoTs' operation and development, and to manage transnational cooperation among IoTs.

### 4.4.2 *National Development Planning*

National policies and strategies are the key factors influencing IoT development, which generally needs the cooperation of government, industry, and other nations. For national IoT development planning, some aspects should be considered by the national IoT management authorities to propel the construction of national IoT:

- Strategy and planning
- Policy support
- Financial support
- Project and technologies support
- Public service platform construction
- Industry chain and ecological environmental construction
- Standards construction
- International cooperation promotion

The development model of national IoT includes different patterns according to the national IoT development strategy plan. For example, national IoT may be designed in a systematic view. It is important to perform comprehensive studies (e.g., architecture, basic theory, and key technologies), and to guarantee the rationality and scalability of national IoT. This means that this systematic view aims to create mature prerequisites for national IoT. Additionally, national IoT can also be designed in a demand-oriented pattern, in which national IoT is led by the practical application demands. For this pattern, IoT development is closely related to specific applications such as smart grid, intelligent medical, smart home, and environmental monitoring. It is hard to determine which development pattern is better, and national IoT should be designed according to the practical situations. In terms of the current status, the latter development pattern is more realistic, as IoT development is driven by demands, and many key issues in IoT will be addressed by practice in the process of IoT exploration.

### 4.4.3 Management of National IoT

The management of national IoT focuses on the management of all the IoTs within the nation. Generally, the scales of national IoT may be different according to the nation's territory area, national development level, and other factors. For example, in nations such as the United States and China, it is not easy to manage national IoT due to the vast territorial area and complexity of national industrial structures. In national IoT, there are two topology-based management schemes:

- *Region-based management scheme.* In this scheme, unit IoTs distributed around the nation are incorporated into local IoTs, which are established based on geographical features. Unit IoTs located in an area are managed by one lM&DC, and the lM&DCs across the nation are under the management of nM&DC. For a regional-based management scheme, the rational partition plan for the local IoTs is important to achieve high management efficiency.
- *Industry-based management scheme.* In this scheme, unit IoTs are managed based on vertical industries in the nation. For example, all the aviation-related IoTs are managed by the aviation iM&DC. The aviation iM&DCs and other iM&DCs are managed by nM&DC.

Due to the high complexity of national IoT management, nM&DC should be armed with high-level intelligence, powerful computing capability, huge storage space, and strong communication ability. In addition to technological support, regulations and laws are also crucial in national IoT management.

## 4.5 Transnational Internet of Things Application

### 4.5.1 Description

With the development of transnational cooperation and commercial trade among multiple nations, transnational IoT is introduced to realize the cooperation of IoTs from different nations. Transnational IoT is efficient for solving international issues. For example, in the cross-border water quality monitoring application, transnational IoT is established by mutual cooperation among different nations to complete the monitoring task. In the following, a case study on the transnational logistics IoT in the Association of Southeast Asia Nations and China Free Trade Area (ACFTA) is discussed to introduce transnational IoT.

### 4.5.2 An Example: Transnational Logistics IoT in ACFTA

The China-ASEAN Free Trade Area (CAFTA), also known as ASEAN-China Free Trade Area (ACFTA), is a free trade area among China and includes the 10 members of the Association of Southeast Asian Nations (ASEAN). The initial framework agreement was signed in 2002 in Cambodia, with the intent of establishing a free trade area among the 11 nations by 2010. CAFTA is the largest free trade area in terms of population, which is about 1.9 billion, and the third largest in terms of nominal GDP. Thanks to policy support from China and ASEAN member nations, the trade cooperation and investment in this area have developed at a fast rate in recent years.

However, there are some difficulties for development, such as the low efficiency of traditional logistics and transportation systems. A transnational logistics IoT with different languages is promising to break the bottleneck and promote the overall development level. The main significant aspects of the transnational logistics IoT in this area are as follows:

- *Overcome the linguistic obstacles.* CAFTA covers 11 nations, which leads to many different languages (i.e., Chinese, Thai, Malay, English, France, Indonesian, Laotian, Burmese, Filipino, and Vietnamese) used in this trade area. The language barrier is one of the most important obstacles for further trade development. It can be solved by the automatic language conversion services provided by transnational logistics IoT.

- *Provide supply chain management and efficient logistics.* With the development of transnational trade, supply chain management brings challenges to traditional logistics. A typical challenge is the promotion of services quality and efficiency. Transnational logistics IoT is promising to address the above challenge through real-time and ubiquitous monitoring and intelligent decision support.
- *Provide a reference for governments.* Transnational logistics IoT can provide a platform for governments to obtain trade information and serve as a reference for governments to develop policy and strategy this area.

Transnational logistics IoT can also promote the development of CAFTA from other aspects, such as providing multibilling and electronic payments, and so forth.

## 4.6 Global Application IoT and a Typical Example

### 4.6.1 Description

Along with the intensification of globalization, the world turns into a global village, and some global application IoTs appear to provide global services or solve some worldwide issues (e.g., environmental protection, ocean protection, and energy crisis). Global application IoT is composed of the IoTs that are needed to accomplish a specific task across the world and the global coordinator, whose responsibility is coordinating the different participants around the globe. Global application IoT will benefit optimized resources allocation in the global range. In the following, global logistics IoT is discussed as an example.

### 4.6.2 Case Study: Global Logistics IoT

The main function of global logistics include multiple aspects, such as security transportation, warehousing, inventory, and management of freight from the source to the destination in the global range.

A significant revolution in global logistics is the adoption of information technology to promote efficiency and reduce costs, such as electronic data interchange (EDI) and computer-based freight management. In recent years, IoT-related technologies, such as ubiquitous sensing (e.g., RFID and global positioning system), ubiquitous and high-bandwidth communicating, and intelligent information processing, have brought a huge upgrade in performance and efficiency to global logistics.

Due to the investment cost and economic gap in different nations, global logistics confronts great challenges, including the following aspects:

- Basic infrastructure is insufficient
- Growing problem of unbalanced container scheduling
- Low efficiency in global logistics chain
- Lag behind the development of new technology

A low-cost and green global logistics IoT can help to overcome the above challenges, but it requires cooperation from different nations. The schematic of global logistics IoT can be regarded in three hierarchies: global infrastructure and sensing, an air-space-ground–based network, and multiple transportation platforms, which are shown in Figures 4.3 to 4.5, respectively.

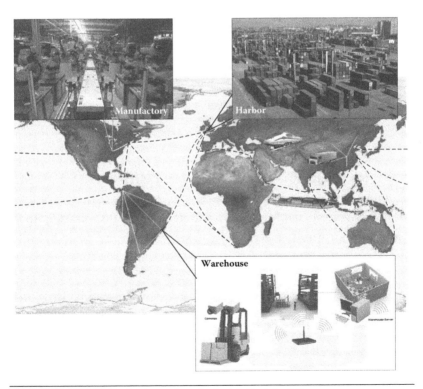

**Figure 4.3**  Ground infrastructure and sensing in global logistics IoT.

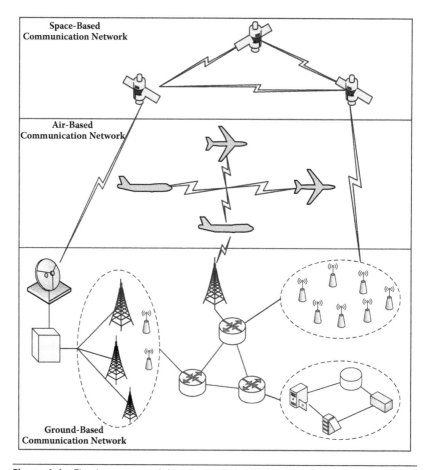

**Figure 4.4** The air-space-ground–based networks in global logistics IoT.

The first hierarchy (Figure 4.3) is ground infrastructure and sensing, including all the infrastructures (e.g., seaports, airports, railway stations, highway facilities, and warehouses), transportation tools (e.g., ships, airplanes, trains, and trucks), and sensing devices (GPS, RFID, and other sensors).

The second hierarchy consists of the air-space-ground–based networks that cover the global range (Figure 4.4). Global logistics IoT is based on communication networks that cover every corner of the globe. Air-space-ground–based networks are integrated by space-based (i.e., satellite), air-based (i.e., airplane), and ground-based (i.e., Internet) communication networks. The selection of different

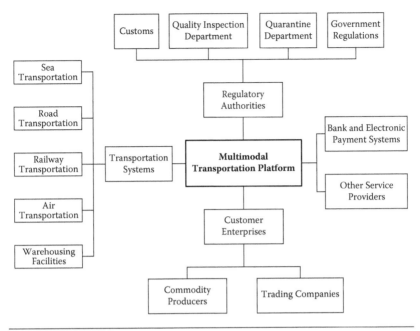

**Figure 4.5** Multimodal transportation platform in global logistics IoT.

kinds of networks can be decided by specific application scenarios and cost.

The third hierarchy refers to the global logistics application with the function to build multimodal transportation platforms. There are several key aspects involved in global logistics multimodel transportation platforms (Figure 4.5): transportation systems (air-based transportation, sea-based transportation, and road/railway-based transportation systems), customer enterprises, regulatory authorities (customs, quality inspection departments, quarantine departments, and other government regulation departments), and other functions, such as bank and payment systems.

The multimodal transportation platform includes road, railway, air transport, and ocean shipping across the world to form a uniform global transportation network. Moreover, other related organizations (e.g., warehouses, agents, enterprises, customs, and inspection/quarantine departments) also participate in global logistics IoT to share information services. The global logistics IoT coordinator manages the coordination among the different participants.

Some core services in global logistics IoT listed as follows, can be used to solve the four challenges that global logistics confronts:

- *Global logistics infrastructure layout and planning decision support* are the services provided to help global logistics infrastructure design and establishment, for example, road, railway, airport, port, warehouse, and information system construction. They can promote the effectiveness of the logistics infrastructure as well as reduce the investment.
- *Global transportation management* is the service of managing the transportation process of freight to realize green, low-cost, and efficient targets (e.g., short delivery time, low transportation cost, low carbon emissions, empty rate, etc.).
- *Intelligent supply chain management* plays an increasingly important role in the process of economic and production globalization, and it penetrates into every link of the commodity life cycle, from material purchasing, intermediate product producing, and product assembling to commodity dispatching for global trade.

### 4.7 Conclusion and Discussion

Ubiquitous IoTs, including local IoT, industrial IoT, national IoT, transnational IoT, and global application IoT, have been described, along with some typical cases. As can be seen from this chapter, the concept of global IoT is not mentioned. The book argues that, similar to the current human society organization, in which a global nation is difficult to form, a unified global IoT will not emerge. Instead, global organizations (or international organizations) responsible for the promotion of interaction and interconnection among multiple nations will appear. This paradigm reflects IoT social attributes and satisfies the requirements of information security for different nations. We can think about the issue from another aspect: though the physical world on the earth is integral, the existence of different nations is independent, and in addition, different regions and industries within a nation are also mutually separated; and though the global communication networks are basically interconnected, when mapping things from the physical world to the cyber world, the social attributes that objectively exist in the physical world (e.g., national attributes, industrial attributes, and regional attributes) will also be reflected in the cyber world.

# References

1. Ning, H., and Z. Wang. 2011. Future Internet of Things architecture: Like mankind neural system or social organization framework? *IEEE Communication Letters* 15: 461–463.
2. Naphade, M., G. Banavar, C. Harrison, J. Paraszczak, and R. Morris. 2011. Smarter cities and their innovation challenges. *Computer* 44: 32–39.
3. Lee, J., S. Baik, and C.C. Lee. 2011. Building an integrated service management platform for ubiquitous cities. *Computer* 44: 56–63.

# 5

# RESOURCE MANAGEMENT

## 5.1 Introduction

Internet of Things (IoT) aims to realize the interconnections among ubiquitous things with the considerations of cyber, physical, and social aspects. In order to address such interconnections in heterogeneous networks, resource management becomes an essential issue.

In the Internet, traditional resources may exist as physical resources and cyber resources, which mainly refer to physical and cyber components of limited availability in computer systems, and can be accessed to support different applications. To a certain degree, external physical components (e.g., devices and equipment) connected to a computer system belong to physical resources, and internal cyber components (e.g., file data, network connections, computing capabilities, and memory storage) belong to cyber resources. In the Internet, cyber resources are essential components during network connections and data interactions; and physical resources are supplementary components to provide necessary hardware support.

In IoT, ubiquitous things are connected into networks, and it turns out that resources have more generalized aspects. In addition to the traditional resources, more physical things also belong to the physical resources, such as sensors, actuators, advanced metering infrastructure (AMI), and locators. Such physical objects and the attached abstract components are involved in IoT to ensure interactive ubiquitous resource cross-sharing and cross-utilization.

Things include not only physical things (e.g., object, behavior, tendency, and physical event), but also cyber things (e.g., entity, cyber action, cyber event, and service). In IoT, things refer to both physical and cyber resources, and resources cover both physical things and cyber things. Accordingly, things and resources can be regarded as almost equivalent in IoT.

Generally, resources have two basic features: existence and availability. The former means that resources can exist or be created, such as information/service-related software infrastructures or supporting hardware infrastructures. The latter refers to resources that may be used by one or more users in an application. Resources may have the following additional features:

- *Authority.* Resources are assigned different access authorities, and may be used, shared, and transferred by authorized users via intranetworks and internetworks. Therefore, a distributed and hierarchical management mode can provide diverse resource utilization.
- *Functionality.* Resources should support particular functions by performing a single or multiple tasks [1]. For example, in radio frequency identification (RFID) systems, a tag is assigned or associated with sensitive information, and such information is regarded as a resource for further network access and data inquiry. During wireless sensing, communication channels are resources for distributed autonomous sensors to support data transmission.
- *Shareability.* Resources can be interoperated by different entities and applications to achieve enhanced resource sharing and utilization in the context of large distributed networks. For instance, in cloud computing and grid computing systems, the resources located on multiple sites are shared and accessed by multiple resource users.
- *Power demand–supply.* In specific applications, resources and power have subtle relationships. In one aspect, resources mainly consume power as an energy demand for functional operation; in another aspect, resources themselves can also provide power as an energy supply in some cases. For example, in the smart grid, distributed electric vehicles can be regarded as both power demand and power supply to achieve power balance, which may perform charging operations during the off-peak time, and feed power back into the power grid during the peak time.
- *Cyber-physical collaboration.* The interrelationships are established among physical resources and cyber resources, which

can be jointly applied to support a particular application according to the dynamic and hybrid environments.

- *Duty cycling.* Resources have the corresponding duty cycling, referring to the activity cycle and life cycle. It indicates that resources can be created, updated, released, and reloaded according to practical applications.

Accordingly, resource management in IoT mainly includes two aspects: physical resource management and cyber resource management. Therefore, physical resources are usually mapped as cyber resources for further management, which makes cyber resource management become the main aspect of resource management in IoT. In this chapter, regarding ubiquitous resources, the main aspects of resource management are discussed according to resource naming, resource addressing, resource discovery, and resource allocation. Particularly, objects (i.e., identifier [ID] objects and non-ID [nID] objects) as a typical physical resource, coding and resolving are discussed in physical resource management.

In the following, Section 5.2 focuses on the physical objects to discuss coding and resolving. Thereafter, resource management is mainly analyzed for cyber resources: Sections 5.3 and 5.4 introduce the main approaches for resource naming and addressing, and Sections 5.5 and 5.6, respectively, present resource discovery and allocation. In Section 5.7, a resource management scheme is established based on cyber world- and physical world-related context considerations, and Section 5.8 draws a conclusion.

## 5.2 Object Coding and Resolving

### 5.2.1 Object Coding Discussion

In the process of objects' mapping from the physical world to the cyber world, objects' coding is significant to represent objects' information and reduce the data needed for transmission. In this section, object coding is discussed. In the physical world, in addition to identifier-based objects, namely, ID objects, there are also nID objects, including objects unattached to any ID themselves, and objects attached to ID but that are unreadable or illegal. Currently, some kinds of mature object coding systems for ID objects exist. However, existing

ID-based schemes may not be applicable for nID objects. Therefore, object coding for ID and nID objects is introduced here.

*5.2.1.1 Coding for ID Objects*    For ID objects, there are two coding types according to the identifier: nonunique ID and unique ID. For example, a bar code is a typical nonunique code, and an RFID tag is usually assigned with a unique ID (e.g., electronic product code [EPC]). A bar code is a global common identification code, and is used in the EAN.UCC uniform identification system. EPC is a product identification code and is stored in the RFID tag. When ID objects are sensed and extra information needs to be added into the ID, coding should be further executed to create a new ID. The assigned code should be able to be indexed to determine the code type.

*5.2.1.2 Coding for nID Objects*    Figure 5.1 shows a proposed nID objects code structure, which includes three main components: location(*t*), unique attributes (UA), and nonunique attributes (NA).

- *Location(t).* Considering nID objects' existence, each object has a unique location attribute at a certain moment in a coordinate system. Location(*t*) means space-time information for one object. If the location is accurate and the detection

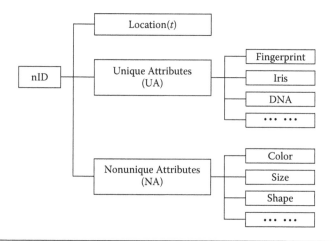

**Figure 5.1**    The nID objects code structure.

interval is short enough to uniquely identify the object, objects' information at different times can be associated. In this case, their context information can also be associated.

- *UA.* UA refers to an object's unique attributes that can be used to identify the object uniquely. For instance, human biometric recognition attributes (e.g., fingerprint, iris, DNA, and face) belong to UA. Therefore, a fingerprint is a typical UA, and fingerprint identification is often employed in many important cases to identify a person uniquely.

- *NA.* NA refers to an object's nonunique attributes that cannot be used alone to identify the object uniquely, including color, size, shape, and velocity. NA can be used along with other attributes to perform identification. For example, two cars that are the same color can also be differentiated by combing the information of location, size, or shape in some cases.

Therefore, location(*t*), UA, and NA information are incorporated into nID code, assigned to the corresponding nID objects. Different attributes can be incorporated in various applications, and the relations among objects can also be added.

*5.2.1.3 Combined Coding for Objects with ID and nID*   As objects may be attached to an ID when assigned a nID, codes for objects may consider the coexistence of ID and nID. The combination code should be composed by all or parts of the information, including its ID or nID. The object coding rule should facilitate resolving so that code can be resolved according to different requirements. The code structure should indicate the priority of resolving processes and be as simple as possible to reduce data transmission and storage. Compatibility is another significant factor that should also be seriously considered when constructing a combination code. Correspondingly, combined resolving is also needed according to corresponding coding approaches.

*5.2.2 Resolving Discussion for nID Objects*

Object Name Service (ONS) is a typical object resolving method for ID objects, which will be detailed in Section 5.4. In this section, resolving for nID objects is mainly discussed. The resolving process refers to obtaining the corresponding readable information from the nID code so that physical objects can be matched to their corresponding identity and attributes in the cyber world. Since an object's different attributes exist separately, and multiple sensing technologies are applied, multiple resolving methods may be used to resolve a nID code.

As introduced in Section 5.2.1.2, a nID code consists of location($t$), UA, and NA. Correspondingly, in this section resolving for the three components is illustrated, including space-time information resolving for location($t$), unique attribute resolving for UA, and nonunique attribute resolving for NA.

*5.2.2.1 Space-Time Information Resolving*    A resolving process of its space-time information example is shown in Figure 5.2. It can be seen that the goal of space-time information resolving can be reached when the space-time information exists uniquely and is unanimous and continuous. Different resolving methods are needed for different space-time formats. For instance, if the space-time information is in a global positioning system (GPS) format, the GPS resolving method should be applied.

*5.2.2.2 Unique Attributes (UA) Resolving*    When UA exists, UA resolving can be used—an example is shown in Figure 5.3.

Since different formats may be used for various UA, corresponding resolving methods shall be designed for UA. For the person's fingerprint, as an example, fingerprint resolving methods such as cluster analysis, principal component analysis (PCA), and nonlinear mapping (NLM) can be used.

*5.2.2.3 Nonunique Attributes (NA) Resolving*    There are also various resolving methods for NA. NA can be used by combining other attributes for identification. The priority of the resolving processes depends on the concrete requirements, and may be combined and integrated for object identification.

## 5.3 Resource Naming

In addition to the above-mentioned physical objects, resources also have other existence forms. For example, the resource may be a

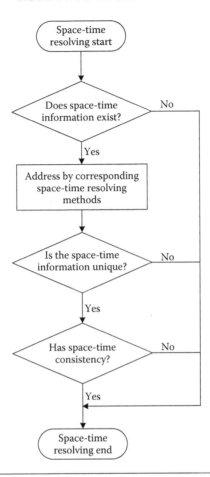

**Figure 5.2**  An example for a space-time information resolving process.

back-end database in a distributed system, object information in a storage system, or the computing capabilities or memory storage in a cloud/grid computing system. Resource naming refers to the resource description based on formal languages, and it is important to achieve formal representation of such varied resources. In order to address the different types of resources, resource naming becomes important to achieve formal representation of such varied resources [2].

In IoT, resource description refers to the physical and cyber resources in formal languages. An efficient resource description method can provide strong support for resource management. Heterogeneous resources may have different descriptive information with different formats and representations, and may also be indexed by different

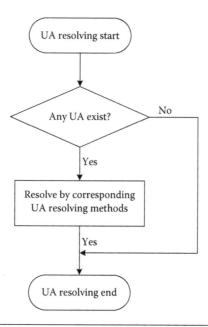

**Figure 5.3**    An example for the UA resolving process.

keywords referring to various attributes [3]. For instance, a uniform resource name (URN) is defined in the Internet to serve as a location-independent resource identifier, and to map the shared namespaces into URN-space. Here, ontology can be introduced to establish a reasonable resource description framework for both physical and cyber resources.

Ontology is a formal language to represent specific domain knowledge as a set of concepts within a domain and the corresponding relationships. The variants of ontology provide a compatible understanding among different applications. Meanwhile, ontology can describe the heterogeneous data in semantic contexts, and address the data integration with unambiguous conceptualizations. The typical ontology languages include Resource Description Framework (RDF), RDF Schema (RDFS), and Web Ontology Language (OWL), which provide the normative syntax to describe entity classes/concepts, properties, and relationships. For the ontology used in resource description, semantic conflict is an important obstacle to heterogeneous ontology languages. Considering the importance of compatibility and interoperation in heterogeneous networks, semantic reconciliation becomes a major challenge for resource representation techniques. In the integration among different ontologies, metadata heterogeneity and instance heterogeneity are two major issues that should be considered [4]. Metadata heterogeneity concerns the name- and structure-related information description conflicts, and instance heterogeneity refers to instance representation conflicts. Additionally, typical semantic conflicts, including naming conflicts and abstraction conflicts, should be considered [5,6].

- *Naming conflicts* refer to the relationships of "object, attribute, instance," and include the synonyms and homonyms among concepts or properties of resources. Synonyms mean that similar or identical terms represent similar concepts, and homonyms refer to similar or identical terms that do not represent synonymous concepts.
- *Abstraction conflicts* may be caused by different attributes during modeling the concept from the physical world into the cyber world. Abstraction conflicts mainly consider the abstraction mapping relationship between two elements according to the aspects of class, generalization, aggregation, and computed function.

Based on ontology, RDF is introduced to provide functions of resource classification, indexing, keyword searching, and semantic analyses on metadata. RDF was originally developed by the World Wide Web Consortium (W3C), and this method can also be used to describe the things in future IoT. RDF is based on Extensible Markup Language (XML), which is a common syntax for the exchange and processing of metadata [7,8]. XML syntax is a profile of Standard Generalized Markup Language (SGML), designed for the Web to alleviate the implementation of the parser. XML syntax also guarantees features, such as vendor independence, extensibility, validation, and the ability to represent complex structures. RDF further extends the general XML syntax and model to provide unambiguous semantic expression, and to enable consistent encoding and exchange of standardized metadata. Concretely, RDF applies the common conventions to facilitate modular interoperability among heterogeneous metadata sets, in which standard mechanisms for representing semantics should be established based on a simple, yet powerful and rigorous, data model. Additionally, RDF provides both human-readable and machine-processable vocabularies to improve reuse and extension of metadata semantics among heterogeneous information. Vocabularies are the set of properties/attributes and metadata, and are defined by resource description communities to standardize the declaration of vocabularies.

An *RDF triple* contains three components: subject, predicate, and object. The general format of an RDF statement is subject-predicate-object, in which the *subject* represents resources, the *predicate* represents all relative properties, and the *object* represents values. Note that the subject must be resources, the predicate must be properties, but the object may be both resources and literals. A set of triples is defined as an RDF graph, in which a subject is expressed as a *node*, a predicate is expressed as an *arc*, and an object is expressed as a node. The set of *nodes* of an RDF graph is the set of *subjects* and *objects* of triples in the graph. RDF should consider human-friendly syntax, data integration/aggregation, nonexistent triples, bandwidth-efficient protocol, literal search, yes–no queries, addressable query results, and sorting results [9].

Physical Markup Language (PML) [10] is another XML-based markup language used to describe physical resources and the corresponding relationships and interactions. PML can be applied to describe resources' inherent attributes of physical things, and can also present resources ascribed by humans. The main purpose of PML is to establish a general and standard method for formal modeling of objects, processes, and environments in the physical world. Based on PML, data structures and formats should be designed considering heterogeneous networks to provide efficient objects classification and generalization. Due to some degree of regularity and organization of physical objects, PML mainly uses a hierarchical organizational structure as a data configuration. Therefore, PML includes a special data structure name to contain an exact name of an entity, and the name element includes multiple attributes to distinguish the different name representations.

## 5.4 Resource Addressing

Resource addressing is applied to locate the required resources by applying certain mechanisms [11]. In IoT, resource addressing includes cyber resource addressing and physical resource addressing.

Cyber resource addressing is similar to the addressing scheme in the Internet, and aims to access resources via domain names and an IP address–based scheme. Physical resource addressing includes two aspects: one is the physical objects' mapping from the physical world to the cyber world, and the other refers to the same as the cyber resource addressing.

The Domain Name System (DNS) is a typical resource addressing mechanism in the Internet, which is a typical hierarchical naming system to connect computers, services, or resources into the Internet or other private networks. Therefore, a domain name is applied as an identifier to define a realm of autonomy, authority, or control on the Internet. Domain names are formed by the rules and procedures of the DNS. Generally, a domain name represents an Internet Protocol (IP) resource, and can be applied in various networking contexts and application-aware naming and addressing purposes. Uniform resource locator (URL) is defined as a unique address for a document and other resources on the Internet, and applied to access a Web site. URL includes a protocol identifier and a resource name, in which the resource name indicates the IP address or domain name where the resource is located. During resource addressing, a resource should be assigned with a unique available identifier—there are three typical addressing schemes in the Internet:

- *Universal Description, Discovery, and Integration* (UDDI) is a platform-independent, XML-based registry to realize self-presentation on the Internet. UDDI is sponsored by the Organization for the Advancement of Structured Information Standards (OASIS), for enabling businesses to publish service listings and resource discovery. The UDDI scheme applies a Universally Unique Identifier (UUID) for resource identification, and is based on the Transmission Control Protocol/Internet Protocol (TCP/IP), Hypertext Transfer Protocol (HTTP), XML, and Simple Object Access Protocol (SOAP) to establish a unified service description format and service discovery protocol.
- *Electronic Numbering Mapping* (ENUM) aims to map the DNS E.164 Number to a uniform resource identifier (URI), and it includes two aspects: (1) creating a domain name from

a telephone network (TN) and resolving it to an Internet address (a URI) using DNS, and (2) hosting ENUM domain names in the *E164.ARPA* domain.

• *Handle system* is based on a uniform resource name (URN), to achieve assigning, managing, and resolving persistent identifiers for cyber resources. The scheme includes an open set of protocols, a namespace, and a reference implementation of the protocols. The protocols enable a distributed system to store identifiers (e.g., names and handles) of arbitrary resources, and resolve the handles into the information that is necessary to locate, access, contact, authenticate, and use resources.

Additionally, Internet Protocol version 6 (IPv6) is developing to address the problem of IPv4 running out of addresses, and it is a revision of the Internet Protocol with extremely large address spaces. Such address expansion can accommodate more nodes, devices, and users, and is flexible for allocating addresses and routing traffic.

For physical resource addressing, ONS is a typical approach to realize the interconnection between the physical world and cyber world. ONS, presented by EPCglobal, is applied to access an object's information and its related services by EPC. Here, EPC is a universal identifier that provides a unique identity for a tagged physical object. ONS as an automated networking service realizes the resource addressing in IoT, and also has similar functions to point each computer to Web sites. The main design idea is first to encode EPC into a fully qualified domain name (FQDN), and then to use DNS infrastructure to query for additional information. Concretely, in the case that a reader identifies a tag, the code is transmitted to an ONS on local networks or the Internet via middleware to find the stored information on the product. During resource addressing, ONS points middleware to a server where a file about that product is stored. The middleware retrieves the file, and the information about the product in the file can be forwarded to an inventory or other applications. Furthermore, EPC Information Services (EPCIS) is designed to enable EPC-related data sharing within and across enterprises, and the EPCIS standard defines standard interfaces to enable EPC-related data to be identified and subsequently to be queried with service operations and an associated data model. Such data interaction is mainly based on persistent back-end databases. Meanwhile, application-to-application resource sharing may occur without needing a persistent database.

### 5.5 Resource Discovery

Resource discovery is an essential component for searching and finding suitable resources (e.g., sensor nodes) to satisfy application requirements. The existing resource discovery mechanisms can be classified into two main categories [12,13]: peer-to-peer (P2P) architectures and directory-based architectures.

P2P architectures are based on the distributed mechanisms, in which network entities negotiate one-to-one with each other to discover the available and required resources (e.g., services). There are two basic resource discovery mechanisms in P2P systems: pull mode and push mode.

- *Pull mode.* In pull mode, users transmit a discovery message to networks by broadcast or multicast communications, and require the matched resources for specific requirements. Providers respond to the challenged query by transmitting a description of the service or resource. For instance, the Service Discovery Protocol (SDP) is used in pull mode–based Bluetooth, as well as for on-demand *ad hoc* networks in the pull mode. In the pull mode, resource information can be updated and notified along with the back-end resources.
- *Push mode.* In push mode, providers advertise periodically by broadcasting or multicasting the location and attributes of resources and services, so that users can build a local database with all the resources available on the network. The back-end resource information can be aggregated from resources in a periodic interval.

Directory-based architectures mainly have a centralized or distributed database to aggregate and index the resource information. The resource providers register their resources/services in the directory, and resource users query the directory to obtain the required information. According to network topology, resource discovery mainly has three models: the centralized model, distributed model, and hierarchical model [14–16].

- *Centralized model.* The centralization model refers to the allocation of all queries processing capability in a single node. The main characteristics of a centralized approach include high controllability and efficiency. All lookup and update queries are sent to a single entity in the system. The centralized architecture is based on a central directory that aggregates information from every provider, and responds to queries from every user. Central directory architecture is a simple solution, and easy to administrate, but the directory can represent a bottleneck and a single point of failure, which causes the whole system's failure. Therefore, such a solution is suitable for small-scale networks, and a centralized model has inherent limitations for overloading the central server, and the model may not adapt well to dynamic network conditions.
- *Distributed model.* There is no centralized control in the distributed model, in which complete autonomy, authority, and query processing capability are distributed over all resources in the system. Note that no entities in the distributed mode are more important than others. In the case that any entity is compromised, the comprised entity will not disturb other entities in the system. In the distributed model, several directories cooperate in a P2P mode to maintain a distributed database of information about resources and services. Directories can exchange information with all other directories by multicasting communications so that each directory maintains a complete database about all resources and services. Information exchange among directories in different clusters can be achieved using a P2P scheme, instead of using a lower advertising frequency than that within a cluster, although clustered solutions are more scalable and suitable for large-scale networks, in which complex algorithms should be designed to manage clusters and guarantee cluster stability.

- *Hierarchical model.* Hierarchical organization has several advantages, including scalability, adaptability, and availability. A tree-like structure is introduced to establish the resource discovery mode, in which only direct links in a hierarchy are from the parent nodes to their child nodes. With the hierarchical architecture, the network is divided into domains with a hierarchical structure, and directories have a parent–child relationship. This solution is fully scalable, but it enforces a rigid hierarchical network organization, which does not fit well in *ad hoc* environments.

During resource discovery, a distributed hash table (DHT) is usually applied as a distributed resource discovery strategy, and provides a lookup service similar to a hash table, in which the pairwise secrets are stored in a DHT, and any participating node can efficiently retrieve the value associated with a given key. The maintenance of the mapping from keys to values is performed by distributed nodes in such a way that a change in the set of participants causes a minimal amount of disruption. This allows a DHT to scale to an extremely large number of nodes and handle continual node arrivals, departures, and failures. A typical resource discovery scheme has been established by SENSEI [17] to link the resources and the corresponding resource descriptions with potential users who look for particular functionalities. Therefore, three main components (i.e., resource publication, resource lookup, and resource database) are included. In SENSEI's resource scheme, a resource creation interface is defined to be provided by the resource host to enable the dynamic new resource creation. The resource discovery challenges are as follows:

- *Heterogeneous.* The component discovery service should support discovery of heterogeneous components, which belong to different distributed computing models (i.e., Java RMI, NET, and CORBA), and apply different communication networks (IP network and wireless sensor network [WSN]).
- *Activeness.* Activeness means that a user looking for a resource will initiate the request, for which the resource provider responds. The resource providers should be available and actively listen for the user's requests.

- *Scalability.* Scalability refers to the resource organizations being easily extended and able to enhance the system resource by adding new functionality at minimal effort.
- *Multilevel matching.* There should be support for matching components at multiple levels, such as syntactic, semantic, protocol, and quality of service (QoS). This multiple-level matching helps to improve query matching.
- *Reliability.* Reliability is defined as the ability of a system or component to perform its required functions under stated conditions for a specified period of time. The component discovery service should be reliable so that it consistently discovers the best components that match the given query. The discovery service should neither fail nor compromise the quality of the component matching process.
- *Security.* The component discovery architecture should be secure. This is mainly because the entities that form the component discovery architecture are in an open environment that suffers from severe threats.

## 5.6 Resource Allocation

Resource allocation focuses on distributing resources to realize optimal allocation on the available resources. Resource allocation in the Internet aims at establishing a ubiquitous interconnection among the available resources in the networks, and focuses on realizing pervasive seamless and transparent access to heterogeneous resources and services. It is significant to present an adaptive resource reservation strategy according to the dynamical networks and application requirements, and an optimal resource allocation scheme is necessary to address underprovisioned or overprovisioned scenarios. There are several algorithms to be applied in resource allocation, mainly including artificial intelligence, theory of random graphs, and P2P-based approaches [18–21].

- *Artificial intelligence* (AI): Artificial intelligence–based resource allocation approaches include mainly two types: game theory and heuristic methods (e.g., ant colony optimization and genetic algorithms).

Game theory is an effective strategy for resource allocation, bandwidth sharing, energy balance, and pricing models,
in which the Nash equilibrium state is achieved among the
competing users under the shared resources and services. The
Nash equilibrium refers to that in which the optimal outcome
of a game is one where no player has an incentive to devi-
ate from the chosen strategy after considering an opponent's
choices [22]. It turns out that an individual can receive no
incremental benefit from changing actions, assuming other
players remain constant in their strategies. Note that a game
may have multiple Nash *equilibriums* or none.

Ant colony optimization (ACO) [23] is also an efficient
algorithm inspired by the foraging behavior of ant colo-
nies, and can be applied for dynamical resource allocation
and optimal resource dispatching. Genetic algorithm (GA)
is another approach applied to address resource optimization. It is noteworthy that for an online decision on optimal
resource scheduling, the performance analysis of GA-based
approaches needs further research. GA is based on a search
heuristic mode inspired by the mechanics of natural selection
and natural genetics (e.g., inheritance, mutation, selection,
and crossover), to realize optimization of resource allocation. Additionally, particle swarm optimization (PSO) is a
population-based stochastic optimization technique [24]. It
combines the social psychology principles in social cognition,
human agents, and evolutionary computations.

- *Theory of random graphs.* Random graphs provide an important paradigm that may be used to realize the network
  connectivity, interoperation, and optimal resource distribution. The distributed network structure should be
  considered, and it generates regular resource allocation
  networks to achieve distributed and cooperative load trade-
  off. Another strategy is regarded as self-configuring and
  self-optimizing, which is inspired by Erdos-Renyi (ER)
  random graphs [25]. Such connectivity distribution of the
  resources satisfies a random graph. Thereby, the load distribution becomes equitable across all nodes with computing

resources. Additionally, IoT network environments should consider the resource allocation with homogeneous nodes and heterogeneous nodes.

- *P2P-based approaches.* Interdomain resource scheduling is important for difficult provisioning of the same QoS requirements and strict threads/processes concurrency requirements across multiple domains. P2P-based approaches address resource allocation in a single domain by using a typical broker. The resource monitor may need to use the same information in all the domains even if the computing resources belong to different domains. It is known that the topological structure of the underlying physical network has significant impacts on the resource utilization of the P2P overlay network [26]. Meanwhile, P2P overlay routing may increase traffic congestion at the Internet backbone since the current traffic engineering algorithms for Internet service providers (ISPs) do not consider the traffic demands [27].

## 5.7 Resource Management Scheme in U2IoT

In unit and ubiquitous IoT (U2IoT), resources are usually context sensitive, and therefore context information is relevant for resource management. Hereafter, context information is discussed according to physical- and cyber-related information, and a resource management scheme is established for U2IoT.

### 5.7.1 Context Information

Context-aware computing [28] has received great attention for acquiring various contexts from different context providers, interpreting contexts through context reasoning, and delivering contexts in both push and pull modes. Initial efforts on context-aware service creation focused on an infrastructure-based solution. A model-driven approach facilitates the creation of context modeling to tackle context awareness in the application layer. The captured low-level static and dynamic contexts are aggregated by these devices to provide another set of deduced high-level contexts to build context-aware resource services. In U2IoT, the context mainly includes three aspects: physical context, cyber context, and physical-cyber context.

The physical context mainly considers the context information during physical things mapping into cyber things. The physical context includes the subclasses of object, behavior, physical event, and tendency. Therefore, object, behavior, and physical event further have the mandatory subclasses of time and location. The detailed typical physical context descriptors are shown in Figure 5.4.

The cyber context mainly considers the context information during cyber things mapping into physical things. Figure 5.5 shows the typical cyber context descriptors, in which the cyber context includes the four main subclasses of entity, cyber action, cyber event, and service.

The physical-cyber context mainly considers the context information during physical things mapping into cyber things, and then the cyber things remapping into the physical things. The physical-cyber context mainly considers the subclasses of network awareness and object/entity. The detailed typical physical-cyber context descriptors are shown in Figure 5.6.

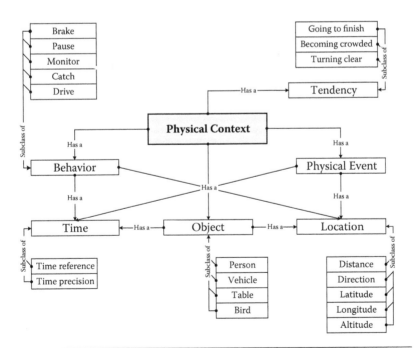

**Figure 5.4**  The typical physical context descriptors.

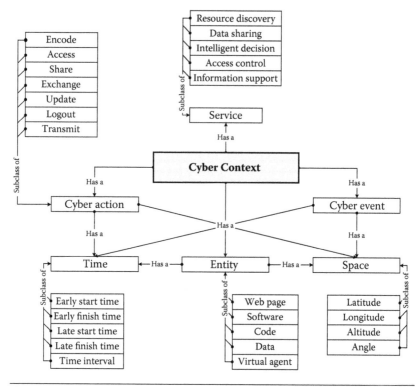

**Figure 5.5** The typical cyber context descriptors.

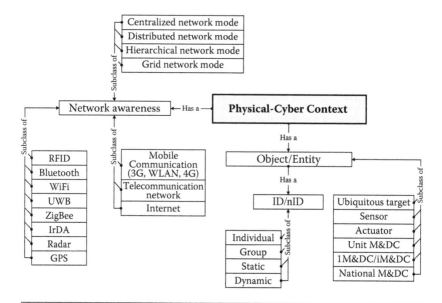

**Figure 5.6** The typical physical-cyber context descriptors.

*5.7.2 Resource Management Scheme for U2IoT*

A resource management scheme is established for U2IoT with the considerations of resource management in unit IoT and ubiquitous IoT. Concretely, resources in unit IoT (called unit resources) mainly include the resource-constrained sensors and actuators, unit management and data center (M&DC), and corresponding abstract resources, which provide basic functions and services for an application. Resources in ubiquitous IoT (called ubiquitous resources) mainly include physical and cyber forms of local, industrial, and national management and data centers (lM&DCs, iM&DCs, and nM&DCs) and other abstract resources in local IoT, industrial IoT, and national IoT. In the meantime, additional service selection and adaptation management are applied to support the resource management for the sensor and actuator resources [29].

*5.7.2.1 Resource Management in Unit IoT*   Unit resources mainly refer to the available resources in unit IoT, in which resources are under intelligent management to achieve self-optimization functions for the sensors, actuators, and M&DCs.

A universal management mode can be applied by resource components that implement service matching and binding services. When sensors receive a service request to access data, the sensors may challenge the service registry to obtain the available services. If the service is available, it will bind the service for internal resource supports. Otherwise, the service request will be transmitted to the upper management and data center for external service acquiring. In the case that the service selection component has selected a service provider, the service manager binds the available service to the appropriate request. Note that services in the sensors and actuators are implemented by the self-organized resource component, and the same resources may be concurrently used by multiple applications. The self-adaptive resource access mode is applied for unit resources. The self-adaptive mode has full-fledged service specifications and contextual information gathered by sensors, in which each service's functioning parameters can be autonomously changed according to specific network scenarios. The self-adaptive mode applies the adaptation control loop to adapt service behavior by polling the system state–related components. Therefore, the resource components mainly include battery capability, process overhead, communication load, and available memory. During resource management, the system state–related components perform a comparison on the current system state against the existing adaptation policies, and the required adaptation is launched upon reaching a threshold. Furthermore, other abstract resources are managed by an upper service manager.

Unit M&DC can also be applied to manage the distributed sensors and actuators in unit IoT, in which unit resources are managed by the service selection component. Unit resources provide services for the bottom sensors and actuators, and also request service from ubiquitous IoT. Unit IoT maintains a service directory for its resources, and matches the service request and available services for applications.

*5.7.2.2 Resource Management in Ubiquitous IoT*   Ubiquitous resources refer to physical and cyber resources in local IoT, industrial IoT, national IoT, and global IoT applications–related resources. The local resources and industrial resources are relatively independent, and interact with each other to provide enhanced services and functions. Cloud management is introduced for IoT to provide anything as a service (XaaS), in which cloud computing may have three service delivery modes, including software as a service (SaaS), platform as a service (PaaS), and infrastructure as a service (IaaS). The combined use of these three modes is referred to as the service-platform-infrastructure (SPI) model [30,31].

- SaaS provides the service provider's applications running in a cloud infrastructure, which refers to the ability for a user to use on-demand software. The user has no need of management or control of the software infrastructure (e.g., storage, servers, and networks).
- PaaS provides the capability for an individual to use the applications without needing to maintain the hardware and software, which build service providers' platforms to create applications running in the cloud infrastructures.
- IaaS provides the service provider's hardware resources, including the storage (e.g., data replication, backup, and archiving),

the server (e.g., computing requirements), and the connectivity domains (e.g., network load balancing and firewalls).

Additionally, XaaS also includes software as a service (SaaS), communications as a service (CaaS), network as a service (NaaS), and monitoring as a service (MaaS). Such cloud resource management realizes the resource optimal allocation and utilization.

In U2IoT, three network-based interfaces are suitable for resource management, including network resource interface, network service interface, and network interaction interface [32]. Concretely, network resource interface is defined to achieve configuration of the multiple physical resources, such as the wireless and wired infrastructures. The network service interface is used to provide service for applications by invoking network resources, in which network services can be measured by the capabilities, such as network delay, throughput, routing, and coverage areas. Network interaction interfaces are used to exchange information among different entities and heterogeneous networks.

## 5.8 Conclusion

In IoT, resources management mainly focuses on the management of physical resources and cyber resources. A particular resource should be formally named after its creation with objective existence consideration, be addressed and discovered for utilization and sharing with availability consideration, and be optimally allocated with efficiency consideration. Furthermore, a resource management scheme is established according to unit resources and ubiquitous resources, to achieve heterogeneous resources that can be managed in such a hierarchical structure.

# References

1. Oteafy, S. M. A., and H. S. Hassanein. 2012. Towards a global IoT: Resource re-utilization in WSNs. In *2012 International Conference on Computing, Networking and Communications*, 617–622.
2. Xu, K. 2010. Research on the common technology of network resource management. Ph.D. dissertation, Beijing University of Post and Telecommunications.

3. Daouadji, A., K. K. Nguyen, M. Lemay, and M. Cheriet. 2010. Ontology-based resource description and discovery framework for low carbon grid networks. In *2010 1st IEEE International Conference on Smart Grid Communications*, 477–482.

4. Tang, J., B. Y. Liang, and J. Z. Li. 2005. Toward detecting mapping strategies for ontology interoperability. Presented at the *14th International World Wide Web Conference*.

5. Naiman, C. E., and A. M. Ouksel. 1995. A classification of semantic conflicts in heterogeneous database systems. *Journal of Organizational Computing* 5: 167–193.

6. Banlue, K., N. Arch-int, and S. Arch-int. 2010. Ontology-based metadata integration approach for learning resource interoperability. In *2010 6th International Conference on Semantics Knowledge and Grid*, 195–202.

7. W3C. 2004. RDF semantics. http://www.w3.org/TR/rdf-mt (accessed August 10, 2012).

8. Miller, E. J. 2001. An introduction to the resource description framework. *Journal of Library Administration* 34: 245–255.

9. W3C. 2005. RDF data access use cases and requirements. http://www.w3.org/2001/sw/DataAccess/UseCases#req (accessed August 10, 2012).

10. Brock, D. L. 2011. The physical markup language—A universal language for physical objects. http://wew.autoidlabs.org/uploads/media/MIT-AUTOID-WH-003.pdf.

11. Ning K., X. Li, and B. Yan. 2008. A model supporting any product code standard for the resource addressing in the Internet of Things. In *1st International Conference on Intelligent Networks and Intelligent Systems*, 233–238.

12. Cardosa, M., and A. Chandra. 2010. Resource bundles: Using aggregation for statistical large-scale resource discovery and management. *IEEE Transactions on Parallel and Distributed Systems* 21: 1089–1102.

13. Moreno-Vozmediano, R. 2006. Resource discovery in ad-hoc grids. In *International Conference on Computational Science*, 3994:1031–1038.

14. Ranjan, R., A. Harwood, and R. Buyya. 2008. Peer-to-peer-based resource discovery in global grids: A tutorial. *IEEE Communications Surveys and Tutorials* 10: 6–33.

15. Xiong J., S. Cai, and L. Zhang. 2008. Research of resource discovery model based on P2P in grid environment. In *Chinese Control and Decision Conference*, 363–368.

16. Bandara, H. M. N. D., and A. P. Jayasumana. 2012. Evaluation of P2P resource discovery architectures using real-life multi-attribute resource and query characteristics. In *2012 IEEE Consumer Communications and Networking Conference*, 634–639.

17. SENSEI. Resource directory cookbook. https://ncit-cluster.grid.pub.ro/trac/Sensei-WP5-Public/wiki/ResourceDirectory (accessed August 10, 2012).

18. Arfeen, M. A., K. Pawlikowski, and A. Willig. 2011. A framework for resource allocation strategies in cloud computing environment. In *2011 IEEE 35th Annual Computer Software and Applications Conference Workshops*, 261–266.

19. Zaki, A.N., and A.O. Fapojuwo. 2011. Optimal and efficient graph-based resource allocation algorithms for multiservice frame-based OFDMA networks. *IEEE Transactions on Mobile Computing* 10: 1175–1186.

20. Gao, J., S. A. Vorobyov, and J. Hai. 2010. Cooperative resource allocation games under spectral mask and total power constraints. *IEEE Transactions on Signal Processing* 58: 4379–4395.

21. Abosi, C. E., R. Nejabati, and D. Simeonidou. 2010. A novel service-oriented resource allocation model for future optical Internet. In *2010 12th International Conference on Transparent Optical Networks (ICTON)*, 1–4.

22. Nash equilibrium. http://www.investopedia.com/terms/n/nash-equilibrium.asp#axzz1yhWttf6z (accessed August 10, 2012).

23. Dorigo, M., and G. D. Caro. 1999. The ant colony optimization meta-heuristic. *New ideas in optimization*, 11–32. New York: McGraw-Hill.

24. Cruz, J., G. Chen, D. Li, and X. Wang. 2004. Particle swarm optimization for resource allocation in UAV cooperative control. In *AIAA Guidance, Navigation, and Control Conference*, 2549–2559.

25. Erdös, P., and A. Rényi. 1960. On the evolution of random graphs. *Publication of the Mathematical Institute of the Hungarian Academy of Sciences* 5: 17–61.

26. Liu, G. L., H. P. Peng, L. X. Li, F. Sun, and Y. X. Yang. 2012. Improving resource utilization in hierarchy network by optimizing topological structure. *European Physical Journal B* 85: 63.

27. Chen H., G. Zhian, and D. Ye. 2009. Pharos: An ISP-P2P cooperation network resource allocation architecture. In *International Symposium on Computer Network and Multimedia Technology*, 1–6.

28. Liu, J., and W. Tong. 2010. Dynamic service model based on context resources in the Internet of Things. In *2010 6th International Conference on Wireless Communications Networking and Mobile Computing*, 1–4.

29. Cid, P. J., N. Matthys, D. Hughes, S. Michiels, and W. Joosen. 2010. Resource management middleware to support self managing wireless sensor networks. In *2010 4th IEEE International Conference on Self-Adaptive and Self-Organizing Systems Workshop*, 251–255.

30. Somasundaram, T. S., and K. Govindarajan. 2011. Cloud monitoring and discovery service (CMDS) for IaaS resources. In *2011 3rd International Conference on Advanced Computing*, 340–345.

31. Hendryx, A. 2011. Cloudy concepts: IaaS, PaaS, SaaS, MaaS, CaaS and XaaS. http://www.zdnet.co.uk/blogs/the-sanman-10014929/cloudy-concepts-iaas-paas-saas-maas-caas-and-xaas-10024679/ (accessed August 10, 2012).

32. Shi, Y., M. Sheng, and F. He. 2011. A resource management and control model supporting applications in the Internet of Things. In *2011 4th International Conference on Cyber, Physical and Social Computing*, 721–725.

# 6

# LOOP CONTROL
# IN ACTUATION

Actuation decides and activates a mechanical or electronic event to modify the contextual situations in the physical world, with the goal of accomplishing the expected results [1]. A series of steps in an actuation is called the actuation loop.

According to whether there is feedback, the actuation loop can be classified into two categories: open actuation loops and closed actuation loops. Open actuation loops refer to those in which there is no direct feedback from the outcome of the actuation, and the closed actuation loops refer to those with feedback. In Internet of Things (IoT), most loops belong to the closed actuation loops, in which the certain action to modify the contextual situations will repeat until the expected result is achieved.

In IoT, loop control in actuation refers to a series of functions, including the decision of the actuation loop's logic, components, and process, and the maintenance of the actuation loop's execution.

- *Decision of the actuation loop's logic, components, and process.* Before the actuation is initiated, the actuation loop logic is designed with expected results of the users or the actuation loop itself, and the loop components, together with the process, are chosen based on the knowledge of the resources, including sensors, actuators, and networks. The knowledge on resources mainly contains their function, condition, attribute, and availability. Resource discovery, naming, and addressing are the fundamentals to addressing a huge number of actuations and the complicated environment in IoT. Stability is another key principle in designing an actuation loop.

- *Maintenance of the actuation loop's execution.* It aims to maintain the actuation loop's normal execution and adapt the loop to the internal limits (e.g., time delay), as well as the external interferences (e.g., loop interaction and actuation loop conflicts). The time delay, loop interaction, actuation loop conflicts, and their corresponding resolutions are introduced as follows.

  1. Time delay consists of the network transfer delay and the computation time for signal coding and processing. Time delay may degrade an actuation's performance and even cause actuation instability. Time synchronization technologies can also mitigate the time delay.
  2. Loop interaction refers to multiple actuation loops suffering a disturbance if one parameter is changed in another actuation loop [2]. That is, the actuation loops are relatively independent, but they will affect others due to the parameters. For example, the same hardware or a parameter used in an actuation loop will affect another parameter in another actuation loop. Some approaches have been proposed to address the loop interaction, such as relative gain array of the dynamic interaction [3] and utilization of steady-state information of the process to control variables [4].
  3. Actuation loop conflicts can be classified into two categories. One is that there are many requests sent to the same actuator at the same time [5]. There are many methods to solve various conflicts, such as assigning priority of user queries, first-in-first-out (FIFO), majority value of the queries, average value of the queries, and so forth. The other is mainly caused by the limitations of resources (e.g., energy, bandwidth, and capacity) among the loops. For example, in a bandwidth-limited condition, there are many actuation loops to be activated, but due to the limitation of bandwidth, all the actuation loops cannot be simultaneously activated. The activation order can be determined according to the relationship of the actuation loops and their priority.

There are some other key issues on the actuation loop control, mainly including access control, security, and heterogeneous networks integration. Security and access control need to be enabled to guarantee that only authorized users are allowed to access certain actuation services. Meanwhile, the actuation loop may involve multiple heterogeneous networks with different frequency bands and different protocols, and it can be challenging for the loop control to deal with the heterogeneous networks.

# References

1. Hauswirth, M., S. Krco, N. Stojanovic, M. Bauer, R. Nielsen, S. Haller, N. Prasad, V. Reynolds, and O. Corcho. 2011. An architectural blueprint for a real-world Internet. In *The future Internet*, 67–80. Lecture Notes in Computer Science 6656. Berlin, Heidelberg, Germany: Springer.
2. Rahman, A., M. A. A. S. Choudhury. 2011. Detection of control loop interactions and prioritization of control loop maintenance. In *2011 International Symposium on Advanced Control of Industrial Processes*, 48–53.
3. Bristol, E. 1966. On a new measure of interaction for multivariable process control. *IEEE Transactions on Automatic Control* 11: 133–134.
4. Tung, L. S., and T. F. Edger. 1981. Analysis of control-output interactions in dynamic systems. *American Institute of Chemical Engineers Journal* 27: 690–693.
5. Rossi, M., P. Barnaghi, S. Meissner, V. Huang, M. Bauer, S. Gessler, M. Strohbach, C. Villalonga, A. Petcu, J. B. Vercher, and F. L. Aguilar. 2009. Integrating the physical with the digital world of the network of the future. http://www.ict-s ensei.org/image s/Docume nts/sensei_wp2_d2.3%20v2.pdf (accessed June 12, 2012).

# 7

# SESSION MANAGEMENT

## 7.1 Introduction

In the Internet, session management is the process used to track and maintain users' activities during their interaction with a computer. It identifies the user's identity, manages the user's login, and tracks the user's activity across sessions.

In Internet of Things (IoT), session management [1] manages the interactions between ubiquitous resources and resource users. It is especially important to manage longer-lasting interactions with dynamic characteristics, particularly for sessions with multiple resources. Session management can help resource users shield complexity to improve operability.

IoT realizes the connection of the physical world and the cyber world. Furthermore, the session participants in IoT are much wider than those in the Internet. In addition, as IoT can realize the combination of heterogeneous networks, the session in IoT needs to satisfy the heterogeneous networks. Therefore, session management brings new issues and challenges in IoT.

In IoT, session management can be classified into two types. One is single-session management, which has only one resource included. The other is multisession management, which has more than one resource included.

The remainder of this chapter is organized as follows: Section 7.2 presents two key issues of single-session management. Multisession management is discussed in Section 7.3; and some challenges about session management are listed in Section 7.4.

## 7.2 Single-Session Management in IoT

Similar to the Internet, single-session management in IoT can be divided into five steps according to the session life cycle: apply, create, register, act, and release [2].

During the five steps, resource joining and quit management and time management are two important parts in terms of the session security, session exception management, and so on. These key issues in single-session management are introduced as follows.

- *Resources joining and quit management.* For resources joining in a session, there are two modes: active and passive. For the former mode, the resources ask the resource user for permission to join in the session, and for the latter mode, the resource is invited by the resource user to join in the session. In one session, the two modes can coexist. For resources quitting the session, they need to ask the resource user for permission. The resource is not allowed to leave the session without permission in the normal situation. In particular cases, if a resource leaves a session without permission, the resource user should find an alternative resource to continue this session; otherwise, the session should be terminated.

- *Time management.* When the goal of a session is achieved, the resource user will end this session. However, the resources may not be able to determine whether the session has ended, which will cause the degrading of resource utilization. There are two ways for the resource to terminate a session. One is the relative timeout: if the resource has not been used for a period of time, the resource will be released from the session. The other is the absolute timeout: the resource will quit the session after a certain period of time. It can make the sessions more secure [3]. The two time management approaches can be used in one case. In addition, in some special cases, such as monitoring systems, the session time is kept to realize real-time management.

## 7.3 Multiple-Session Management in IoT

Multiple-session management mainly includes three aspects: session conflict management, resource deployment, and security. Session conflict management is more important since it is essential for the other two aspects, which is to manage the conflict where more than one resource user wants to have interactions with the same exclusive resource. Here, three typical session conflicts, including mutual exclusion, deadlock, and collision, and their corresponding solutions are introduced.

- *Mutual exclusion* refers to multiple sessions wanting to use the same exclusive resource. The exclusive resource is the resource that can only be used by one resource user at a time. In this case, the priority comparison of the resource users is introduced to solve the conflict. If the conflict occurs in the condition that the resource users with different priorities want to request the same resource, the session with highest priority is first. If the conflict occurs among resource users with the same priority, the order of resource users requesting the resource is decided by the weight of each resource user. The current weight of certain resource users can be determined by influencing factors such as distance, related attributes, and previous weight.
- *Deadlock* occurs in exclusive resources when a resource is in a session and other sessions also want to request this resource. Silberschatz et al. [4] introduced a typical deadlock. Suppose that there are two sessions in interactions:
    - Session 1: A resource user $I$ is in an interaction with a resource $A$.
    - Session 2: A resource user $II$ is in an interaction with a resource $B$.
  If $I$ wants to make an interaction with $B$, and $II$ wants to make an interaction with $A$, the two sessions are waiting for each other and involved in a deadlock state. Some solutions are proposed to deal with the deadlock conflict. For example, the banker algorithm proposed by Dijkstra in 1968 is the classic approach to prevent the deadlock. Efficient deploying of the resource development in an orderly fashion is also a common solution.
- *Collision* happens when multiple resource users establish interactions with the same resource. In this condition, the resource is involved in more than one session, and data in

different sessions will compete to transmit. If a resource is challenged by two or more data packets from different sessions, the collision will occur, and it may further cause channel blocking. Space division multiple access (SDMA), frequency division multiple access (FDMA), code division multiple access (CDMA), and time division multiple access (TDMA) are mainly used to achieve anticollision in wireless communication. For instance, CDMA-based anticollision protocols (e.g., ALOHA-based protocols and tree-based protocols) can be applied in radio frequency identification (RFID) systems [5].

## 7.4 Challenges

In session management, additional challenges should be addressed in both the physical world and cyber world, such as session management among heterogeneous networks, session management, and session management of large-scale mobile nodes.

# References

1. Gluhak, A., M. Hauswirth, S. Krco, N. Stojanovic, M. Bauer, R. Nielsen, S. Haller, N. Prasad, V. Reynolds, and O. Corcho. 2011. An architectural blueprint for a real-world Internet. In *The future Internet*, 67–80. Lecture Notes in Computer Science 6656. Berlin, Heidelberg, Germany: Springer.
2. Espinosa, J. M., O. Nabuco, and K. Drira. 2001. A UML model for session management in collaborative design for space activities. In *Proceedings of 8th European Concurrent Engineering Conference (ECEC'2001)*, 170–174.
3. Nazmul, F. 2001. Secure session management. Master diss., Aalto University.
4. Silberschatz A., P. B. Galvin, and G. Gagne. 2006. *Operating system principles*. 7th ed. New Delhi: Wiley India Pvt. Ltd.
5. Jacobsen, R., K. F. Nielsen, P. Popovski, and T. Larsen. 2009. Reliable identification of RFID tags using multiple independent reader sessions. In *Proceedings of 2009 IEEE International Conference on RFID*, 64–71.

# 8

# SPACE-TIME CONSISTENCY AND LOCATION PRIVACY

## 8.1 Introduction

Time and space are basic characteristics of objects in the physical world, and the consistent space-time data are significant for objects' modeling, discovery, and services when they are mapped from the physical world to the cyber world. Different technologies, such as radio frequency identification (RFID), global positioning system (GPS), infrared localization technology, and cameras, are available to obtain objects' space-time data. However, the obtained data are usually nonuniform, inconsistent, and discontinuous due to the limitations of different technologies [1]. In Internet of Things (IoT), space-time data are required to be accurate, comprehensive, and continuous. Therefore, the study on consistency and space-time registration becomes noteworthy.

Several studies have worked to enable the consistency of space-time data, in which space-time registration receives wide attention in the field of multiple-sensor fusion systems [2–4]. Nabaa and Bishop [2] proposed a homogeneous sensor registration solution to the radar tracking problem in aircraft. Li et al. [3] put forward a space-time registration method for heterogeneous sensors of mobile radars and Electronic Support Measures (ESM). Fuiorea et al. [4] presented some registration algorithms to estimate sensors' location in a wireless sensor network (WSN). Zhou et al. [5] discussed space-time consistency in a distributed visual environment to deal with message transmission delay and clock asynchrony. Additionally, Zhong and Chang [6] adopted space-time consistency to achieve reliable object tracking over long sequences in video region track systems. However, space-time consistency-related issues in IoT are still open challenges, and it

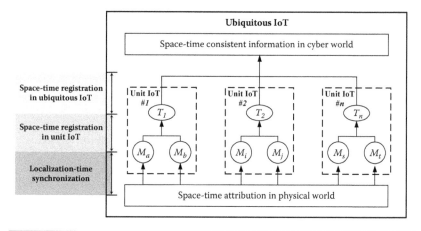

**Figure 8.1**   Space-time registration in unit IoT and ubiquitous IoT.

is significant to introduce space-time registration into heterogeneous networks to achieve consistent data integration.

Figure 8.1 shows the space-time registration in unit IoT and ubiquitous IoT (U2IoT), which is to promote the accuracy and consistency of the objects' space-time data based on U2IoT [7]. In Figure 8.1, $M_a$, $M_b$, $M_i$, $M_j$, $M_s$, and $M_t$ represent the measurements (note that the number of the measurements in each Unit IoT is more than two) of objects in the physical world, and are collected by the technologies in unit IoTs. $T_1$ is the fused data from $M_a$ and $M_b$ in *Unit IoT* #1 (similarly, $T_2$ is the fused data from $M_i$ and $M_j$ in *Unit IoT* #2, and $T_n$ is the fused data from $M_s$ and $M_t$ in *Unit IoT* #n). The consistent space-time data can be obtained by using the data from unit IoTs (#1, #2, ..., #n) in the cyber world.

Time synchronization and localization refer to the mapping process from objects' space-time attributes in the physical world to measurements in the cyber world, which are the foundation of space-time registration. After them, there are two levels of space-time registration. One is space-time registration for unit IoT, and the other is the space-time registration for ubiquitous IoT. Correspondingly, in Figure 8.1, the space-time registration for unit IoT is the process from $M_a$ and $M_b$ to $T_1$ (and from $M_i$, $M_j$ to $T_2$), and the space-time registration for ubiquitous IoT is the process from $T_1$ $T_2$, ..., $T_n$ to the final consistent space-time data.

After space-time registration, the consistent space-time data of objects not only provide convenient location-based services to objects, but also bring threats to individual location privacy. The location privacy has unique characters of personality, quality of service (QoS), and dynamics. There are four main types of attacks to location privacy. Various approaches have been proposed for location privacy preservation, but location privacy is still an open issue in IoT.

In the following, Section 8.2 presents time synchronization, localization, and the space-time registration for unit IoT. Section 8.3 introduces space-time registration for ubiquitous IoT. The space-time consistency in U2IoT is discussed in Section 8.4. A case study is discussed in Section 8.5, and Section 8.6 finally draws a conclusion.

## 8.2 Space-Time Registration in Unit IoT

Four kinds of significant techniques, including time synchronization, object localization, time registration, and space registration, will be discussed in unit IoT. Therein, time synchronization and object localization are the preconditions for space-time registration. Based on time synchronization, localization technologies are used to obtain objects' space-time data with the same time standards. And time and space registration is essential to achieve consistent space-time data.

### 8.2.1 Time Synchronization

Time synchronization is the process of exchanging the local clock data of each node to maintain internal time consistency of the whole system. It is the basic requirement to ensure the data accuracy and consistency. Here, the typical time synchronization schemes and the corresponding advantages and limitations will be introduced.

Time synchronization is a traditional research topic. The earliest and most typical time synchronization issue is how to synchronize a remote clock to the reference clock. The traditional time synchronization algorithms like Network Time Protocol (NTP) [8] and GPS [9] are widely used in wired distributed systems. However, they also have obvious defects. For instance, NTP has high requirements for bandwidth and energy consumption, and GPS devices have limitations on size and cost. Wireless networks such as WSN have limited bandwidth and energy consumption, and the node in this network is designed to be miniature and inexpensive. Therefore, NTP and GPS are impractical for synchronizing this kind of network. Many new time synchronization algorithms are designed for WSN afterward.

The wireless network–based time synchronization algorithms can be generally divided into three categories: the receiver-receiver mode, sender-receiver mode, and pair-wise mode. Reference Broadcast Synchronization (RBS) [10], Timing-Sync Protocol for Sensor Networks (TPSN) [11], and Flooding Time Synchronization Protocol (FTSP) [12], respectively, apply the mentioned three synchronization modes for the time synchronization of WSN. Concretely, RBS synchronizes the separate stamped time when two adjacent nodes receive the beacons from the beacon node. TPSN adopting the sender-receiver synchronization mode is similar to RBS in accuracy and scope. FTSP combines the advantages of TPSN and RBS. It eliminates the delay influence of the sending nodes, estimates the uncertain delay of the receiving node, and minimizes the uncertainty of the propagation delay to improve the precision of time synchronization. Additionally, Sichitiu and Veerarittiphan [13] put forward the Tiny and Mini synchronization algorithms, and Greunen and Rabaey [14] proposed the tree-based synchronization algorithm. The Tiny and Mini synchronization algorithms are relatively simple and have low energy consumption, and can be used in large-scale networks. The tree-based synchronous algorithm can adjust its precision according to the bandwidth and energy supply of the network, and it has good extensibility and low operation requirements. Among the algorithms introduced above, the Tiny, Mini, and RBS algorithms can only achieve internal time synchronization, and they lack good external interface of the time reference, which brings great difficulty to the systematic and global time synchronization in IoT.

### 8.2.2 Object Localization

The localization of objects based on time synchronization is the foundation of mapping the objects from the physical world to the cyber world. The earliest technology in modern localization is global navigation satellite systems such as GPS. It is widely applied in earth measurement, navigation, and logistics. But its high power consumption, high cost, and big size limit its application in the localization of objects in IoT. In severe environments (e.g., city buildings), it will bring the urban canyon effect and make GPS unavailable. Thus, several local and indoor localization technologies have subsequently been developed, such as RFID, third-generation (3G) cellular network, Wi-Fi, and other sound/video-based positioning technologies.

The accuracy and cost vary for different localization technologies, and become the major consideration for choosing suitable localization technology. Each localization technology has its optimal application environments and functions. Most technologies are market-oriented products for particular applications. For example, WhereNet [15] focuses on the localization of the industrial production line. Ekahau [16] adapts to hospital and family safety systems. The EasyLiving project [17] is designed for localization in office rooms.

### 8.2.3  Time Registration for Unit IoT

Time registration for unit IoT is the process to eliminate the transmission delay and the inconsistency of the sampling cycles of the sensors, and to adjust the measurement sequence to the same time level. Here, time registration of the heterogeneous sensors is introduced.

There are many time registration methods, such as least squares, interpolation and extrapolation, the curve-fit method, and the 3-point parabola interpolation method. Among them the least squares algorithm [18] and the interpolation and extrapolation algorithm [19] are most widely used as mainstream algorithms. The least squares algorithm requires that the sensors must have the same initial sampling time point, and the synchronous cycle is equal to the maximum one among all sensors' sampling cycles. The interpolation and extrapolation algorithm can be used when the ratio of the sampling cycles of sensors is not an integer.

### 8.2.4  Space Registration for Unit IoT

Space registration for unit IoT has two aspects: one is converting the measured data to the reference frame or the reference expression, and the other is estimating and eliminating the registration biases of measured data. Space registration is particularly essential when the object is identified by multiple sensors at the same time. Similarly, space registration consists of homogeneous registration and heterogeneous registration. Heterogeneous space registration for unit IoT will be discussed, and it is also suitable for the homogeneous sensors.

For consistent expression of the object location data, a reference frame is necessary for unit IoT. But the applied technologies may adopt different frames (e.g., polar coordinate, orthogonal coordinate, and Cartesian coordinate) or expressions. So, the first step in space registration should be the conversion of frames and expressions.

The second step of space registration is the estimation and elimination of the registration biases. The major sources of registration biases include system bias and position bias. System bias is caused by the defect of each sensor, and position bias refers to the bias of the initial position of the sensor. Registration bias is systematic and constant. It can be estimated by a variety of space registration algorithms, such as least squares, maximum likelihood estimation, and the Kalman filter.

## 8.3 Space-Time Registration for Ubiquitous IoT

Space-time registration for ubiquitous IoT is the process of getting the final consistent space-time data in the cyber world from the data of unit IoTs. Different from the space-time registration in unit IoT, more factors should be considered for space-time data in ubiquitous IoT, including the time reference for time registration and the location model for space registration.

### 8.3.1 Time Registration for Ubiquitous IoT

The time reference determines the internal time of unit IoT. For ubiquitous IoT, time registration in unit IoT is not enough due to the different time references. Thus, time registration for ubiquitous IoT considers more on the time reference. One unit IoT may adopt the local time as its time reference, while another unit IoT may adopt the time of another time zone as its time reference. Time references in different industries may also be different and may be used in certain unit IoT. The different kinds of time references and the inconsistency among them bring time bias to ubiquitous IoT. In ubiquitous IoT, the purpose of time registration is to mainly eliminate the time bias caused by the differences in the time reference, and adjust the internal time of unit IoTs to ensure the global time synchronization.

### 8.3.2 *Space Registration for Ubiquitous IoT*

Different location expressions and models are usually used by localization technologies, and the location data are represented in different forms in unit IoTs. The key point of space registration for ubiquitous IoT is to achieve effective location modeling, and establish interconversion between different location models.

In general, the location models can be categorized into two classes: symbolic location models and geometric coordinate location models. The symbolic coordinate is used by cellular networks (e.g., Global System for Mobile Communications [GSM]), wireless local area networks (WLANs), and other wireless indoor localization technologies (e.g., RFID and infrared). The typical geometric coordinate–based location model is GPS, in which the data refer to a point in a plane or three-dimensional space. The topological properties allow the distance calculation between points. If there is no additional data, symbolic coordinates may not be able to provide any reasoning about the distance and inclusion.

After interconversion among different models, a series of the space-time data of the object can be obtained. The remaining work in the space registration for ubiquitous IoT is to estimate the optimized trajectory of the object with consistency in space and time, and the Kalman filter algorithm can be used in this process.

### 8.4 Space-Time Consistency Discussion in U2IoT

In U2IoT, the real-time localization and tracking of objects are useful in the fields of logistics, safety, health, and other location-based services. The location data of a moving object are a continuous trajectory, so the time coordinates should be given as well as the space coordinates. Space-time consistency in IoT is the consistency of mapped space-time data of an object in the cyber world and its real space-time distribution in the physical world. This requires that time synchronization, object localization, time registration, and space registration be achieved. In order to ensure space-time consistency, the following three requirements should be considered:

- *Consistent to the real attribution.* The space-time data collected by heterogeneous sensing technologies to map the object from the physical world to the cyber world should be consistent to the object's real information. This consistency must adapt to the different objects, applications, and environments. Different applications have different requirements on space-time data, accuracy levels, and space relationships. Hence, appropriate technologies are required to satisfy the scope, precision, and cost requirements in the specific applications. Such requirements need reliable localization technologies and data fusion technologies to provide consistent data.

- *Mutual understanding and the same time-space connotation.* The space-time data of the same object obtained by various localization technologies in IoT should have mutual understanding and the same connotation in the cyber world. The object may be detected by different technologies at the same time, and the expression and accuracy of the detected data may be different, so that interconversion is needed for data sharing and combined detection. The same connotation means that the different data must point to one object and a unique trajectory in the cyber world. Different object expressions need to be understood and utilized by other technologies to construct space-time data. This understanding is the basic requirement of data sharing and the scalability of the system. This requirement focuses more on the interconversion of different detection technologies, and covers time synchronization, time registration, and space registration.

- *Continuous trajectory.* The object data obtained by sensing technologies are generally discrete, while their real space-time information is continuous. So, the closest and continuous trajectory for the object is needed for exploring. It is the holistic requirement of space-time consistency in IoT. This is more about using data processing to derive the object's trajectory as precisely as possible.

Social factors greatly affect IoT from various aspects such as the adopted time standards and space model. Objects' social role can be classified from the three aspects according to the located places: nation, industry, and locale. The nation that one object belongs to will affect the time reference and space model that the unit IoT uses. Different industries may also use different time standards and space models, and local IoT will have its characteristic time reference and space model. In U2IoT, this issue can be solved appropriately with the three defined kinds of management and data centers (M&DCs): nM&DC for national IoT, iM&DC for industrial IoT, and lM&DC for local IoT. By distinction of the three kinds of M&DCs, the social attributes are originally considered for ubiquitous IoT. After assigning the specific data, the time reference and space model can be generally used to analyze and realize the space-time consistency. For instance, by identifying the social attribute in ubiquitous IoT, the time reference can be determined, and then the time in unit IoT can be transferred to the other time standards for other unit IoTs.

## 8.5 A Case Study in an Airport

A case at an airport is shown to illustrate the connotation of space-time consistency in IoT in Figure 8.2. Assume that in the airport scenario, local IoT consists of several unit IoTs, such as the ticket check system, safety check system, and monitor system. When a person enters the airport, his space-time characteristics can be detected by the multiple systems, and the corresponding space-time consistency should be considered in both unit IoT and ubiquitous IoT.

The person's information is recorded when he buys the ticket, which contains sensitive data such as the ticket holder's ID number and flight information (e.g., time, seat number, departing place, and destination). In addition, an identity card, passport, and driver's license can also store the person's information to represent the person's identity. Thus, a person's individual data can be associated with the corresponding cyber identifier by such physical cards.

As shown in Figure 8.2, when a person is identified by multiple systems at the airport, the space-time data can be obtained and

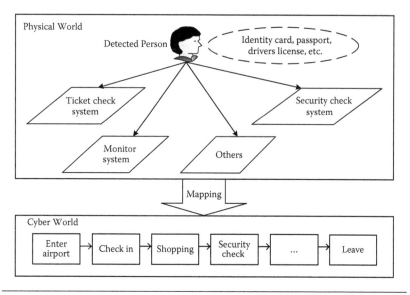

**Figure 8.2** A multiple-sensor–based identification system at the airport.

mapped from the physical world to the cyber world along with the information disclosure. For example, when the ticket system identifies the person during ticket checkin, the time data can be extracted to remind him of the departure time by reading the stored data in the ticket. Such services require time synchronization as the precondition. When the person passes the safety check system, the check time and place, namely, the person's space-time data, can also be obtained. The data can be stored as his relevant data via the corresponding identity. Similarly, for the monitor system, the detection space-time data referring to the person's tracking and position (e.g., entering the airport, going shopping, and leaving the airport) are also mapped into the cyber world. Hence, a series of space-time data are obtained, and can be used to monitor and analyze the person's location-related information, such as the person's trajectory and habits.

As the person is identified by multiple systems in U2IoT, space-time registration is required to achieve data consistent for further processing. If the person identified by the systems is confirmed as the same person, the achieved space-time data can be associated to the person's identity and jointly used to provide location-based or time-based services. The space-time data can also facilitate for the probability analysis that he appears in other scenarios. For instance, it can be used to exclude a suspect in a criminal investigation, as the person's activity range can be derived by certain space-time data. If more space-time data are collected, the ideal condition is that the person's trajectory can be obtained, and his attributes identified at different times are aggregated so that comprehensive attributes can be obtained by associating the obtained space-time data.

## 8.6  Location Privacy

The consistent space-time data of objects provides convenient and personalized services to objects, but also the divulgence of space-time data brings severe threats to objects' location privacy. Location privacy refers to the ability to prevent other parties from learning an object's current or past location. In other words, objects whose location is being measured should have the right to control who can know it, and other parties that get the location data legally also have the obligation of protecting the location privacy.

### 8.6.1  Main Characteristics of Location Privacy

Space-time data are one of the most important aspects of object attributes. If an object's space-time data are obtained by attackers, the sensitive information (e.g., personal interests, social relationship, and living habits) may be deduced and revealed. Such sensitive information disclosure may lead to privacy intrusion, and even criminal offense, such as kidnapping. In IoT, services are closely correlated with space-time data in most applications. This makes location privacy an important issue in future IoT.

There are two unique characteristics for location privacy:

- Location privacy is closely related to the QoS. The space-time data are provided to applications for location-based services. The precision of space-time data decides the quality of the delivered service. But, in some cases, more precision means more threats to the location privacy. So there is an implicit conflict between location privacy and service quality.
- Location data are extremely dynamic, and the divulgence of location data could be continuous. The location of the object is ever changing, so the collected location data are dynamic and

need to be detected frequently. The data exchange between objects and service providers is frequent. This characteristic brings convenience to the attacks and increases the threat on location privacy.

Based on the above characteristics, the attacks to location privacy can probably be summarized as the following types:

- *Observation.* Attackers can obtain location data by configuring devices in a sensitive environment or attaching them to the object.
- *Eavesdropping.* The location data, requests, and responses can be obtained by eavesdropping on the communication channel.
- *Spread.* The illegally obtained but sensitive location data may be traded from one to another illegal party.
- *Inference.* Location data aggregated by the above methods can be used to deduce other sensitive information of the objects. For example, the identity of an object can be inferred by tracking its moving pattern.

### 8.6.2 Location Privacy-Preserving Mechanism

The different approaches that exist for protecting location privacy mainly include three categories: policies, anonymity and pseudonymity, and obfuscation strategies.

#### 8.6.2.1 Privacy Policy

In the process of getting location-based service, objects have to reveal location data in some circumstances, such as customs, where identity data are required for ticket checking. Thus, privacy policy provides the privacy preservation against abuses of individual data. Privacy policy approaches attempt to ensure three aspects: legal services provider, location data quality, and service providing with conditions. Standards organizations have proposed some solutions: GeoPriv of the Internet Engineering Task Force (IETF), Privacy Preferences Project (P3P) of the World Wide Web Consortium (W3C), and Personal Digital Rights Management (PDRM).

However, the policy-based approaches only solve some of the location privacy problems. The existing policies for location privacy protection often lag behind technological and economic developments.

*8.6.2.2 Anonymity and Pseudonymity*  Anonymity concerns the dissociation of real identity data of an object from its location data. Pseudonymity is a particular anonymity mechanism, in which a pseudonym is generated to hide the real identifier. There are two typical approaches adapting anonymity and pseudonymity: $k$-anonymity [20] and mix zone [21].

- *k-Anonymity.* If the data for each object contained in a release cannot be distinguished from at least $k - 1$ individuals whose data also appear in the release. The only data to identify an object from a release can be its birth date and gender. There are $k$ objects satisfying the requirement. However, $k$-anonymity does not provide privacy when the sensitive data lack diversity in an equivalence class, or attackers have background knowledge.
- *Mix zone.* In mix zone networks, the infrastructure provides an anonymous service. The infrastructure can delay and reorder messages from subscribers within a mix zone, and confuse an observer. Based on a mix zone, there should be enough subscribers in the mix zone to provide an acceptable level of anonymity.

The anonymity and pseudonymity approaches can protect objects' real identity information, but these approaches have obvious disadvantages in location privacy preservation. For example, data mining technology can deduce the object's identification data using the location data. Furthermore, anonymity and pseudonymity are obstacles to authentication and personalization, which are widely used in applications.

*8.6.2.3 Obfuscation*  Obfuscation refers to the process of degrading the quality of the object's location data, which is similar to anonymity to hide data in order to protect privacy. The crucial difference between obfuscation and anonymity is their type of hidden data. Anonymity aims to hide an individual's real identity, while obfuscation is an explicitly spatial and temporal approach to location privacy that aims to allow a person's identity to be revealed.

There are three main typical mechanisms to degrade the quality of location data: inaccuracy, imprecision, and vagueness. Inaccuracy means that when providing location to the service provider, there are several locations, but only one position among the locations is accurate. Imprecision means that the provided location data are not the position where the user stands but some guideposts nearby. Vagueness means that the providing data may be an area in which the object stands.

### 8.6.3  Challenges and Open Issues

Due to the complexity of location privacy in IoT, several challenges should be considered:

- Achieving trade-off of location privacy and location awareness. Providing better access to the location-related data of individuals, while still enabling objects to preserve the control of the users and uses of their location data.
- Analyzing the possible attacks and establishing the robust attack model. Most existing approaches to protect location privacy have not taken full account of the possible attacks, resulting in their weak resilience to the different kinds of attacks. Robust attack models for location privacy need to be established based on the study of possible attacks.
- Achieving scalability of the location privacy protecting solutions. Most proposed solutions can only serve a small number of objects. However, in IoT, the number of objects and devices is huge, as well as the demand of location privacy protection. The mass data and ubiquitous communications will also be an obstacle to the scalability of location privacy protecting solutions.

### 8.7  Conclusion

Space-time consistency is a basic requirement for IoT, which is significant for the objects' mapping from the physical world to the cyber world. In order to satisfy this requirement, time synchronization and object localization should be introduced to obtain accurate space-time data, and space-time registration should be considered to provide consistent data. Then to explain the connotation of space-time consistency in IoT, a case in an airport is discussed. The consistent space-time data also bring threats to location privacy, and how to protect location privacy in IoT needs intensive consideration and research.

# References

1. Ma, H. 2011. Internet of Things: Objectives and scientific challenges. *Journal of Computer Science and Technology* 26: 919–924.
2. Nabaa, N., and R. H. Bishop. 1999. Solution to a multisensor tracking problem with sensor registration errors. *IEEE Transactions on Aerospace and Electronic Systems* 35: 354–363.
3. Li, W., H. Leung, and Y. Shou. 2004. Space-time registration of radar and ESM using unscented Kalman filter. *IEEE Transactions on Aerospace and Electronic Systems* 40: 824–836.
4. Fuiorea, D., V. Gui, D. Pescaru, and C. Toma. 2007. Using registration algorithms for wireless sensor network node localization. In *SACI '07: 4th International Symposium on Applied Computational Intelligence and Informatics*, 209–214.
5. Zhou, S., W. Cai, B.-S. Lee, and S. J. Turner. 2004. Time-space consistency in large-scale distributed virtual environments. *ACM Transactions on Modeling and Computer Simulation (TOMACS)* 14: 31–47.
6. Zhong, D., and S.-F. Chang. 2001. Long-term moving object segmentation and tracking using spatio-temporal consistency. In *Proceedings of 2001 International Conference on Image Processing*, 2: 57–60.
7. Ning, H., and Z. Wang. 2011. Future Internet of Things architecture: Like mankind neural system or social organization framework? *IEEE Communication Letter* 15: 461–463.
8. Mills, D. 1992. Network time protocol (version 3): Specification, implementation and analysis. Technical report, University of Delaware. https://ebook.tools.ietf.org/html/rfc1305 (accessed June 12, 2012).
9. Hofmann-Wellenhof, B., H. Lichtenegger, and J. Collins. 2001. *Global positioning system: Theory and practice*, 365. 5th ed., vol. 33. American Geophysical Union. Vienna: Springer-Verlag.
10. Elson, J., L. Girod, and D. Estrin. 2002. Fine-grained time synchronization using reference broadcasts. In *Proceedings of the 5th Symposium on Operating Systems Design and Implementation (OSDI 2002)*.
11. Ganeriwal, S., R. Kumar, and M. Srivastava. 2003. Timing sync protocol for sensor networks. In *Proceedings of the 1st ACM International Conference on Embedded Networked Sensor Systems*, 138–149.
12. Maróti, M., B. Kusy, G. Simon, and Á. Lédeczi. 2004. The flooding time synchronization protocol. In *Proceedings of 2nd ACM International Conference on Embedded Networked Sensor Systems*, 39–49.

13. Sichitiu, M. L., and C. Veerarittiphan. 2003. Simple, accurate time synchronization for wireless sensor networks. *IEEE Transactions on Wireless Communications and Networking* 2: 1266–1273.
14. Greunen, J. V., and J. Rabaey. 2003. Lightweight time synchronization for sensor networks. In *Proceedings of the 2nd ACM International Conference on Wireless Sensor Networks and Applications (WSNA)*, 11–19.
15. ZEBRA Technologies. Industrial machinery. http://www.zebra.com/us/en/-solutions/industry/manufacturing/industrial-machinery.html (accessed August 18, 2012).
16. Ekahau. Healthcare tracking solutions. http://www.ekahau.com/ (accessed August 18, 2012).
17. Brumitt, B., B. Meyers, J. Krumm, A. Kern, and S. Shafer. 2000. Easyliving: Technologies for intelligent environments. *Handheld and Ubiquitous Computing* 97–119.
18. Blair, W. D., T. R. Rice, and A. T. Alouani. 1991. Asynchronous data fusion for target tracking with a multi-tasking radar and optical sensor. In *Proceedings of the 2nd SPIE Conference on Tracking and Pointing*, 234–245.
19. Baoshu, W., and L. Fenshe. 1998. Multi-target tracking algorithm research based on data fusion. *Journal of Xidian University* 25: 269–272.
20. Gedik, B., and L. Liu. 2008. Protecting location privacy with personalized *k*-anonymity: Architecture and algorithms. *IEEE Transactions on Mobile Computing* 7: 1–18.
21. Beresford, A. R., and F. Stajano. 2003. Location privacy in pervasive computing. *IEEE Transactions on Pervasive Computing* 2: 46–55.

# Security and Privacy

## 9.1 Introduction

In Internet of Things (IoT), ubiquitous things are associated with cyber, physical, and social considerations [1,2]. Security and privacy issues become particularly more noteworthy. Several open issues in security and privacy should be considered. For example: How do we design appropriate security solutions for different applications? What advanced security mechanisms are applied in interconnection among mass things? How do we maintain a balance between things' security requirements and supporting infrastructures' hardware limitations? How do we achieve a trade-off between individual privacy preserving and information sharing? These security-related issues influence future IoT development, making security and privacy critical issues.

Several solutions have been presented for IoT security and privacy issues, including security architectures and recommended countermeasures [3–7], specific communication and sensing techniques [8–12], cryptographic mechanisms [13–17], and practical applications and scenarios [18–20]. The previous security studies can be categorized into three aspects: system security, network security, and application security.

- *System security* mainly considers the whole system to identify the security requirements and challenges, to design security frameworks, and to provide recommended security measures.
- *Network security* focuses on wireless and wired communication networks (e.g., radio frequency identification [RFID], wireless sensor networks [WSNs], and Internet Protocol [IP] network) to design key distribution algorithms, authentication protocols, advanced signature algorithms, and access control mechanisms.

- *Application security* serves applications (e.g., intelligent transportation and smart grid) and addresses practical problems to satisfy particular scenario requirements.

In IoT, security and privacy are important to ensure reliable interactions in the physical world and cyber world. In the following, Section 9.2 introduces major security challenges in U2IoT (i.e., unit and ubiquitous IoT). Furthermore, Section 9.3 establishes a security model with information, physical, and management considerations, and Section 9.4 proposes a hybrid authentication and hierarchical authorization scheme for U2IoT to realize security protection and privacy preservation. Section 9.5 presents an entity activity cycle based security solution for future IoT. Finally, Section 9.6 draws a conclusion.

## 9.2 Security Challenges in U2IoT

### 9.2.1 Security Requirements

There are four main security requirements in IoT, including data confidentiality, data integrity, and data availability (CIA triad); authority; nonrepudiation; and privacy preservation.

#### 9.2.1.1 CIA Triad

The CIA triad refers to the basic security requirements:

1. *Confidentiality*. Protect data from unauthorized disclosure.
2. *Integrity*. Ensure correctness or accuracy of data.
3. *Availability*. Ensure that there is no denial of authorized access to network elements, information flow, services, and applications.

Cryptographic algorithms should be designed to achieve such a CIA triad in the heterogeneous networks infrastructure. Additional security requirements should also be considered:

- *Forward and backward unlinkability*. Ensure the interrogations during prior and later sessions of unlinkability, and ubiquitous things cannot be correlated with their corresponding physical, cyber, and social considerations.
- *Dynamic session freshness*. Applies session freshness mechanisms into the data integrity check to achieve dynamic sessions.

- *Self-identification and nonself-identification.* Ensure that an authorized self object/entity can access the network resources and services, and eliminate any nonself object/entity.

*9.2.1.2 Authority* Authority refers to authentication and authorization. The former ensures that only legal things can access network resources, and excludes any illegal object/entity from the networks. The latter realizes classified access control among legal things. Meanwhile, additional mechanisms are also considered in U2IoT.

- *Intelligent access control.* Uses heterogeneous authentication and identification for access control on legal information interoperation.
- *Compatible certificate authority.* Authenticates object/entity and grant authority to access system resources.
- *Hierarchical authentication.* Establishes hierarchical authentication, individual/group authentication, and source/terminal authentication.

*9.2.1.3 Nonrepudiation* Nonrepudiation is traditionally defined as providing available proofs to prevent any object/entity from denying a performed particular behavior/action related to the exchanged messages, to ensure the availability of evidence that can be presented by a trusted third party (TTP), and to prove that an object/entity's behavior or action has occurred before. Moreover, social factors are attached to an object/entity's identity, which are applied for compatible social computing and behavior/action supervision.

*9.2.1.4 Privacy Preservation* Privacy refers to individual sensitive information, which may be derived from the observation of network activities, and should be protected with the privacy-utility trade-offs. In IoT, privacy preservation has additional considerations:

- *Transparency.* Lets a user (individual user and group user) know which object/entity contains the related data, when and where the object/entity has used the data, and how the object/entity realizes the specific function.
- *Traceability.* Lets a user know whether the network and service information have ever connected.

*9.2.2 Security Attacks*

In U2IoT, malicious threats during an interaction are classified into four attack categories: gathering, imitation, blocking, and privacy disclosure. Therefore, the sensor-actuator layer and network layer directly suffer from the gathering, imitation, and blocking attacks, and the application layer mainly confronts the imitation, blocking, and privacy disclosure attacks. In the service integration layer, national management layer, and international coordinator layer, attacks similar to those in the application layer also suffer. Note that such attacks also have correlations (e.g., a gathering attack may lead to imitation and further cause privacy disclosure).

*9.2.2.1 Gathering*  Gathering refers to the data collection–related attacks, including skimming, tempering, eavesdropping, and traffic analysis.

- *Skimming* is an unauthorized access of a quick reading on a target (e.g., RFID tag), and the target's sensitive data are directly read without obtaining authority.
- *Tampering* is an unauthorized data modification or deletion to achieve deliberate data destruction and corruption.
- *Eavesdropping* is unauthorized listening and intercepting via the communication channels of an authorized transmission to record the exchanged data among legal things.
- *Traffic analysis* detects or monitors the exchanged data packets and communication stream, and deduces information from the communication patterns.

*9.2.2.2 Imitation*  Imitation refers to the attacks of data/identity cheating, including spoofing, cloning, replay, and Sybil attack.

- *Spoofing* means that an illegal object/entity imitates a legal data source to transmit duplicate data, in which the object/entity may be disguised as another object/entity by falsifying data and thereby gaining illegal interests.
- *Cloning* refers to an attacker duplicating a legal object/entity's valid data, and the obtained data can be rewritten into an equivalent object/entity.

- *Replay* occurs when a valid data transmission is intercepted during the former deliveries, then is repeated or delayed by the originator or another object/entity.
- *Sybil attack* represents a reputation system being subverted by creating multiple pseudonyms to forge identities in peer-to-peer (P2P) networks.

*9.2.2.3 Blocking*   Blocking refers to the active attacks of system or communication channel interferences, including denial of service (DoS), jamming, and malware.

- *DoS* is caused by flooding data streams with false addresses, which interfere in normal communication to overwhelm the system resource, and to render it inoperative.
- *Jamming* interdicts communication channels with an electronic device, and disrupts the object/entity's function by using wireless signals in the same frequency band.
- *Malware* includes computer viruses, worms, Trojan horses, most rootkits, spyware, dishonest adware, and other malicious or unauthorized programs. Additionally, other attacks (e.g., blackhole, sinkhole, and wormhole) are also regarded as malware attacks, which apply malicious nodes to interfere with the normal routing path selection and communication.

*9.2.2.4 Privacy Disclosure*   Privacy disclosure refers to sensitive information revelation, including individual privacy disclosure and group privacy disclosure.

- *Individual privacy disclosure* refers to speculation of an individual user's information, such as locations, interests, and behavior/actions. It correlates sensitive data with the user's real identity.
- *Group privacy disclosure* includes commercial espionage, in-group/out-group unauthorized access, and trusted domain disclosure.

Table 9.1 summarizes the major attacks against security and recommended countermeasures.

**Table 9.1** Security Attacks and Recommended Countermeasures

|  | ATTACK | IMPACT | COUNTERMEASURE |
|---|---|---|---|
| Gathering | Skimming | Quickly read the transmitted messages for data abuse | Encryption, steganography, and anonymous data transmission |
|  | Tampering | Modify or delete the messages for data cheating | Hash function, cyclic redundancy check (CRC), and message authentication code (MAC) |
|  | Eavesdropping | Collect raw data to determine the exchanged communication data, collect the target's sensitive data, and determine traffic patterns | Encryption, identity-based authentication, concealed data aggregation, and anonymous data transmission |
|  | Traffic analysis | Difficult to detect in the open interfaces | Network forensics, and update keys periodically |
| Imitation | Spoofing | Impersonate as a legal object/entity to obtain the trust and authority for further cheating purposes | Identity-based authentication, key predistribution (e.g., topology-aware group key agreement), digital signature (e.g., RSA and ElGamal), digital certificate, and secure communication based on Internet Protocol Security (IPSec) |
|  | Cloning | Data reproduction | Physically unclonable function (PUF) and secure distributed data storage |
|  | Replay | Record and store the data of former sessions to involve the current session communication | Timestamp, time synchronization, time-variant nonce, pseudorandom number, dynamic session identifier, and serial number |
|  | Sybil attack | Impersonate as multiple things to establish communication with neighbor nodes, and to become a routing node for collusion attack | Secure routing, distributed storage, data aggregation, voting, fair resource allocation, and misbehavior detection |
| Blocking | Denial of service (DoS) | Exhaust the system resource to make the normal communication unavailable | Use a firewall, switches, and router control; broaden bandwidth; and quickly check mechanism |
|  | Jamming | Electromagnetic interference or interdiction | Antijamming, active jamming, and Faraday cage |

**Table 9.1 (Continued)** Security Attacks and Recommended Countermeasures

| | ATTACK | IMPACT | COUNTERMEASURE |
|---|---|---|---|
| | Malware | Disturb the system to make it unavailable | Antivirus program, firewall, intrusion detection, and active defense mechanism |
| Privacy disclosure | Individual privacy disclosure | Derive an individual user's identity, location, social attribute, and other private information | Aggregated proof establishment, periodical anonymous data transmission, concealed data aggregation (CDA), and advanced digital signature (e.g., blind/group/ring signature) |
| | Group privacy disclosure | Evaluate a group user's commercial interests, and deduce its affiliated individual's sensitive data | Zero-knowledge proof, selective disclosure, and data distortion and equivocation |

## 9.3 The Security Framework for U2IoT

A systematic security framework that integrates the awareness and inter-activity of the cyber world, physical world, and social world is proposed for U2IoT, as shown in Figure 9.1. The proposed security framework considers the aspects of information, physical, and management, and realizes the unison of the cyber world, physical world, and social world to address the security and privacy issues in three perspectives.

- *Information security* mainly considers basic and advanced security/privacy issues in the cyber world. Awareness of information data is interpreted and represented by things,

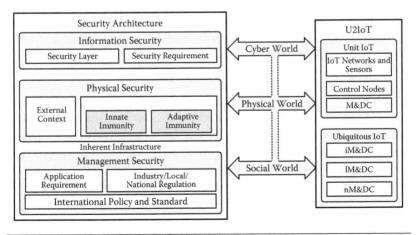

**Figure 9.1** The security framework for U2IoT.

and authentication algorithms, security protocols; interaction functions are also included for intelligent information interactions.

- *Physical security*, including external context and inherent infrastructure, is inspired by artificial immunity, and ensures that things should be adaptable to dynamic semantic contexts with innate and adaptive immunities against malicious attacks. It relates to environmental monitoring, motion detection, and perimeter control. Artificial immunity is applied to resist passive attacks (e.g., eavesdropping) and active attacks (e.g., spoofing and replay).

- *Management security* provides the recommended strategies for hierarchical classified scenes with rationality and compatibility, including the recommended application requirements; local, industry, or national regulations; and international policy/standards to guide activities and events in human society.

### 9.3.1 Information Security

Information security protects both raw data and contextualized information, in which intelligence and compatibility should be considered.

- *Intelligence* means that an object/entity should own the capabilities, including self-learning, self-adapting, and self-reasoning, to adapt itself to dynamic semantic contexts. In nondeterministic channels and open interfaces, virtual intelligent things should be autonomously interconnected in U2IoT. Intelligence makes objects/entities have strong efficacies to adapt dynamic environments, including cyber interactions, social connections, and human participation.

- *Compatibility* means that an object/entity has appropriate interconnection and interoperability mechanisms to adapt to heterogeneous data formats, interfaces, channels, and networks in U2IoT. The supplemental requirements address advanced criteria for information interaction. Meanwhile, compatibility can be promoted to scalability, expansibility, and modularity among the multicontext-based heterogeneous things.

The two above-mentioned requirements are jointly applied for information security: (1) to ensure diverse things to own artificial intelligence and autonomous security control against the strong attackers, and (2) to ensure heterogeneous things, networks, and applications to establish reliable interconnection without compromising any communication data and individual privacy.

### 9.3.2 Physical Security

Physical security is denoted in the external context and inherent infrastructure, in which a human-like security-immune safeguard is implemented.

*External context.* Simple context and complex context are specified by Wang et al. [16], in which the former determines the basic identity, location, and object/entity status by a single parameter, and the latter refers to geographical structures, traceability information, and environment. Both contexts are refined to support creating, debugging, and integrating applications in ubiquitous IoT, and providing a controlled interface for unit IoTs. In U2IoT, the borders of the external context merge—even vanish—and the obscure contexts spanning from an object/entity, or an environment to social relationships, should support the hierarchical applications. The intrusion detection algorithm is particularly significant for acquiring context information for monitoring sensors, discovering control node breaches, and other potential vulnerabilities.

*Inherent infrastructure.* Inherent infrastructure is an artificial immune security system. Computational intelligence is applied to analyze the inherent infrastructure, which belongs to a sensor-based system inspired by principles and processes of the natural immune system. Typical algorithms (e.g., clonal selection, negative selection, and immune network) exploit the immune system's features (e.g., detection, learning capacity, and memory) to constitute innate immunity and adaptive immunity. Physical security issues such as intrusion detection, adaptive disposition, context-driven feedback, and error recovery can be addressed based on the following immunity-inspired mechanisms:

- *Innate immunity.* Innate immunity provides basic defenses against external invasions in a real-time environment, and is triggered by the intelligent pattern recognition mechanisms upon identifying abnormal or malevolent attacks. Costimulation signals are transmitted to distributed control nodes via unit IoT, and then reactions of rejection are performed by management centers. During defense operations, activation thresholds are defined to ensure detection optimization, and fuzzy diagnosis can also be applied for imperfect detection. Note that the innate immune defense is nonspecific, which means that U2IoT responds to the various attacks in a general scheme. Such a system cannot afford long-lasting immunity against a certain attack. The innate immune system is dominant to confront the dynamic contexts and continuously refreshing threats.

- *Adaptive immunity.* Adaptive immunity refers to acquired resistance, where an attack is marked as a specific signature. Selective response requires recognizing a nonself object/entity during an attack prototype presentation. If U2IoT has been infected by the same or similar invasion, a specific memory module would be aroused to eliminate damage by generating an improved response to recover the system into a secure state. Adaptive immunity executes fuzzy diagnosis to variations of the same former attack, and optimal stimulation such as subsidiary vaccination is available by updating each management and data center's (M&DC) profile database.

According to the innate and adaptive immunities [21], there are three main features that can also be considered in IoT physical security.

- *Multithreaded and hybrid configuration.* U2IoT may apply multithreaded security algorithms to the parallel network architecture that comprises a diverse set of components. The components are organized in hybrid mode, in which both centralized and distributed configurations are included. For unit IoT, the allocation of sensing and query processing is performed by M&DC. Industrial IoTs and local IoTs are relatively independent, which commonly construct national IoT. In U2IoT, such multithreaded and hybrid configurations are present throughout all the networks, sensors-actuators, and M&DCs.
- *Multilayered and autonomous organization.* There is no single security mechanism that offers complete immunity. Therefore, multilayered protection should operate independently for enhanced

safeguards. During the layered organization, U2IoT autonomously makes decisions by detecting potential attacks and proposing feasible solutions based on artificial immune algorithms.

- *Heterogeneity*. U2IoT should be accessible by a large number of heterogeneous things with different networks, channels, interfaces, and hardware/software capabilities. Such heterogeneity of things adds complexity to its security situations, which allows for a certain attack to simultaneously act on multiple things in different IoTs, but the attack cannot act on all of the involved IoTs. Immune protection ensures that the entire heterogeneous components cannot be corrupted due to the same attacker.

### 9.3.3 Management Security

Due to the limitations of technological approaches, appropriate management should be coupled with the implementation of information security and physical security. Security strategies working on human factors should be considered to ensure that cyber data are adapted to the physical contexts. The related management aspects are discussed as follows.

*Application requirements* provide generic/specific protection for distributed sensors and actuators, and serve unit IoTs to offer project management, risk assessment, software design, and system certification. For example, customized requirements are assigned to describe authorized/unauthorized utilization toward an individual or organization. Additionally, application requirements should also be consistent with privacy preservation, which realizes that the sensitive data can be exchanged, stored, and shared without revealing any privacy.

*Industry, local, and national regulations* mainly serve industrial M&DC (iM&DC), local M&DC (lM&DC), and national M&DC (nM&DC) to provide suitable rules and guidance, and apply legal/disciplinary approaches to avoid offenses. Therein, industry regulation provides approaches to achieve security objectives for a special industrial authority. For instance, in chemical hazards medical management, some parameters (e.g., temperature and vibrations) should be regulated to guarantee system security, and abnormal configurations should cause an automatic warning. As a result, local regulation should be developed according to the local customs, and adopt human-istic concerns to design, implement, and maintain local IoTs. National regulation aims to manage nationwide local IoTs and industrial IoTs, and formal memoranda of agreements need to be shared among multiple nations.

*International policy* considers national cooperation and coordi-nation during connectivity and consistency of national IoT and transnational IoT. International standards should be addressed by international organizations to promote security confidence and ensure interoperability. It indicates that inter-national frameworks with reasonable enforcement policies should be designed for long-term security planning.

## 9.4 A Proposed Hybrid Authentication and Hierarchical Authorization Scheme

Among the mentioned security mechanisms, authentication and authorization can provide efficient security protection and privacy preservation to resist the confidentiality- and integrity-related attacks. In U2IoT, hybrid authentication and hierarchical authentication can be designed according to the heterogeneous networks.

Suppose that there are $\{T, S, MC\}$ in unit IoT, and $\{MC, lMC/iMC, nMC\}$ in ubiquitous IoT, in which $MC$ has two variants $\{MC_l, MC_i\}$ under $\{lMC, iMC\}$'s jurisdictions. Each object/entity has the corresponding identify flag, pseudonym, and preshared secrets. For $\{T, S\}$, they have an additional group identifier. Four types of keys $\{k_{au}, k_{se}, k_{pu}, k_{pr}\}$ are assigned for encryption/signature; therein, $\{k^1_x, k^2_x, k^3_x, k^4_x\}$ $(x = \{au, pu, pr\})$ are respectively appointed to $\{T, S\}$, $\{S, MC\}$, $\{MC, lMC/iMC\}$, and $\{lMC/iMC, nMC\}$, and $\{k^1_y, k^2_y\}$ $(y = \{se\})$ are respectively assigned to $\{T, MC\}$ and $\{lMC, iMC\}$. The notations are introduced in Table 9.2. In U2IoT, $\{T, S, MC, lMC/iMC, nMC\}$ can be categorized into the following four aspects:

- The *sensor–target aspect* includes multiple general sensors $(S)$ and ubiquitous targets $(T)$, which may be different according to the detailed communication scenarios. For example, $\{S, T\}$ respectively refer to the reader and tag in RFID systems.

**Table 9.2** Notations

| NOTATION | DESCRIPTION |
|---|---|
| $nMC$ | The nM&DC in national IoT. |
| $IMC, iMC$ | The IM&DC and iM&DC in local/industrial IoT. |
| $MC$ | The M&DC in unit IoT. {$MC_j$, $MC_i$} are two variants under {$IMC$, $iMC$}'s jurisdictions. |
| $S, T$ | The sensor and target in unit IoT. |
| $T_p, T_a$ | The passive target and active target in unit IoT. |
| $k_{au}, k_{se}$ | The authentication key and secret key (one-time pad). |
| $k_{pu}, k_{pr}$ | The pairwise public key and private key. |
| $F, PID, gid$ | The identify flag, pseudonym, and group identifier. |
| $S_{[x,y]}, S_{[y,x]}$ | The shared pairwise secrets between $x$ and $y$. |
| $p^x_y$ | The pointer that points from $x$ to $y$; it satisfies that $p^x_y = p^z_y + p^x_z$, and the available pointer makes {$x, y$}'s authority sharing. |
| $ts, r$ | The timestamp and random number. |
| $Cert, Sig(.)$ | The certificate and signature. |
| $E(.), H(.)$ | The encryption and hash function. |

- The *unit management aspect*, acting as the mediacy layer, includes the unit management centers (i.e., $MC$s). MCs are organized into different groups and are under the corresponding local/industrial IoT's jurisdictions.
- The *local and industrial management aspect* mainly comprises the local and industry management centers (i.e., $iMC$ and $IMC$), which have relatively independent authorities on a certain $MC$.
- The *national management aspect* includes a top trusted national management center ($nMC$) to manage national IoT.

In the following, a security scheme is proposed based on the layered communication model, and it includes two protocol suites to guarantee unit IoT and ubiquitous IoT. In the scheme, six protocols are proposed as follows:

- The in-group hybrid authentication protocol in unit IoT (P1)
- The out-group centralized authorization protocol in unit IoT (P2)
- The centralized authentication protocol in ubiquitous IoT (P3)
- The distributed authority transfer protocol in ubiquitous IoT (P4)
- The centralized authority transfer protocol in ubiquitous IoT (P5)
- The distributed authority sharing protocol in ubiquitous IoT (P6)

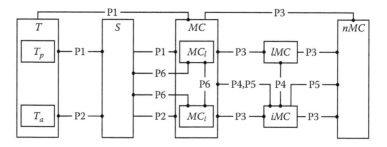

**Figure 9.2** The proposed authentication and authorization scheme.

Therein, P1 to P2 and P3 to P6 are jointly applied to realize hybrid authentication and authority management in unit IoT and ubiquitous IoT. Figure 9.2 illustrates the interrelation of the six protocols, and the verification points (marked as black dots). For instance, in P1, $T$ and $S$ verify each other to establish the mutual authentication, and $MC$ as a trusted entity only verifies $S$ without being verified by $S$. Assume that the channel between $\{T, S\}$ belongs to the sensor-actuator–based networks, and the channels among $\{MC, lMC/iMC, nMC\}$ belong to computer networks.

For the trust model, $nMC$ is an only entity trusted by all the other things (i.e., $T, S, MC, lMC/iMC$), and there are no other direct trusting relationships. In unit IoT, $MC$ is regarded as a trusted entity by $\{T, S\}$, which are under $MC$'s default jurisdiction. $\{lMC, iMC\}$ have relatively independent jurisdictions on the corresponding $\{MC_l s, MC_i s\}$ in ubiquitous IoT.

The attacker may (1) impersonate a legal entity (except the trusted entity, e.g., $nMC$) to modify the intercepted messages, (2) eavesdrop and record the exchanged messages in the former sessions, and replay them in the current session, and (3) perform tracking and traffic analysis to monitor the ongoing communication.

The attacker cannot (1) obtain preshared secrets, keys, or identifiers, and distort the timestamp of the exchanged messages; (2) extract the pseudonym via the intercepted messages, and generate the consistent pseudonyms; or (3) acquire the pseudorandom generation algorithm, hash function, and encryption/signature algorithms.

Note that the proposed security scheme mainly considers the open security challenges of authentication and authorization in U2IoT, and it is a security draft solution based on typical cryptographic operators (e.g., timestamp, pseudonym, and hash function). Other detailed cryptographic algorithms can be directly applied in the scheme to support enhanced security efficacy.

### 9.4.1 The Security Protocol Suite in Unit IoT (UnSPs)

In unit IoT, $\{T, S, MC\}$ are considered to establish the authentication and authorization protocol suite (UnSPs). $T$ may act as a passive target $T_p$ or an active target $T_a$ to establish communication. The wireless channels between $T$ and $S$ are suffering from serious attacks, and the channels between $S$ and $MC$ can be regarded as secure.

#### 9.4.1.1 The In-Group Hybrid Authentication Protocol in UnSPs
The in-group hybrid authentication protocol considers the authentication among $\{T_p/T_a, S, MC\}$, in which $\{T_p/T_a, S\}$ belong to the same group under $MC$'s jurisdictions. During the authentication, $\{T_p/T_a, S\}$ first establish mutual authentication in the distributed mode, and afterward MC further verifies $\{T_p/T_a, S\}$ in the centralized mode.

- Case 1: The authentication among $\{T_p, S, MC\}$ is shown in Figure 9.3a.

  Phase 1 ($S$ authenticating $T_p$). $S$ generates a random number $r_S$, extracts the pseudoidentify flag $F_S$, and transmits $r_S \| F_S$ to $T_p$. Upon receiving the query, $T_p$ generates $r_{Tp}$, extracts

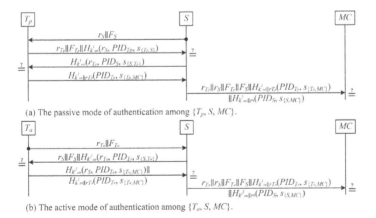

(a) The passive mode of authentication among $\{T_p, S, MC\}$.

(b) The active mode of authentication among $\{T_a, S, MC\}$.

**Figure 9.3** The in-group hybrid authentication protocol in UnSPs.

$F_{Tp}$, and computes $H_{k^1_{au}}(r_S, PID_{Tp}, s_{\{Tp,S\}})$, in which $k^1_{au}$ is a shared authentication key, and $s_{\{Tp,S\}}$ is a shared secret by $\{T_p, S\}$. Thereafter, $T_p$ replies $r_{Tp}||F_{Tp}||H_{k^1_{au}}(.)$ to $S$. When $S$ receives the message, $S$ first ascertains $T_p$'s identity by $F_{Tp}$, then extracts $\{PID_{Tp}, s_{\{S,Tp\}}\}$ and locally recomputes $H_{k^1_{au}}(r_S, PID_{Tp}, s_{\{Tp,S\}})$. Therein, the pairwise secrets $\{s_{\{Tp,S\}}, s_{\{S,Tp\}}\}$ satisfy the bijection function. Then, $S$ verifies $T_p$ by checking whether the recomputed hash value equals the received hash value. If it holds, $S$ will regard $T_p$ as a legal target; otherwise, the protocol will terminate.

Phase 2 ($T_p$ authenticating $S$). $S$ computes the hash value $H_{k^1_{au}}(r_{Tp}, PID_S, s_{\{S,Tp\}})$ and transmits it to $T_p$. Upon receiving the message, $T_p$ extracts $\{PID_S, s_{\{Tp,S\}}\}$, obtains $s_{\{S,Tp\}}$ by $s_{\{Tp,S\}}$, and recomputes $H_{k^1_{au}}(r_{Tp}, PID_S, s_{\{S,Tp\}})$ to verify $S$. If it holds, $T_p$ will regard $S$ as a legal sensor; otherwise, the protocol will terminate. $T_p$ further extracts $s_{\{Tp,MC\}}$ to compute $H_{k^1_{se}||rTp}(PID_{Tp}, s_{\{Tp,MC\}})$ by the randomly wrapped secret key $\{k^1_{se}||r_{Tp}\}$, and transmits it to $S$.

Phase 3 ($MC$ authenticating $\{T_p, S\}$). $S$ computes $H_{k^2_{au}||rS}(PID_S, s_{\{S,MC\}})$ and transmits the cascaded value $r_{Tp}||r_S||F_{Tp}||F_S$ and $H_{k^1_{se}||rTp}(.)||H_{k^2_{au}||rS}(.)$ to $MC$. Thereafter, $MC$ ascertains $\{T_p, S\}$'s identities by $\{F_{Tp}, F_S\}$, and then it extracts $\{PID_{Tp}, PID_S, s_{\{Tp,MC\}}, s_{\{S,MC\}}\}$ to recompute the hash values to verify $\{T_p, S\}$. If both hold, $MC$ will regard $\{T_p, S\}$ as legal things to establish the trusting relationships; otherwise, the protocol will terminate.

- Case 2: The authentication among $\{T_a, S, MC\}$ is shown in Figure 9.3b.

Phase 1 ($T_a$ authenticating $S$). $T_a$ generates $r_{Ta}$, extracts $F_{Ta}$, and transmits $r_{Ta}||F_{Ta}$ to challenge $T_a$. Upon receiving the message, $S$ generates $r_S$, extracts $\{F_S, s_{\{S,Ta\}}\}$, and computes $H_{k^1_{au}}(r_{Ta}, PID_{Ta}, s_{\{S,Ta\}})$. Thereafter, $S$ transmits $r_S||F_S||H_{k^1_{au}}(.)$ to $T_a$. $T_a$ further recomputes $H_{k^1_{au}}(r_{Ta}, PID_{Ta}, s_{\{S,Ta\}})$ to verify $S$. If it holds, $T_a$ will regard $S$ as a legal sensor; otherwise, the protocol will terminate.

Phase 2 ($S$ authenticating $T_a$). $T_a$ computes the hash values $H_{k^1_{au}}(r_S, PID_{Ta}, s_{\{Ta,MC\}})$ and $H_{k^1_{se}||rTa}(PID_{Ta}, s_{\{Ta,MC\}})$, and transmits $H_{k^{'1}_{au}}(.)\|H_{k^{'1}_{se}\|rTa}(.)$ to $S$. Upon receiving the message, $S$ recomputes $H_{k^{'1}_{au}}(r_S, PID_{Ta}, s_{\{Ta,MC\}})$ to verify $T_a$. If it holds, $S$ will regard $T_a$ as a legal target; otherwise, the protocol will terminate.

Phase 3 ($MC$ authenticating $\{T_a, S\}$). $S$ further extracts $\{PID_S, s_{\{S,MC\}}\}$ to compute $H_{k^{'2}_{au}\|rs}(PID_S, s_{\{S,MC\}})$, and transmits $r_{Ta}\|r_S\|F_{Ta}\|F_S\|H_{k^{'1}_{se}\|rTa}(.)\|H_{k^{'2}_{au}\|rs}(.)$ to $MC$. Through passing the final authentication on $\{T_a, S\}$, the trusting relationships are established.

*9.4.1.2 The Out-Group Centralized Authorization Protocol in UnSPs* The out-group centralized authorization protocol considers the authorization among $\{T_p/T_a, S, MC\}$, in which $\{T_p/T_a, S\}$ belong to the different groups with $MC$'s jurisdictions. It means that $\{S, MC\}$ have different authorities on $T_p/T_a$. During the authorization, $S$ first passes $MC$'s verification to obtain the authority on $T_p/T_a$ in the centralized mode; thereafter, $\{T_p/T_a, S\}$ further establish mutual authentication.

- Case 1: The authorization among $\{T_p, S, MC\}$ is shown in Figure 9.4a.

  Phase 1 (challenge-response of $\{T_p, S\}$). $S$ generates $r_S$, extracts $F_S$, and transmits $r_S\|F_S$ to $T_p$. Then, $T_p$ generates $r_{Tp}$,

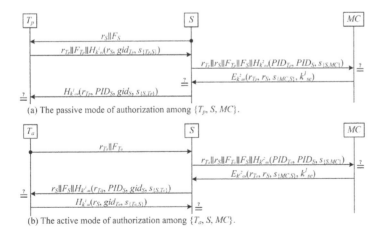

(a) The passive mode of authorization among $\{T_p, S, MC\}$.

(b) The active mode of authorization among $\{T_a, S, MC\}$.

**Figure 9.4** The out-group centralized authorization protocol in UnSPs.

extracts $\{F_{Tp}, gid_{Tp}\}$, computes $H_{k^1_{se}}(r_S, gid_{Tp}, s_{\{Tp,S\}})$, and transmits $r_{Tp}||F_{Tp}||H_{k^1_{se}}(.)$ to $S$. Upon receiving the message, $S$ extracts $\{PID_{Tp}, PID_S, s_{\{S,MC\}}\}$ to compute $H_{k^2_{au}}(PID_{Tp}, PID_S, s_{\{S,MC\}})$, and then transmits $r_{Tp}||r_S||F_{Tp}||F_S||H_{k^2_{au}}(.)$ to $MC$.

Phase 2 ($MC$ authorizing $S$). $MC$ ascertains $\{T_p, S\}$'s identities by $\{F_{Tp}, F_S\}$, and extracts the corresponding values to recompute $H_{k^2_{au}}(PID_{Tp}, PID_S, s_{\{S,MC\}})$. Therein, $s_{\{MC,S\}}$ is used to obtain $s_{\{S,MC\}}$. $MC$ verifies $S$ by comparing whether the recomputed and received hash values are identical. If it holds, $MC$ will regard $S$ as a legal sensor and grant $S$ the authority on $T_p$; otherwise, the protocol will terminate.

Phase 3 ($\{T_p, S\}$'s mutual authentication). $MC$ extracts and wraps $k^1_{se}$ into $E_{k^2_{au}}(r_{Tp}, r_S, s_{\{MC,S\}}, k^1_{se})$ and transmits it to $S$. Upon receiving the message, $S$ performs decryption to obtain $k^1_{se}$, and then $S$ extracts $s_{\{S,Tp\}}$ to obtain $s_{\{Tp,S\}}$, and applies $k^1_{se}$ to recompute $H_{k^1_{se}}(r_S, gid_{Tp}, s_{\{Tp,S\}})$. Thereafter, $S$ verifies $T_p$ by comparing whether the recomputed value equals the received value. If it holds, $S$ will regard $T_p$ as a legal target; otherwise, the protocol will terminate. $S$ proceeds to extract $\{PID_S, gid_S\}$ to compute $H_{k^1_{au}}(r_{Tp}, PID_S, gid_S, s_{\{S,Tp\}})$ and transmits it to $T_p$. When $T_p$ receives the message, it recomputes $H_{k^1_{au}}(r_{Tp}, PID_S, gid_S, s_{\{S,Tp\}})$ to verify $S$. If it holds, $T_p$ will regard $S$ as a legal sensor; otherwise, the protocol will terminate.

- Case 2: The authorization among $\{T_a, S, MC\}$ is shown in Figure 9.4b.

  Phase 1 ($T_a$'s challenge and $MC$ authorizing $S$). $T_a$ generates $r_{Ta}$, extracts $F_{Ta}$, and transmits $r_{Ta}||F_{Ta}$ to $T_a$. Upon receiving the message, $S$ generates $r_S$, extracts $\{F_S, PID_{Ta}, PID_S, s_{\{S,MC\}}\}$, and further computes $H_{k^2_{au}}(PID_{Ta}, PID_S, s_{\{S,MC\}})$. Thereafter, $S$ transmits $r_{Ta}||r_S||F_{Ta}||F_S||H_{k^2_{au}}(.)$ to $MC$. Similarly, $MC$ recomputes the hash value to verify $S$. If it holds, $MC$ will regard $S$ as a legal sensor and $S$ will obtain the authority on $T_a$; otherwise, the protocol will terminate.

  Phase 2 ($\{T_a, S\}$'s mutual authentication). $MC$ transmits $E_{k^2_{au}}(r_{Ta}, r_S, s_{\{MC,S\}}, k^1_{se})$ to $S$. $S$ performs decryption to derive $k^1_{se}$, and extracts $\{PID_S, gid_S, s_{\{S,Ta\}}\}$ to compute $H_{k^1_{au}}(r_{Ta}, PID_S,$ $gid_S, s_{\{S,Ta\}})$. Thereafter, $S$ transmits $r_S \| F_S \| H_{k^1_{au}}(.)$ to $T_a$. Upon receiving the message, $T_a$ locally recomputes $H_{k^1_{au}}$ $(r_{Ta}, PID_S, gid_S, s_{\{S,Ta\}})$ to verify $S$. If $S$ passes the verification, $T_a$ will extract $\{gid_{Ta}, s_{\{Ta,S\}}\}$ to compute $H_{k^1_{se}}(r_S, gid_{Ta},$ $s_{\{Ta, S\}})$ and transmits it to $S$. Thereafter, $S$ also recomputes $H_{k^1_{se}}(r_S, gid_{Ta}, s_{\{Ta,S\}})$ by the formerly derived $k^1_{se}$ to verify $T_a$. If it holds, $S$ will regard $T_a$ as a legal target; otherwise, the protocol will terminate. Until now, $S$ has obtained the authority on $T_a$.

### 9.4.2 The Security Protocol Suite in Ubiquitous IoT (UbSPs)

In ubiquitous IoT, $\{MC, lMC/iMC, nMC\}$ are considered to establish the authentication and authorization protocol suite (UbSPs). Therein, $MC$ has two variants, $MC_l/MC_i$, which are respectively under $lMC/iMC$'s jurisdiction in the local IoT and industrial IoT.

#### 9.4.2.1 The Centralized Authentication Protocol in UbSPs   The centralized authentication protocol (as shown in Figure 9.5) considers the authentication among $\{MC, lMC/iMC, nMC\}$, in which $MC$ and $lMC/iMC$ establish mutual authentication, and $nMC$ is a trusted authority to authenticate $lMC$. Take $lMC$ as an example to introduce the authentication procedure.

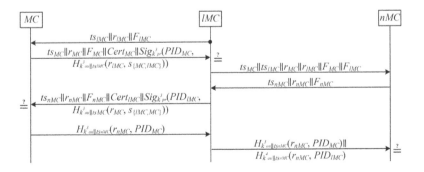

**Figure 9.5**   The centralized authentication protocol in UbSPs.

Phase 1 (*lMC* authenticating *MC*). *lMC* generates $\{ts_{lMC}, r_{lMC}\}$, extracts $F_{lMC}$, and transmits $ts_{lMC}||r_{lMC}||F_{lMC}$ to *MC*. Upon receiving the query, *MC* also generates $\{ts_{MC}, r_{MC}\}$, extracts $\{F_{MC},$ $Cert_{MC}, s_{\{MC,lMC\}}\}$, and computes $H_{k^3{}_{au}||tslMC}(r_{lMC}, s_{\{MC,lMC\}})$. Then, *MC* establishes a signature $Sig_{k^3_{pr}}(PID_{MC}, H_{k^3{}_{au}||tslMC}(.))$ and transmits $ts_{MC}||r_{MC}||F_{MC}||Cert_{MC}$ and $Sig_{k^3_{pr}}(.)$ to *lMC*. Upon receiving the message, *lMC* extracts $PID_{MC}$ and decrypts $Sig_{k^3_{pr}}$ (.) to obtain $H_{k^3{}_{au}||tslMC}(r_{lMC}, s_{\{MC,lMC\}})$, and then recomputes the hash value to verify *MC*. If it holds, *lMC* will regard *MC* as a legal M&DC; otherwise, the protocol will terminate.

Phase 2 (*MC* authenticating *lMC*). *lMC* transmits $ts_{MC}||ts_{lMC}$, $r_{MC}||r_{lMC}$, and $F_{MC}||F_{lMC}$ to *nMC*, and *nMC* replies $ts_{nMC}||r_{nMC}||F_{nMC}$ to *lMC*. *lMC* further extracts $\{PID_{lMC},$ $s_{\{lMC,MC\}}, Cert_{lMC}\}$ to compute $H_{k^3{}_{au}||tsMC}(r_{MC}, s_{\{lMC,MC\}})$, and establishes a signature $Sig_{k^3_{pr}}(PID_{lMC}, H_{k^3{}_{au}||tsMC}(.))$. Thereafter, *lMC* transmits $ts_{nMC}||r_{nMC}||F_{nMC}||Cert_{lMC}||Sig_{k^3_{pr}}(.)$ to *MC*. *MC* extracts $PID_{lMC}$, decrypts $Sig_{k^3_{pr}}(.)$ to derive $H_{k^3{}_{au}||tsMC}(r_{MC},$ $s_{\{lMC,MC\}})$, and extracts $s_{\{MC,lMC\}}$ to recompute the hash value to verify *lMC*. If it holds, *MC* will regard *lMC* as a legal lM&DC; otherwise, the protocol will terminate.

Phase 3 (*nMC* authenticating $\{MC, lMC\}$). *MC* first computes the hash value $H_{k^3{}_{au}||tsnMC}(r_{nMC}, PID_{MC})$ and transmits it to *lMC*. Thereafter, *lMC* computes $H_{k^4{}_{au}||tsnMC}(r_{nMC}, PID_{lMC})$ and transmits the cascaded value $H_{k^3{}_{au}||tsnMC}(.)||H_{k^4{}_{au}||tsnMC}$ (.) to *nMC* for authentication. Upon receiving the message, *nMC* recomputes the two hash values to verify $\{MC, lMC\}$. If they hold, *nMC* will regard $\{MC, lMC\}$ as legal things; otherwise, the protocol will terminate.

*9.4.2.2 The Distributed Authority Transfer Protocol in UbSPs*   The distributed authority transfer protocol (as shown in Figure 9.6) considers the authorization among $\{MC, lMC, iMC\}$, in which the authority on *MC* has been transferred from *lMC* to *iMC*. The authority transfer between local IoT and industrial IoT is achieved in the distributed networks.

Phase 1 (*iMC* authorizing *MC*). *iMC* generates $\{ts_{iMC}, r_{iMC}\}$, extracts $F_{iMC}$, and transmits $ts_{iMC}||r_{iMC}||F_{iMC}$ to *MC*. Upon receiving the message, *MC* generates $\{ts_{MC}, r_{MC}\}$ and extracts

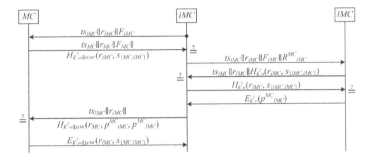

**Figure 9.6** The distributed authority transfer protocol in UbSPs.

$\{F_{MC}, s_{\{MC,iMC\}}\}$ to compute $H_{k'^3_{au}||tsiMC}(r_{iMC}, s_{\{MC,iMC\}})$. Thereafter, $MC$ continues to transmit $ts_{MC}||r_{MC}||F_{MC}||H_{k'^3_{au}||tsiMC}(.)$ to $iMC$. Afterward, $iMC$ ascertains $MC$'s identity and recomputes $H_{k'^3_{au}||tsiMC}(r_{iMC}, s_{\{MC,iMC\}})$ to verify $MC$. If it holds, $iMC$ will regard $MC$ as a legal M&DC; otherwise, the protocol will terminate.

Phase 2 ($\{iMC, lMC\}$'s mutual authentication). $iMC$ first extracts its access request $R^{MC}_{iMC}$ and transmits $ts_{iMC}||r_{iMC}||F_{iMC}||R^{MC}_{iMC}$ to $lMC$. Thereafter, $lMC$ generates $\{ts_{lMC}, r_{lMC}\}$ and extracts $s_{\{lMC,iMC\}}$ to compute $H_{k^2_{se}}(r_{iMC}, s_{\{lMC,iMC\}})$. $lMC$ replies $ts_{lMC}||r_{lMC}||H_{k^2_{se}}(.)$ to $iMC$. Upon receiving the message, $iMC$ recomputes $H_{k^2_{se}}(r_{iMC}, s_{\{lMC,iMC\}})$ to verify $lMC$. If it holds, $iMC$ will regard $lMC$ as a legal lM&DC; otherwise, the protocol will terminate. Afterward, $iMC$ extracts $s_{\{iMC,lMC\}}$ to compute $H_{k^2_{se}}(r_{lMC}, s_{\{iMC,lMC\}})$ and transmits it to $lMC$. Upon receiving the message, $lMC$ extracts $s_{\{iMC,lMC\}}$ to obtain $s_{\{iMC,lMC\}}$, and recomputes $H_{k^2_{se}}(r_{lMC}, s_{\{iMC,lMC\}})$ to verify $iMC$. If it holds, $lMC$ will regard $lMC$ as a legal lM&DC; otherwise, the protocol will terminate. $lMC$ further extracts the pointer $p^{MC}_{lMC}$ to compute $E_{k^2_{se}}(p^{MC}_{lMC})$ and transmits $E_{k^2_{se}}(p^{MC}_{lMC})$ to $iMC$.

Phase 3 ($MC$ authorizing $iMC$). $iMC$ decrypts $E_{k^2_{se}}(p^{MC}_{lMC})$ to obtain $p^{MC}_{lMC}$, and then extracts the pointer $p^{MC}_{iMC}$ to compute $H_{k'^3_{au}||tsMC}(r_{MC}, p^{MC}_{iMC}, p^{MC}_{lMC})$. Then, $iMC$ transmits $ts_{lMC}||r_{lMC}||H_{k'^3_{au}||tsMC}(.)$ to $MC$. Upon receiving the message, $MC$ first extracts $\{p^{iMC}, p^{lMC}_{MC}\}$ to recompute $H_{k'^3_{au}||tsMC}(r_{MC}, p^{MC}_{iMC}, p^{MC}_{lMC})$ to verify $iMC$. If it holds, $MC$ will regard *iMC* as a legal *iM&DC*; otherwise, the protocol will terminate. *MC* further extracts $s_{\{MC,lMC\}}$ to compute $E_{k'^3{}_{pu}||tslMC}(r_{lMC}, s_{\{MC,lMC\}})$, and transmits it to *iMC*. Thereafter, *iMC* decrypts $E_{k'^3{}_{pu}||tslMC}(.)$ to obtain $s_{\{MC,lMC\}}$, which is originally shared by {*MC*, *lMC*}. Note that {*MC*, *iMC*} should perform secret updating to realize the authority transfer from *lMC* to *iMC*, and to avoid *lMC*'s later unauthorized access.

*9.4.2.3 The Centralized Authority Transfer Protocol in UbSPs*   The centralized authority transfer protocol (as shown in Figure 9.7) considers the authorization among {*MC*, *iMC*, *nMC*}, in which *iMC* has obtained authority on *MC* from *lMC*, and then is further authorized by *nMC*. The transferred authority is finally ascertained in the centralized networks.

Phase 1 (*nMC* authorizing *iMC*). *iMC* generates {$ts_{iMC}$, $r_{iMC}$}, extracts {$F_{iMC}$, $R^{MC}{}_{iMC}$}, and further computes $H_{k^4_{pu}}(p^{MC}{}_{iMC}, s_{\{MC,lMC\}})$. Therein, $R^{MC}{}_{iMC}$ represents the access request that *iMC* wants to be authorized by *nMC* to obtain the access authority on *MC*. Thereafter, *iMC* transmits $ts_{iMC}||r_{iMC}||F_{iMC}||R^{MC}{}_{iMC}|| H_{k^4_{pu}}(.)$ to *nMC*. Upon receiving the message, *nMC* extracts $s_{\{MC,lMC\}}$ to recompute $H_{k^4_{pu}}(p^{MC}{}_{lMC}, s_{\{MC,lMC\}})$ to verify *iMC*. If it holds, *nMC* will regard *iMC* as a legal *iM&DC*; otherwise, the protocol will terminate. *nMC* generates {$ts_{nMC}$, $r_{nMC}$}, extracts {$F_{nMC}$, $p^{MC}{}_{nMC}$} to compute $E_{k^4_{pu}}(p^{MC}{}_{nMC})$, and transmits $ts_{nMC}||r_{nMC}||F_{nMC}|| E_{k^4_{pu}}(p^{MC}{}_{nMC})$ to *iMC*.

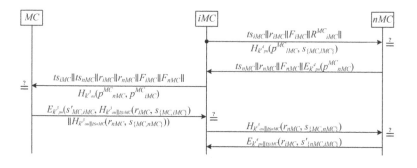

**Figure 9.7**   The centralized authority transfer protocol in UbSPs.

Phase 2 ($\{MC, iMC\}$'s mutual authentication). $iMC$ decrypts $E_{k_{pu}^{'3}}(p^{MC}{}_{nMC})$ to obtain $p^{MC}{}_{nMC}$, and extracts $p^{MC}{}_{iMC}$ to compute $H_{k_{pu}^{'3}}(p^{MC}{}_{nMC}, p^{MC}{}_{iMC})$. Thereafter, $iMC$ transmits $ts_{iMC}$ $||ts_{nMC}||r_{iMC}||r_{nMC}||F_{iMC}||F_{nMC}|| H_{k_{au}^{'3}}(.)$ to $MC$. $MC$ extracts $\{p^{nMC}{}_{MC}, p^{iMC}{}_{MC}\}$ to obtain $p^{MC}{}_{n}\tilde{M}C$, and recomputes $H_{k_{au}^{'3}}$ $(p^{MC}{}_{nMC}, p^{MC}{}_{iMC})$ to verify $iMC$. If it holds, $MC$ will regard $iMC$ as a legal iM&DC; otherwise, the protocol will terminate. Thereafter, $MC$ extracts $\{s_{\{MC,iMC\}}, s_{\{MC,nMC\}}\}$ to compute $H_{k^{'3}{}_{au}||tsiMC}(r_{iMC}, s_{\{MC,iMC\}})$ and $H_{k^{'3}{}_{au}||tsnMC}(r_{nMC},$ $s_{\{MC,nMC\}})$. $MC$ performs secret updating on $s_{\{MC,iMC\}}$ to obtain $s'_{\{MC,iMC\}}$, encrypts $s'_{\{MC,iMC\}}$ into $E_{k_{pu}^{'3}}(s'_{\{MC,iMC\}}, H_{k^{'3}{}_{au}||tsiMC}(.)||$ $H_{k^{'3}{}_{au}||tsnMC}(.)$, and transmits $E_{k_{pu}^{'3}}(.)$ to $iMC$. Upon receiving the message, $iMC$ derives $s'_{\{MC,iMC\}}$, and extracts $s_{\{MC,iMC\}}$ to recompute $H_{k^{'3}{}_{au}||tsiMC}(r_{iMC}, s_{\{MC,iMC\}})$ to verify $MC$. If it holds, $iMC$ will regard $MC$ as a legal M&DC; otherwise, the protocol will terminate.

Phase 3 ($nMC$ authorizing $MC$). $iMC$ forwards the derived $H_{k^{'3}{}_{au}||tsnMC}(r_{nMC}, s_{\{MC,nMC\}})$ to $nMC$. Upon receiving the message, $nMC$ extracts $s_{\{MC,nMC\}}$ and recomputes $H_{k^{'3}{}_{au}||tsnMC}(r_{nMC},$ $s_{\{MC,nMC\}})$ to verify $MC$. If it holds, $nMC$ will regard $MC$ as a legal M&DC; otherwise, the protocol will terminate. $nMC$ continues to extract and update $s_{\{nMC,iMC\}}$ into $s'_{\{nMC,iMC\}}$, and computes $H_{k^{'4}{}_{pu}||tsiMC}(r_{iMC}, s'_{\{nMC,iMC\}})$, Thereafter, $nMC$ transmits $H_{k^{'4}{}_{pu}||tsiMC}(.)$ to $iMC$, and then $iMC$ can obtain $s'_{\{nMC,iMC\}}$ by decryption operation. Until now, $iMC$ has been authorized by $nMC$ on the access authority on $MC$.

*9.4.2.4 The Distributed Authority Sharing Protocol in UbSPs* The distributed authority sharing protocol (as shown in Figure 9.8) considers the authorization among $\{S, MC_i, MC_j\}$, in which $\{MC_i, MC_j\}$ are assigned different authorities on $S$'s identifier, and they have relatively independent authorities to access the authorized subfields. This protocol realizes that $\{MC_i, MC_j\}$ grant their authorities on $S$'s subfields to each other to realize authority sharing without compromising privacy.

Phase 1 ($\{MC_i, MC_j\}$ challenging $MC$). $\{MC_i, MC_j\}$ respectively generate $\{ts_{MCi}, ts_{MCj}\}$ and $\{r_{MCi}, r_{MCj}\}$, extract $\{F_{MCi}, F_{MCj}\}$, and transmit $ts_{MCi}||r_{MCi}||F_{MCi}$ and $ts_{MCi}||r_{MCi}||F_{MCi}$ to $S$.

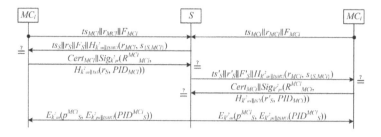

**Figure 9.8**   The distributed authority sharing protocol in UbSPs.

Phase 2 ($\{MC_l, S\}$'s mutual authentication). $S$ generates $\{ts_S, r_S\}$ and extracts $\{F_S, s_{\{S,MCl\}}\}$ to compute $H_{k^2_{au}||tsMCl}(r_{MCl}, s_{\{S,MCl\}})$. Thereafter, $S$ transmits $ts_S||r_S||F_S||H_{k^2_{au}||tsMCl}(.)$ to $MC_l$. Upon receiving the message, $MC_l$ recomputes $H_{k^2_{au}||tsMCl}(r_{MCl}, s_{\{S,MCl\}})$ to verify $S$. If it holds, $MC_l$ will regard $S$ as a legal sensor and the protocol will continue; otherwise, the protocol will terminate. $MC_l$ further extracts $\{Cert_{MCl}, R^{MCl}_{MCl}, PID_{MCl}\}$ to compute $H_{k^2_{au}||tsS}(r_S, PID_{MCl})$, and establishes $Sig_{k^2_{pr}}(R^{MCl}_{MCl}, H_{k^2_{au}||tsS}(.))$. Therein, $R^{MCl}_{MCl}$ is an access request, and represents that $MC_l$ wants to access $MC_l$'s authorized subfields of $S$; meanwhile, it also permits sharing of its authorized subfields with $MC_l$. Thereafter, $MC_l$ transmits $Cert_{MCl}||Sig_{k^2_{pr}}(.)$ to $S$ for authentication. Upon receiving the message, $S$ recomputes $H_{k^2_{au}||tsS}(r_S, PID_{MCl})$ to verify $MC_l$. If it holds, $S$ will regard $MC_l$ as a legal M&DC in local IoT; otherwise, the protocol will terminate.

Phase 3 ($\{MC_i, S\}$'s mutual authentication). Similarly, $S$ generates $\{ts'_S, r'_S\}$, extracts $\{F'_S, s_{\{S,MCi\}}\}$ to compute $H_{k^2_{au}||tsMCi}(r_{MCi}, s_{\{S,MCi\}})$, and transmits $ts'_S||r'_S||F'_S||H_{k^2_{au}||tsMCi}(.)$ to $MC_i$ for authentication. Based on $MC_i$'s verification on $S$, $MC_i$ extracts its access request $R^{MCl}_{MCi}$, computes $H_{k^2_{au}||ts'S}(r'_S, PID_{MCi})$, and establishes $Sig_{k^2_{pr}}(R^{MCl}_{MCi}, H_{k^2_{au}||ts'S}(.))$. Thereafter, $MC_i$ responds with $Cert_{MCi}||Sig_{k^2_{pr}}(.)$ to $S$. Here, $R^{MCl}_{MCi}$ represents that $MC_i$ wants to share its authorized subfields with $MC_l$. Note that $MC_i$ may have no access request or have another access request such as $R^{MCx}_{MCi}$ $(x \neq l)$, which means that $MC_i$ has no interest in $MC_l$'s authorized subfields, or has an interest in another entity. Afterward, $S$ recomputes $H_{k^2_{au}||ts'S}(r'_S, PID_{MCi})$ to verify $MC_i$. If it holds,

$S$ will regard $MC_i$ as a legal M&DC in industrial IoT; otherwise, the protocol will terminate.

Phase 4 ($S$ responding to $\{MC_i, MC_j\}$). $S$ respectively derives $\{R^{MCi}_{MCi}, R^{MCi}_{MCj}\}$ and checks whether the two requests are matched according to a given mapping relationship. If it holds, $S$ will extract the path pointers $\{p^{MCi}_S, p^{MCi}_S\}$ and the partial pseudonyms $\{PID^{MCi}_S, PID^{MCi}_S\}$. $S$ respectively computes $E_{k^2_{au}}(p^{MCi}_S, E_{k^2_{pu||tsMCi}}(PID^{MCi}_S))$ and $E_{k'^2_{au}}(p^{MCi}_S, E_{k'^2_{pu||tsMCi}}(PID^{MCi}_S))$, and transmits $\{H_{k^1_{au}}\}$ to $\{MC_i, MC_j\}$. Thereafter, $\{MC_i, MC_j\}$ derive $\{p^{MCi}_S, PID^{MCi}_S\}$ and $\{p^{MCi}_S, PID^{MCi}_S\}$, and obtain the authorities on each other's authorized subfields.

### 9.4.3 Security Analysis

*9.4.3.1 Authentication* The hybrid authentication mode is applied to establish the mutual trusting relationships in the heterogeneous networks. In P1, $\{T, S\}$ perform mutual authentication, and MC performs additional unilateral authentication on $\{T, S\}$. In P2, P3, and P5, there is a trusted authority in the centralized networks, in which $\{MC, nMC\}$ respectively act as the legal objects in unit IoT and ubiquitous IoT to authenticate or authorize $\{T, S\}$ and $\{MC, lMC, iMC\}$. In P4 and P6, there are no trusted things in the distributed networks; $\{S, MC_i, MC_j\}$ and $\{MC, lMC, iMC\}$ should respectively perform mutual authentication on each other. For the authentication operators, the pairwise values are introduced as the preshared secrets, which are wrapped by the pseudonyms and other session-variant values for authentication. The authentication protocols consider the limitation of the communication channels, and apply lightweight hash functions in the wireless networks and full-fledged encryption/signature algorithms in the computer networks; such an authentication mode realizes the trade-off of security and efficiency.

*9.4.3.2 Authorization* In U2IoT, different things have relatively independent authorities on a certain identifier, and even have different authorities on a subfield of the same identifier. It turns out that the established hierarchical authorization mode can provide classified access control. In P2, $\{S, MC\}$ are appointed different authorities on $T$'s identifier, in which $MC$ has the full authority on $T$, and $S$ has the partial authority. $S$ should pass the verifications by $\{S, MC\}$ to obtain the one-time pad-based secret key for further obtaining the full authority on $S$, in which the group identifier is introduced to indicate the group attribution. In P4 and P5, authority transfer can be realized among $\{MC, lMC, iMC, nMC\}$. Concretely, $lMC$ originally has access authority on $MC$, and the authority is transferred to $iMC$. When $iMC$ has obtained authority on $MC$ from $lMC$, it is further authorized by $nMC$. In P6, $\{MC_i, MC_j\}$ have different authorities to access $S$, and $\{MC_i, MC_j\}$ can achieve authority sharing on specific authorized subfields of $S$'s identifier with privacy consideration. Therein, $\{MC_i, MC_j\}$'s privacy is achieved by introducing the access requests $\{R^{MCi}_{MCi}, R^{MC}_{MCj}\}$.

*9.4.3.3 Session Freshness*   Session freshness is achieved by introducing timestamps and random numbers, which also enhance the randomization of the shared secret-based authentication and authorization modes. In P1 and P2, $\{T_p/T_a, S\}$ respectively generate $\{r_{Tp}/r_{Ta}, r_S\}$ as access queries for session challenging, in which the lightweight pseudorandom number generator (PRNG) is applied as adequate for the resource-constrained communication environments in unit IoT. In P3 to P6, $\{MC, lMC/iMC, nMC\}$ apply the timestamps $\{ts_*\}$ to mark the session identifier. Therein, the timestamps are used for quick checks by verifying whether the received timestamp has appeared in the former sessions, and whether it is within an acceptable time interval. The timestamps and random numbers are also introduced for anonymous data transmission, and the exchanged messages are randomized by such fresh operators. For instance, $\{PID_{Tp}, s_{\{Tp,MC\}}\}$ are wrapped by $\{k^1_{se}, r_{Tp}\}$ into the hash value $H_{k^1_{se}||rTp}(PID_{Tp}, s_{\{Tp,MC\}})$ in P1, and $s_{\{MC,lMC\}}$ is wrapped into $E_{k'^3_{pu}||tslMC}(r_{lMC}, s_{\{MC,lMC\}})$ by applying $\{ts_{lMC}, r_{lMC}\}$ in P4. The session freshness is realized along with the enhanced data integrity.

*9.4.3.4 Privacy Preservation*   Privacy-preserving approaches are applied to protect an individual or group user's sensitive information (e.g., location, interest). The pseudonyms $\{PID_*\}$ are introduced to guarantee that no real identifier is transmitted during the open communication channels, and attackers cannot derive the identity information against the tracking attacks. In P2, the one-time available secret key $k^1_{se}$ is assigned to the out-group $S$ by $MC$, and thus $S$ can temporarily obtain access authority on $T_p/T_a$ without compromising any static sensitive secret. In P6, $\{MC_l, MC_i\}$ transmit the private access requests $\{R^{MCi}_{MCl}, R^{MCl}_{MCi}\}$ to $S$, and the requests are never revealed until $S$ ascertains that both $MC_l$ and $MC_i$ want to share each other's authorized subfields. Such a subtle authority sharing mode realizes that even if either $MC_l$ or $MC_i$ has no interests in the other authorized subfields, the access request cannot reveal any underlying access requests.

## 9.5 Entity Activity Cycle–Based Security Solution

For security and privacy in IoT, entity-based cyber security is an important aspect. In order to address security and privacy issues in future IoT, an entity activity cycle–based security solution is established to achieve security protection and privacy preservation, as shown in Figure 9.9. The solution refers to a suite of cryptographic mechanisms according to an entity's three phases, including the preactive phase, active phase, and postactive phase. Note that "active" is defined according to an entity's communication session. Concretely, the preactive phase refers to the entity being in the preliminary status before it launches a session (e.g., network accessing, target identification, and services addressing), the active phase means that the entity is in the ongoing session with a

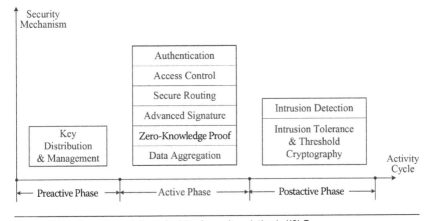

**Figure 9.9** The entity activity cycle–based security solution in U2IoT.

certain function, and the postactive phase refers to the entity being in the inactive state after the current session.

### 9.5.1 In the Preactive Phase

Key distribution and management is a fundamental issue in the preactive phase. The symmetric key management and distribution technique is a basic approach for communication, in which a preinstalled symmetric key or pairwise shared keys are stored in the memory. Meanwhile, an asymmetric key cryptosystem is appropriate to establish a secret key. Identity-based cryptography (IBC) is a typical scheme in WSNs, and the hardness of the bilinear Diffie-Hellman problem (BDHP) and Tate pairing can be applied into key predistribution. Additionally, a group key agreement scheme can be adopted by multiple things to establish dynamic and deterministic keys, in which bilinear pairing and cryptographic algorithms (e.g., elliptic curve cryptography [ECC], threshold broadcast encryption) can be applied to achieve high efficiency. Thus, the shortest path tree (SPT) routing mode and multipath key mode are suitable for the heterogeneous networks and cross-layer communication environments.

### 9.5.2 In the Active Phase

In the active phase, authentication, access control, securing routing, advanced signature, zero-knowledge proof, and data aggregation are introduced.

*9.5.2.1 Authentication* Authentication considers the validity of the interactive things. The traditional authentication modes are mainly based on the shared secrets/keys, entity's identity, and trusted third party (TTP). For authentication operators, ultra-lightweight algorithms such as bitwise logical operators, permutation, and pseudorandom number generators can be applied in the resource-constrained devices (e.g., passive RFID tag); the lightweight algorithms such as hash function, cyclic redundancy check (CRC), and message authentication code (MAC) can be applied to provide enhanced security; and the full-fledged encryption/signature algorithms can be used in the back-end systems. Physical authentication approaches (e.g., physically unclonable function [PUF]) can also be introduced for authentication. Moreover, network access authentication is applied to control the things' access in network services; therefore, an IP-based protocol (i.e., protocol for carrying authentication for network access [PANA]) has been standardized by the Internet Engineering Task Force (IETF). Additionally, the authentication mode should fully consider the heterogeneous, mobile, and large-scale networks; therefore, the tiered multicast message authentication and batch authentication mode becomes noteworthy for unit IoTs.

*9.5.2.2 Access Control*   Access control refers to the authorization among different things with the classified authorities on a certain system resource. The hybrid access control model can be established according to the access control paradigms (e.g., mandatory access control [MAC], discretionary access control [DAC], role-based access control [RBAC], and attribute-based access control [ABAC]). The space-time characteristic is a key factor so that the temporal role-based access control model should be designed with the geographical location information. Semantic-based and attribute-based models are also feasible for Web services-oriented environments. Along with considering the social factors, a trust-oriented access mode can be established according to the virtualization of the things' profiles.

*9.5.2.3 Secure Routing*   Secure routing is represented as dynamic addressing modes, which are traditionally applied along with Internet Protocol Security (IPSec) in computer networks, and are also suitable for mobile *ad hoc* networks (MANETs) and WSNs. The multipath routing and on-demand routing secure protocols can be applied in the heterogeneous sensor networks, and the tree-based, identity-based, and trust-based schemes should be designed to achieve the distributed anonymous data transmission.

*9.5.2.4 Advanced Signature*   Advanced signature mainly includes blind, group, ring, and identity signature algorithms. Therein, proxy blind signature and partially blind signature schemes can apply bilinear pairings for identity verification, and the Advanced Encryption Standard (AES) cryptosystem can also be introduced into the signature establishment. The blind signature can be introduced into certificateless public key cryptography, and the certificateless pairing-based signature scheme has advantages in the computational cost. The background and foreground knowledge-based offline signature identification can also achieve perfect security unlinkability, and the group/ring signature schemes can combine the anonymous authentication mode to enhance data anonymity. The multisignature and identity-based concurrent signature should consider the privacy preservation by the hybrid aggregation scheme.

*9.5.2.5 Zero-Knowledge Proof* Zero-knowledge proof focuses on the authentication that the interaction between the prover and verifier does not reveal any sensitive information, and both interactive and noninteractive modes are included during the verification. Thus, ECC and blind watermark cryptosystems can be used jointly to achieve zero-knowledge identity verification in the resource-constrained applications. Note that Sigma Protocol with different composition modes (e.g., parallel, EQ, OR, AND) can be applied to realize aggregated multiple-proof verification.

*9.5.2.6 Data Aggregation* Data aggregation is applied to achieve privacy preservation, and it realizes that the real-time data of an individual user or a group user cannot reveal sensitive information. The original data aggregation is to aggregate multiple sensing data by performing algebraic or statistical functions to establish a data set for transmission, which has vulnerability on the cluster heads. Concealed data aggregation (CDA) is applied to provide privacy homomorphism (PH) encryption with additive homomorphism to achieve enhanced higher security. Additionally, yoking-proofs or grouping-proofs can be regarded as a data aggregation algorithm, which realizes multiple sensing data, which can be aggregated as a group for further authentication. Meanwhile, hierarchical data aggregation can be applied in the in-network and cross-network aggregations, in which homomorphic encryption and advanced signature algorithms can be jointly added into the aggregation to achieve confidentiality and integrity.

### 9.5.3 *In the Postactive Phase*

In the postactive phase, intrusion detection, intrusion tolerance, and threshold cryptography are introduced.

*9.5.3.1 Intrusion Detection*   Intrusion detection detects malicious attacks and enables the systems and communications in secure status. For heterogeneous networks, adaptive network intrusion detection systems with hybrid detection algorithms become necessary. Artificial immune algorithms can be applied to achieve self- and nonself-identifications, and artificial neural networks (ANNs) can also be based to identify real-time intrusions. Meanwhile, data mining techniques (e.g., data collection and feature selection) provide efficient assists to enhance unreliable node detection.

*9.5.3.2 Intrusion Tolerance and Threshold Cryptography*   Intrusion tolerance refers to secret sharing, and distributes a secret among multiple things, in which each object/entity is allocated a share of the secret. The intrusion tolerance and threshold cryptography realize that multiple things collectively participate in secret management, and even in the case that an object/entity is temporarily inactive or perennially unavailable, other legal things can also perform the normal interaction. Usually, the two mechanisms are used along with other cryptographic algorithms. For example, ECC can be introduced into the secret sharing scheme and threshold signature scheme, a dynamic group key agreement scheme can apply threshold secret sharing to achieve key distribution among multiple things, and a hierarchical secret sharing scheme can be designed according to the hybrid access structures (e.g., multilevel, compartmented, multipartite). Furthermore, fragmentation redundancy scattering (FRS) to harden the tolerance resilience, and segmentation can also be introduced into the overlay secret space for distributed shared memory. Dependable intrusion tolerance (DIT) and hierarchical intrusion tolerance (HIT) should be established for detection-triggered unit IoTs.

### 9.6 Conclusion

In order to provide enhanced security protection and privacy preservation for U2IoT architecture, the security requirements and security attacks are analyzed. Based on the security challenge analysis, an integrated security framework is established with the considerations of information security, physical security, and management security, and a hybrid authentication and hierarchical authorization scheme is presented to guarantee information security. Furthermore, an entity activity cycle–based security solution with a suite of cryptographic mechanisms has been presented as a recommended measure for securing future IoT.

# References

1. Atzori, L., A. Iera, and G. Morabito. 2010. The Internet of Things: A survey. *Computer Networks* 54: 2787–2805.
2. Pan, J., S. Paul, and R. Jain. 2011. A survey of the research on future Internet architectures. *IEEE Communications Magazine* 49: 26–36.
3. Weber, R. H. 2010. Internet of Things—New security and privacy challenges. *Computer Law and Security Report* 26: 23–30.
4. Roman, R., P. Najera, and J. Lopez. 2011. Securing the Internet of Things. *Computer* 44: 51–58.
5. Lampropoulos, K., and S. Denazis. 2011. Identity management directions in future Internet. *IEEE Communications Magazine* 49: 74–83.
6. Heer, T., O. Garcia-Morchon, R. Hummen, S. L. Keoh, S. S. Kumar, and K. Wehrle. 2011. Security challenges in the IP-based Internet of Things. *Wireless Personal Communications* 61: 527–542.
7. Ning, H., and H. Liu. 2012. Cyber-physical-social based security architecture for future Internet of Things. *Advances in Internet of Things* 2: 1–7.
8. Hancke, G. P., K. Markantonakis, and K. E. Mayes. 2010. Security challenges for user-oriented RFID applications within the Internet of Things. *Journal of Internet Technology* 11: 307–313.
9. Yan, T., and Q. Wen. 2011. Building the Internet of Things using a mobile RFID security protocol based on information technology. *Advances in Intelligent and Soft Computing* 104: 143–149.
10. Toumi, K., M. Ayari, L. A. Saidane, M. Bouet, and G. Pujolle. 2010. HAT: HIP address translation protocol for hybrid RFID/IP Internet of Things communication. Presented at the *2010 International Conference on Communication in Wireless Environments and Ubiquitous Systems: New Challenges (ICWUS)*.
11. McCusker, K., and N. E. O'Connor. 2011. Low-energy symmetric key distribution in wireless sensor networks. *IEEE Transactions on Dependable and Secure Computing* 8: 363–376.
12. Chang, K., and J. Chen. 2012. A survey of trust management in WSNs, Internet of Things and future Internet. *KSII Transactions on Internet and Information Systems* 6: 5–23.

13. Roman, R., C. Alcaraz, J. Lopez, and N. Sklavos. 2011. Key management systems for sensor networks in the context of the Internet of Things. *Computers and Electrical Engineering* 37: 147–159.
14. Ren, F., and J. Ma. 2011. Attribute-based access control mechanism for perceptive layer of the Internet of Things. *International Journal of Digital Content Technology and Its Applications* 5: 396–403.
15. Chen, D., G. Chang, D. Sun, J. Li, J. Jia, and X. Wang. 2011. TRM-IoT: A trust management model based on fuzzy reputation for Internet of Things. *Computer Science and Information Systems* 8: 1207–1228.
16. Wang, X., X. Sun, H. Yang, and S. A. Shah. 2011. An anonymity and authentication mechanism for Internet of Things. *Journal of Convergence Information Technology* 6: 98–105.
17. Zhao, G., X. Si, J. Wang, X. Long, and T. Hu. 2011. A novel mutual authentication scheme for Internet of Things. In *2011 International Conference on Modeling, Identification and Control (ICMIC)*, 563–566.
18. Zhou, L., and H. C. Chao. 2011. Multimedia traffic security architecture for the Internet of Things. *IEEE Network* 25: 35–40.
19. Li, X., R. Lu, X. Liang, X. Shen, J. Chen, and X. Lin. 2011. Smart community: An Internet of Things application. *IEEE Communications Magazine* 49: 68–75.
20. Sridhar, S., A. Hahn, and M. Govindarasu. 2012. Cyber-physical system security for the electric power grid. *Proceedings of the IEEE* 100: 210–224.
21. Harmer, P. K., P. D. Williams, G. H. Gunsch, and G. B. Lamont. 2002. An artificial immune system architecture for computer security applications. *IEEE Transactions on Evolutionary Computation* 6: 252–280.

# 10
# ENERGY MANAGEMENT

## 10.1 Introduction

Energy, as a basic factor for both artificial and natural systems, should be elaborately managed to guarantee normal system operation. Energy management finds solutions to address how to provide energy for the system and how to make full use of the energy. However, the specific content of energy management can be different due to various constraints in different scenarios. During ubiquitous things being sensed, controlled, and connected by sensors, actuators, and networks in Internet of Things (IoT), energy management becomes an important open issue due to the limited communication and infrastructure resources as well as the energy crisis. It is noteworthy to achieve energy requirements and sustainability without causing environmental problems for sustainable IoT development.

Energy management is a key topic in traditional networks. For example, in wireless sensor networks (WSNs), energy management is performed to realize persistent network lifetime by energy harvesting technology and dynamic power management technology. In the information and communications technology (ICT) sector, energy management mainly considers reducing energy demand through a series of technologies (e.g., low-power consumption circuits, simplified system structures, virtualization, and efficient air conditioning systems) to reduce energy consumption in communication systems and data centers. In recent years, a renewable energy supply for ICT equipment has been attracting more attention because of its advantages, such as its ease to deploy in places without power grids and reduction of greenhouse gas (GHG) emissions. Differing from traditional energy management, energy management in IoT should be reconsidered according to IoT characteristics (e.g., ubiquitous sensing,

**173**

network of networks, and intelligent processing). Concretely, IoT is thought to be a network of networks, a network of applications, a network of services, and even a network of everything, and the energy should be managed and organized from both single-application and multiple-application aspects.

Due to the ubiquitous features, energy supply issues may be unprecedentedly complicated. Moreover, the development of IoT will lead to a fast increase of data load to the networks, which in turn will cause increasing energy demand. For instance, the network energy consumption of Japan in 2025 is estimated to be 13 times that in 2006 [1], and 1/10 of Japan's total power output [2]. Note that energy consumption in accessing, switching/routing, and data processing will be climbing at a faster speed, along with the ubiquitous things connected to the networks. In addition, energy supplied for ICT is partly provided by fossil fuels, which are harmful to the environment. Thus, energy management in IoT should overcome such severe difficulties to achieve green IoT for sustainable development.

Energy management schemes should be particularly designed according to the IoT architecture. In this section, energy management of IoT is discussed based on unit and ubiquitous IoT (U2IoT) architecture. In U2IoT architecture, energy management should satisfy the following requirements:

- *Support for heterogeneity.* Heterogeneity is an obvious characteristic of IoT, which mainly includes heterogeneity of devices, networks, services, and energy.
- *Support for dynamic characteristics.* Dynamic topology, service, and power supply usually exist in wireless sensing and networking scenarios. As an important power supply, distributed energy sources (such as solar power, wind power, etc.) will be extensively used in IoT. With the utilization of distributed energy sources, dynamic energy management should be designed to be adapted to the unstable and unpredictable features of these energy sources.
- *Support for social attributes.* Social attributes should be considered during energy interaction in the physical world and cyber world. Energy management of IoT should support social attributes to achieve significant energy conservation.

- *Ubiquitous management.* The ubiquitous characteristic mainly refers to the pervasive IoT components, such as sensor nodes, radio frequency identification (RFID) tags/readers, communication gateways, and data centers. Energy management should cover the entire range of IoT components to realize ubiquitous management.
- *Self-management operation.* In future IoT, some characteristics such as self-organization, self-recovery, and intelligent control should be considered. These characteristics require human intervention-free operation, which can greatly release human labor from managing ubiquitous things in future IoT.

In the following, Section 10.2 discusses energy management of unit IoT from the technical aspects of supply management, demand management, and supply-demand balance management. Section 10.3 focuses on the nontechnical energy management of ubiquitous IoT. Section 10.4 draws a conclusion.

## 10.2 Energy Management in Unit IoT

Unit IoT generally consists of a large amount of sensors-actuators, communication networks, and management and data centers (M&DCs), and the scale of unit IoT can range from several nodes to millions of nodes. The main task of energy management in unit IoT includes three aspects: energy supply management, energy demand management, and supply-demand balance management.

- *Energy supply management* refers to obtaining energy with the considerations of particular constraints.
- *Energy demand management* refers to reducing energy consumption through applying technologies such as low energy consumption silicon computing/communicating technologies and sleep/low-power mode technologies.
- *Supply-demand balance management* keeps the balance between energy supply and energy demand in unit IoT components (e.g., sensors and actuators, networking devices, and data centers), and to eliminate/migrate the effects caused by the mismatching of energy supply and demand.

*10.2.1 Energy Supply Management in Unit IoT*

Unit IoT is composed of three layers: the sensor-actuator layer, network layer, and application layer. Due to the fact that the energy supply in the network infrastructures and data center is mainly based on the power grid, energy supply management of unit IoT is introduced in two aspects: supply management of sensors and actuators, and supply management of network communications and data centers.

- *Supply management of sensors and actuators* mainly refers to technologies that provide energy for sensors and actuators in unit IoT. Energy supply in the sensor-actuator layer can be classified into mobile energy supply and fixed energy supply. In some cases (e.g., wireless monitoring application), the fixed power line–based energy supply is extremely constrained due to the mobility and ubiquitous features of sensors and actuators. As a result, self-powered and battery-based energy supply modes are suitable in powering sensors and actuators for unit IoT. In the self-powered energy supply mode, the key technologies mainly include solar energy harvesting [3], radio frequency energy harvesting [4], mechanical energy harvesting [5], and other technologies (e.g., thermal energy harvesting [6] and wind generating [7]). For the battery-based energy supply mode, innovative energy storage materials-based technology can be applied to promote battery performance (e.g., energy storage capacity, life cycle, and energy density). It is noteworthy that super-capacity as a newly emerged energy storage device is promising for use as the primary energy storage to power self-powered sensors and actuators in unit IoT. A fixed energy supply mainly provides energy to the fixed sensors and actuators by the power grid, and can also be used as a backup energy source.
- *Supply management of network communications and data centers* mainly focuses on providing energy to the network infrastructures and data centers of unit IoT. Currently, a significant aspect of energy supplies is based on the power grid. For the current power grid, it is important to improve the access of renewable energy and reduce the proportion of fossil-based energy in order to realize sustainable development. An innovation to

achieve this goal is the smart grid, which applies IoT-related technology in integrating distributed renewable energy into the power grid to make electricity cleaner [8]. Furthermore, the smart grid aims at delivering electricity from varied suppliers to distributed consumers to save energy, to reduce transmission loss, and to increase energy reliability and transparency [9]. Recently, distributed energy supplies for network infrastructures and data centers have become an increasing trend in the consideration for sustainable development.

### 10.2.2 Energy Demand Management in Unit IoT

Energy demand management refers to reducing energy consumption during operations. According to the three-layer model of unit IoT, energy demand management can be classified into the following three aspects:

- *Demand management of sensors and actuators.* Based on the main functions of sensors and actuators in unit IoT, sensor- and actuator-related energy demand management will be discussed from the aspects of sensing and actuating, short-range communicating, and processing.
  1. In some particular applications (e.g., video surveillance systems), sensors or actuators may consume a large part of the total energy input. The technologies that can be used to reduce energy consumption of sensing and actuating components mainly include adopting a new sensor-actuator manufacturing process (such as nanotechnology, microelectromechanical systems, etc.) and applying a sleep mode in sensing activities.
  2. Short-range communications are another energy consumer in sensors and actuators, particularly in WSNs. Due to energy scarcity, energy demand management needs to be implemented in both hardware and software modes. Energy-efficient short-range communication can be achieved through radio sleeping and data reducing for WSNs. Radio sleeping means putting the radio into an energy saving mode, or turning off the radio when there is no communication activities. Radio sleeping can be

achieved through two different approaches, which refer to topology control and sleep/awake protocol. For example, topology control can be applied in ant colony optimization and virtual grid-based methods [10,11]. Sleep/awake protocol reduces the energy demand of communication through dynamically switching the radio between sleeping mode and active mode. Zheng et al. [12] classified sleep/awake protocols into three classes based on the wake-up trigger: on-demand, synchronous, and asynchronous. Data reducing lowers the energy demand of communication by reducing the traffic load. In the sensor-actuator layer, sensing data of the physical world and cyber world take an important part of the transmitted data. For the sensing data of the physical world, data prediction models (e.g., [13–15]) can be built to reduce data transmitted in the networks. For the sensing data of the cyber world, data reducing can be achieved by related coding schemes.

3. A significant part of energy in the sensor-actuator layer is consumed by data processing. Lower-power circuit technology is promising in reducing energy consumption of processing, but it is difficult to make further breakthroughs. Two simpler and feasible technologies can be used to achieve energy savings in processing: dynamic voltage and frequency scaling (DVFS) and dynamic power management (DPM) [16].

- *Demand management of network communications.* IoT is endowed with the meaning of network of networks, which means the fusion of networks. For network communication, demand management for mobile communication networks and Internet are discussed in this section. For mobile communication networks, a radio base station (RBS) is the most energy-greedy part of wireless access networks [17]. In order to reduce the energy consumption of RBS, energy-efficient solutions have been proposed at the device level, such as energy-efficient amplifiers [18] and energy-efficient antennas [19], as well as at the network level, such as femtocell and relaying [20] and turning off RBS [21]. For the

Internet, energy demand from network infrastructures has been climbing at a high speed. The most energy-intense parts of the Internet are high-performance routing and switching devices, and new technology such as optical packet switching (OPS), performance adjusting, and node sleeping can be used to reduce their energy demand. Driven by IoT, where ubiquitous things are connected into networks, the development progress of the next-generation Internet has been accelerated. It is important to take sustainable factors into consideration during the whole designing and implementing process of the next-generation Internet.

- *Demand management of M&DCs.* Energy consumption of data centers can be summarized as energy consumed by either IT equipment (e.g., computer, server, and storage system) or non-IT facilities (e.g., cooling equipment, uninterrupted power systems, and lighting systems). For IT equipment, demand management can be implemented in hardware and software directions. Hardware-oriented demand management includes low-power circuits, dynamic voltage and frequency scaling (DVFS), and lower-power mode scheduling. Barroso et al. [22] studied energy proportion computing in solving the mismatch between energy efficiency and workload of the server, and found that we can save a lot of energy through tuning the consumption power based on the computing load. CPUs of computing servers adopt proportional computing technology more aggressively than other subsystems (e.g., dynamic random access memory [DRAM] and hard disk). Software-oriented directions include operating system based, virtual machine based, and so on. For example, Lebeck et al. [23] provided a study on a memory subsystem in an operating system (OS). This study directs memory accesses to certain memory banks and proposes turning off unused memory banks to save energy. Von Laszewski et al. [24] proposed a scheduling algorithm for dynamically distributing virtual machines in a DVFS-enabled cluster environment. It is noteworthy that hardware- and software-oriented demand management have to be combined with each other to achieve good performance. Non-IT facilities account for a large percentage of the total energy feed into the data center and have large potential in reducing total energy consumption. In order to reduce energy wasted in IT cooling devices, it is reasonable to distribute cooling air based on the workload or the generating heat of the devices. Smart cooling, proposed by Patel et al. [25], can reduce energy consumption in cooling based on the above principle. Thermal-related energy efficiency can also be achieved by optimizing the formation of hot and cold aisles, introducing free cooling, and adopting high-efficiency air conditioning equipment. In addition to air conditioning, possible measures, including high-efficiency uninterruptible power supply (UPS) and transformers, can also help in reducing energy consumption [26].

### 10.2.3 Supply-Demand Balance Management in Unit IoT

Supply-demand balance management in unit IoT is the comprehensive solution to the mismatching of energy supply and energy demand. It is different from the supply or demand management in the following aspects:

- *Function.* As was explained above.
- *Scope.* Supply-demand balance realizes its function with a much wider scope than supply management or demand management. Therein, supply-demand balance takes measures on both the supply side and the demand side. Moreover, in order to gain the maximum management effect, it is important to implement management mechanisms on a network level.

As the proportion of renewable energy in the total energy supply of IoT increases, the dynamicity of the energy supply becomes more and more obvious, which has pushed supply-demand balance management to be more important in energy management for IoT. For the sensors and actuators in unit IoT, distributed, self-powered energy supply has been adopted as an important energy supply mode, and supply-demand balance management has been comprehensively researched in the single-node level. Therein, an easy way is using an energy buffer (e.g., rechargeable battery or super-capacitor) to realize supply-demand balance. Another supply-demand balance management way in single-node-level sensors and actuators is adaptive energy management, which includes energy monitoring, prediction, and performance adjustment of nodes. Related research can be found in Kinoshita et al. [27] and Hsu et al. [28] for energy prediction and adaptive performance adjustment, respectively. For network communications and data centers of unit IoT, the direct and efficient method of supply-demand balance management is also energy buffering technology. However, with the increase of renewable energy access, the strengthened dynamicity of energy supply and energy demand has forced the network and computing infrastructures to take more aggressive energy supply-demand balance management measures. Moreover, the high cost and low efficiency, together with other inconveniences of energy buffering systems, have added pressure to the development of these measures. As a result, some meaningful research for improving supply-demand balance management in unit IoT networking and computing infrastructure has been done. For example, Bolla et al. [29] proposed that through virtualization of the physical resources, the workload of the nodes in the backbone network can be migrated to other nodes without causing loss of the present problem. This research provided the foundation of energy supply-demand balance management in the network layer of IoT. A study performed by Le et al. [30] investigates cost-aware and energy-aware load distribution across multiple data centers. The study evaluates the potential cost and carbon savings for data centers located in different places and partly powered by green energy, and the research achieved significant GHG emission reduction.

## 10.3 Energy Management in Ubiquitous IoT

Ubiquitous IoT is composed of multiple unit IoTs that are managed or coordinated by specific higher-level M&DCs. Different from energy management of unit IoT, which only controls and manages the energy issues in unit IoT (e.g., sensors, actuators, communicating and switching devices, and data centers) from the technical aspect, energy management in ubiquitous IoT considers both technical and nontechnical aspects.

For the technical aspect, attention should be paid to building energy-aware IoT that integrates the end user into the energy management mechanism. It has been proven that energy management involving the end user is an effective method to reduce energy consumption in many scenarios (e.g., smart grid). In energy-aware IoT, the price of services required by a user is affected by both the energy amount and situation. For example, when large-scale solar energy is connected to the power grid, the same service required by the user on a sunny day may be much cheaper than that required on a cloudy day because energy on a sunny day can be more easily gained than on a cloudy one.

For nontechnical aspects, energy management mechanisms should be considered at different levels (i.e., international, national, industrial, and local levels) due to the complexity of ubiquitous IoT. Energy management in different levels has different features, and complies with the upward-compatible rule, which means that energy management mechanisms in lower levels need to be compatible with those in higher levels. In the following, energy management mechanisms are discussed according to different levels.

International/global-level coordination refers to energy management mechanisms that are commonly adopted by different nations around the world. As IoT is relatively new and emerging, many aspects of it have not been determined, including energy management. However, since IoT is based on current IT/ICT systems, international/global energy management of IoT can be developed from current energy management mechanisms. An example that can be used for reference of international/global-level energy management is Energy Star [31]. Energy Star is an international standard that was originally proposed by the U.S Environmental Protection Agency and Department of Energy to reduce energy consumption of IT-related products (such as computers and printers). Thus far, this standard has been adopted by many areas in the world, such as Canada, Australia, the European Union, Japan, the Netherlands, and Taiwan, and the product range of Energy Star has been largely enriched. Energy Star promotes energy efficiency and reduces $CO_2$ emission by labeling products that satisfy specific energy requirements. Some audit and calculation methods and tools were developed by Energy Star for the determination of energy efficiency, such as the energy performance rate, portfolio manager [32], an online tool to identify the energy performance rate and guidelines for energy reform. Other innovative programs for ICT energy management at the international/global level have been launched, such as Aligning Energy Efficiency Regulations for ICT Products. It was developed by a Strategic Approach Workshop [33], which was organized by the Asia-Pacific Economic Cooperation (APEC) Subcommittee on Standards and

Conformance and the APEC Expert Group on Energy Efficiency and Conservation (EGEEC).

National-level management refers to the energy management mechanisms that are developed by national authorities. There are several aspects that the related national authorities can consider to make national-level energy management for IoT, such as tax policy, financial support, operational model support, technical support, laws and regulations, standards, and so on. Moreover, an energy management contract is promising in promoting nationwide energy efficiency. However, for some nations, due to obstacles such as lack of financial support and industrial standards, the energy management contract (EMC) is difficult to conduct in a short time. So, national-level strategies and supports are needed.

Industrial-level management refers to energy management schemes that are based on the characteristics of a specific industry. A classical method to implement industrial-level energy management is industrial energy regulation, which is developed through the cooperation of an industry. The development of an energy management mechanism at the industrial level can be boosted by related government authorities (e.g., environmental ministries) and implemented by the cooperation of the whole industry.

Local-level management refers to the energy management schemes that are based on the characteristics of a specific region. The energy management mechanism at the local level can be developed and implemented by local management organizations (e.g., local government) and other participants according to the regional regulations.

Energy management of ubiquitous IoT not only manages energy from technical aspects, which directly manage the energy-consuming components, but also manages energy from other aspects, such as laws and regulations, standards, and economic strategies. The technical aspect of ubiquitous IoT energy management is similar to that of unit IoT, and the nontechnical aspect should be considered from different levels such as the global, national, industrial, and local levels.

## 10.4 Conclusion and Discussion

In this chapter, energy management is discussed based on unit IoT and ubiquitous IoT. For unit IoT, existing energy management technologies are reviewed, which enable green sensing, communicating, and computing. Meanwhile, nontechnical mechanisms are discussed in ubiquitous IoT. In future IoT, energy management should be considered in the network level or social factor due to the infrastructure complexity, component heterogeneity, and dynamics of energy supplement.

IoT is destined to be related to energy not only because energy is the basis for its operation, but also because it can be used to manage energy for various industries (e.g., power industry, logistics industry, and transportation industry). With the help of IoT, every energy-related participant (e.g., power plants, distributed energy generation systems, energy transmission systems, energy distribution systems, energy consuming systems, and human beings) can be connected to form the Internet of Energy (IoE). IoE can be regarded as a form of IoT, which means that IoE is a special IoT conceptual scheme aimed at energy management during the whole energy lifetime, from energy generation to end-user utilization. IoE is to evolve the traditional power grid into the following three aspects: improving energy usage efficiency, adding information and intelligence to the power grid, and increasing renewable energy access to the power grid [34]. It turns out that IoE should be a network that covers and manages energy not only in space dimensions (e.g., manage energy supply and demand in different areas) but also in time dimensions (e.g., preserve energy for future utilization when energy is sufficient).

# References

1. Alagoz, F., and G. Gur. 2011. Energy efficiency and satellite networking: A holistic overview. *Proceedings of the IEEE 99*, 1954–1979.
2. Mitsuaki, K., and C. Akira. 2009. Approaches to green network. *FUJITSU Scientific and Technical Journal* 45: 398–403.
3. Dutta, P., J. Hui, J. Jeong, S. Kim, C. Sharp, J. Taneja, G. Tolle, K. Whitehouse, and D. Culler. 2006. Trio: Enabling sustainable and scalable outdoor wireless sensor network deployments. In *Proceedings of the 5th International Conference on Information Processing in Sensor Networks*, 407–415.
4. Buettner, M., B. Greenstein, A. Sample, J. R. Smith, and D. Wetherall. 2008. Revisiting smart dust with RFID sensor networks. In *Proceedings of 7th ACM Workshop on Hot Topics in Networks (Hotnets-VII)*, 1–6.
5. Shen, D., J. H. Park, J. H. Noh, S. Y. Choe, S. H. Kim, H. C. Wikle, and D. J. Kim. 2009. Micromachined PZT cantilever based on SOI structure for low frequency vibration energy harvesting. *Sensors and Actuators A: Physical* 154: 103–108.

6. Starner, T., and Y. Maguire. 1998. A heat dissipation tutorial for wearable computers. In *2nd International Symposium on Wearable Computers*, 140–148.

7. Park, C., and P. H. Chou. 2006. AmbiMax: Autonomous energy harvesting platform for multisupply wireless sensor nodes. In *Proceedings of 3rd Annual IEEE Communications Society Conference on Sensor and Ad Hoc Communications and Networks (SECON '06)*, 1: 168–177.

8. Huang, A. Q., M. L. Crow, G. T. Heydt, J. P. Zheng, and S. J. Dale. 2011. The future renewable electric energy delivery and management (FREEDM) system: The energy Internet. *Proceedings of the IEEE 99*, 133–148.

9. Saint, B. 2009. Rural distribution system planning using smart grid technologies. In *Proceedings of IEEE Rural Electric Power Conference*, B3–B8.

10. Lee, J., B. Choi, and J. Lee. 2011. Energy-efficient coverage of wireless sensor networks using ant colony optimization with three types of pheromones. *IEEE Transactions on Industrial Informatics* 7: 419–427.

11. Xu, Y., J. Heidemann, and D. Estrin. 2001. Geography-informed energy conservation for *ad hoc* routing. In *7th Annual International Conference on Mobile Computing and Networking*, 70–84.

12. Zheng, R., J. C. Hou, and S. Lui. 2006. Performance analysis of power management policies in wireless networks. In *IEEE Transactions on Wireless Communications* 5: 1351–1361.

13. Chu, D., A. Deshpande, J. M. Hellerstein, and W. Hong. 2006. Approximate data collection in sensor networks using probabilistic models. In *Proceedings of 22nd International Conference on Data Engineering (ICDE06)*, 48–59.

14. Tulone, D., and S. Madden. 2006. PAQ: Time series forecasting for approximate query answering in sensor networks. In *Proceedings of 3rd European Conference on Wireless Sensor Networks (EWSN06)*, 21–37.

15. Goel, S., and T. Imielinski. 2001. Prediction-based monitoring in sensor networks: Taking lessons from MPEG. *ACM Computer Communication Review* 31: 82–98.

16. Sinha, A., and A. Chandrakasan. 2001. Dynamic power management in wireless sensor networks. *IEEE Design and Test of Computers* 18: 68–74.

17. Chen, T., Y. Yang, H. Zhang, K. Haesi, and K. Horneman. 2011. Network energy saving technologies for green wireless access networks. *IEEE Wireless Communications* 18: 30–38.

18. Moon, J., J. Son, J. Kim, I. Kim, S. Jee, Y. Y. Woo, and B. Kim. 2010. Doherty amplifier with envelope tracking for high efficiency. In *2010 IEEE MTT-S International Microwave Symposium Digest (MTT)*, 23–28.

19. Bougard, B., G. Lenoir, A. Dejonghe, L. Van der Perre, F. Catthoor, and W. Dehaene. 2007. Smart MIMO: An energy-aware adaptive MIMO-OFDM radio link control for next-generation wireless local area networks. *EURASIP Journal on Wireless Communications and Networking* 2007: 1–18.

20. McLaughlin, S., P. M. Grant, J. S. Thompson, H. Haas, D. I. Laurenson, C. Khirallah, Y. Hou, and R. Wang. 2011. Techniques for improving cellular radio base station energy efficiency. *IEEE Wireless Communications* 18: 10–17.

21. Conte, A., A. Feki, L. Chiaraviglio, D. Ciullo, M. Meo, and M. A. Marsan. 2011. Cell wilting and blossoming for energy efficiency. *IEEE Wireless Communications* 18: 50–57.

22. Barroso, L. A., and U. Holzle. 2007. The case for energy-proportional computing. *Computer* 40: 33–37.

23. Lebeck, A. R., X. Fan, H. Zeng, and C. Ellis. 2000. Power aware page allocation. *SIGPLAN Not* 35: 105–116.

24. Von Laszewski, G., L. Wang, A. J. Younge, and X. He. 2009. Power-aware scheduling of virtual machines in DVFS-enabled clusters. In *IEEE International Conference on Cluster Computing and Workshops*, 1–10.

25. Patel, C. D., C. E. Bash, R. Sharma, M. Beitelmal, and R. Friedrich. 2003. Smart cooling of data centers. In *Proceedings of ASME Conference*, 129–137.

26. Wang, L., S. Khan, and J. Dayal. 2011. Thermal aware workload placement with task-temperature profiles in a data center. *Journal of Supercomputing* 1–24.

27. Kinoshita, K., T. Okazaki, H. Tode, and K. Murakami. 2008. A data gathering scheme for environmental energy-based wireless sensor networks. In *Proceedings of 5th IEEE Consumer Communications and Networking Conference*, 719–723.

28. Hsu, J., S. Zahedi, A. Kansal, M. Srivastava, and V. Raghunathan. 2006. Adaptive duty cycling for energy harvesting systems. In *Proceedings of 2006 ACM International Symposium on Low Power Electronics and Design*, 180–185.

29. Bolla, R., R. Bruschi, A. Cianfrani, and M. Listanti. 2011. Enabling backbone networks to sleep. *IEEE Network* 25: 26–31.

30. Le, K., R. Bianchini, M. Martonosi, and T. D. Nguyen. 2009. Cost- and energy-aware load distribution across data centers. In *SOSP Workshop on Power Aware Computing and Systems (HotPower'09)*, 1–5.

31. U.S. Environmental Protection Agency and U.S. Department of Energy. 1992. Energy Star. http://www.energystar.gov (accessed September 7, 2012).

32. U.S. Environmental Protection Agency and U.S. Department of Energy. 1992. Energy Star. http://www.energy star.gov/index.cfm ?c=small_busin ess.sb_spp_gui delines (accessed September 7, 2012).

33. Asia Pacific Economic Cooperation. 2012. Boosting energy efficiency through industry-government collaboration. http://www.apec.org/Press/Features/2012/0816_ict.aspx (accessed September 7, 2012).

34. BDI. 2011. Internet of Energy ICT for energy markets of the future. http://www.bdi.eu/bdi_english/download_content/Marketing/Broch ure_Internet_of_Energy.pdf (accessed September 7, 2012).

# 11

# SPECTRUM MANAGEMENT

## 11.1 Introduction

Radio spectrum refers to a range of frequencies over which electromagnetic signals can be transmitted. It is an essential and finite resource to provide various services, such as mobile telecommunications, global positioning system (GPS) localization, broadcasting, aeronautical and marine communications, radar detection, and so on. An increasing number of services are using radio spectrum, and the spectrum demands of each service have increased enormously, such as the growing use of mobile phones and GPS devices. Therefore, as a public resource, it is used to obtain the greatest economic benefits and to serve the maximum number of users. And efficient spectrum management is needed to satisfy the tremendous spectrum demand on the finite radio spectrum.

Spectrum management is the procedures of planning, coordinating, and managing spectrum utilization, and aims to enable spectrum-dependent devices to access the spectrum in a contested spectrum environment without causing unacceptable interferences [1]. Spectrum management includes multiple elements, such as legal and regulatory foundations, spectrum planning, licensing, spectrum authorization, spectrum monitoring, electromagnetic compatibility (EMC), electromagnetic interference (EMI) analysis and resolution, and so on.

The development of spectrum management can be divided into three phases: traditional spectrum management, modern spectrum management, and future spectrum management for IoT. Traditional spectrum management practice is predicated on the spectrum being a finite resource that frequencies are assigned by issuing licenses to specific users for specific purposes, limiting access to and use of radio spectrum. It had worked well for many years, but recently the spectrum has been under pressure from rapidly increasing demands of wireless services and changing patterns of spectrum utilization. The improvement of spectrum management is so urgent and significant that many technologies and strategies have been proposed. A strategic plan and framework for future spectrum management was introduced by the National Telecommunications and Information Administrator [1]. The proposed schemes are significant guides for the spectrum management of other nations and global spectrum coordination. The International Telecommunication Union (ITU) has also published many reports [2,3] to help the spectrum management of its member states, in which the national spectrum management framework and strategies are particularly introduced. Meanwhile, researchers have been working on the hottest topics in spectrum management [4,5]. Many technical reforms in spectrum management are described [4], mainly including spectrum trading [6], dynamic spectrum access [7], and cognitive radio [8]. However, the increasing IoT has brought new challenges to modern spectrum management, and some possible efficient schemes can be drawn based on advantages of IoT. Thus, the study of spectrum management adapting to IoT development is urgent too. And the concept, vision, demands, and challenges of spectrum management in future IoT should be clarified.

In summary, modern spectrum management attempts to overcome the disadvantages of the traditional one. But with the development of IoT, modern spectrum management is facing trouble in dealing with the increasing spectrum demand and the new requirements of spectrum utilization. In the following, Section 11.2 reviews modern spectrum management from three aspects: spectrum management systems, equipment, and technologies. The vision, challenge, and scheme of spectrum management in future IoT are discussed in Section 11.3. Section 11.4 draws a conclusion.

## 11.2 Spectrum Management System, Equipment, and Technology

For efficient spectrum management, the national spectrum management regulatory framework and its spectrum management system are fundamental. They determine the characteristics and basic components of spectrum management in this nation. Therein, spectrum monitoring and management equipment are the essential tools to preserve normal spectrum utilization. The application of some new technologies increases spectrum demands, while others can help to manage spectrum resources. Technological innovations will play important roles in the improvement of spectrum management. In this section, a brief overview of the national spectrum management systems, equipment, and technologies is given.

### 11.2.1 National Spectrum Management System

Driven by the enormous economic opportunities presented by the growth of wireless communications and technological changes, a number of nations have developed spectrum management systems to plan and manage spectrum utilization. In this section, three spectrum management systems proposed by Turkey, the United Kingdom, and Canada are introduced.

- *Turkey.* The development of a spectrum management system in Turkey takes advantage of the university facilities and has made impressive progress. In Turkey, the Communications and Spectrum Management Research Center (ISYAM) [9] is the core institution of the national spectrum management, which is also a research center of Bilkent University. ISYAM provides various administrative and technical solutions, including projects for radio and TV spectrum planning in Turkey and the National Frequency Management System (NFMS) [10]. NFMS is a distributed architecture including a national control center and several regional monitoring centers. NFMS's main functions cover various elements, including radio signals supervision, spectrum attribution measurement, and interference analysis.
- *United Kingdom.* In the United Kingdom, the spectrum management system tends to apply market mechanisms. Ofcom, as the independent regulator and competition authority for its communications industries, was set up to encourage and promote optimal utilization of the radio spectrum in the interests of all citizens and stakeholders. Ofcom believes that market mechanisms, such as spectrum trading, liberalization, administered incentive pricing, and auctions, can work better than command-and-control–based traditional spectrum management [11]. And Ofcom's Spectrum Information System (SIS)

[12] provides information on how to use the radio spectrum, including the spectrum authorization plan, the details of spectrum allocation/registration, types of wireless telegraphy act licenses, and details of tradable licenses.

- *Canada.* In Canada, the spectrum management system takes advantage of market forces, and it encourages and entrusts the stakeholders to take part in national spectrum management with the advantages of management capabilities of each industry. Three organizations are involved: Industry Canada, Canadian Heritage, and Canadian Radio-Television and Telecommunications Commission (CRTC). Therein, Industry Canada is the lead department of spectrum management [13]. In 2007, Industry Canada conducted a public consultation on a revised spectrum management framework that would rely on more market forces. The spectrum licenses can be obtained by means such as spectrum votes, spectrum auctions, and spectrum trading. In some industries (e.g., railway, broadcasting, telecommunication, and civil aviation), the industrial organizations and associations are entrusted to manage the industrial spectrum with a special license for certain frequency utilization.

### 11.2.2 Spectrum Monitoring and Management Equipment

Spectrum management requires spectrum monitoring and management equipment as an essential component. Measuring the spectrum occupancy is indispensable for planning allocations of frequencies. Monitoring all emissions, measuring their technical characteristics, and locating their sources by using direction finders are key parts of daily spectrum management. Several devices are introduced for spectrum monitoring and management, as follows.

Rohde & Schwarz provides variable solutions such as the ARGUS-IT spectrum monitoring and management system [14] for spectrum monitoring and management tasks proposed by ITU, from stand-alone systems to completely automated nationwide networks.

Glowlink presents a solution called the Model 1000 Satellite Spectrum Monitoring System [15] to provide the network operator with powerful automated and interactive measurement tools for monitoring and troubleshooting satellite network traffic. It is designed to address the increasing complexity and demands of satellite communications. Other satellite spectrum monitoring systems such as the Sentinel [16] can monitor, evaluate, and decrease EMI.

TCI designs the Model 725 Spectrum Monitoring System [17] to provide spectrum monitoring and direction finding (DF). The system utilizes TCI's field-proven angle of arrival (AOA) DF technique and is TDOA-ready to supplement DF performance in diverse and complex radio frequency (RF) environments. TCI's single-band, passive antenna solutions can provide high-quality monitoring and direction finding measurements of signals from 20 to 3000 MHz without cost or time-consuming field calibration.

Agilent is another important spectrum monitoring and management equipment producer, and its N6841A RF Sensor [18] provides an extremely cost-effective way to improve spectrum awareness. The RF Sensor is enclosed in a weatherproof case allowing wide-area, close-proximity signal monitoring, detection, and location. It can be used for frequency regulators needing ITU-R spectrum monitoring systems and interference detection, location systems, and government and industry frequency managers needing spectrum monitoring for test range management.

### 11.2.3  Technological Innovation and Spectrum Management

New technologies not only increase the spectrum demands, but also provide opportunities to enhance spectrum management. As shown in Figure 11.1, technologies such as wireless local area networks (WLANs),

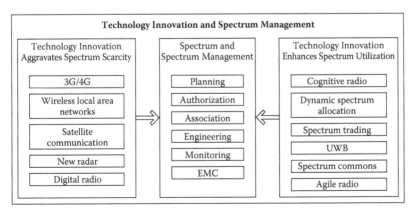

**Figure 11.1**  Technology innovation and spectrum management.

satellite communication, third-generation telecommunication (3G)/ fourth-generation telecommunication (4G), and communication in the high frequency aggravate the spectrum scarcity. However, in order to break technology-specific restrictions imposed by the traditional spectrum allocation, the flexible and dynamic mechanism can be improved by technical innovations, including spread spectrum, dynamic spectrum allocation, ultra-wide bandwidth (UWB), and agile radio.

Among the new technologies to enhance spectrum utilization, dynamic spectrum allocation (DSA) is a promising technology to deal with the spectrum scarcity problem caused by the traditional inflexible spectrum allocation policies. DSA considers the fact that spectrum demands vary in time and space, which results in a substantial fraction of the spectrum potentially being wasted at the given time and space. So the assigned spectrum blocks in DSA may vary according to different demands to get the most efficient spectrum utilization, which is based on the cognitive radio (CR) and is regarded as its application. The CR can switch the spectrum to an unused frequency band according to the characteristics and situation of the spectrum. In this process, the transmitter and receiver parameters will be reconfigured, and similarly, the CR will reselect appropriate communication protocol parameters and modulation schemes to use. In summary, CR can figure out which frequency is idle in a given band, and pick one or more to transmit/receive data.

## 11.3 The Vision, Challenge, and Scheme of Spectrum Management in IoT

### 11.3.1 Spectrum Management Visions and Challenges

Spectrum management in future IoT will be quite different from the modern one. In order to satisfy the ubiquitous connection of the objects in IoT, all electronic devices and systems should have permission to the spectrum. The vision of spectrum management by the National Telecommunications and Information Administration [1] is discussed as "understandable, agile, seamless and integrated," which means that access to the spectrum should be a basic right for all spectrum-dependent devices, and it mainly serves the global information grid of the United States.

It is believed that spectrum management in future IoT should provide flexible, dynamic, and coordinated spectrum access for every authorized, qualified, and reasonable electronic device or other spectrum resource user.

- *Flexible* means that the spectrum management should have the ability to satisfy the tremendous spectrum demand of the multiple spectrum-dependent devices by planning the spectrum efficiently and normalizing the devices with spectrum standards and spectrum management protocols.
- *Dynamic* means the spectrum allocation will vary in time and space based on the regional and temporal spectrum use knowledge. And to obtain optimized spectrum utilization, the dynamic access relies on instant and accurate awareness of the spectrum situation and intelligent reconfiguration and allocation of the idle and available reuse spectrum.
- *Coordinated* means that all spectrum-related operations should respect each other and avoid interference with other authorized spectrum-dependent devices. It refers to a multilayered spectrum harmony, including regional, national, and international spectrum coordination, and is an important requirement for efficient spectrum utilization.

Spectrum management should also be decentralized into multiple spectrum management centers that can perform autonomously. Meanwhile, a network to integrate these centers is needed to manage the spectrum cooperatively. However, there is a huge gap between the current spectrum demand and the vision of the spectrum management. These are the challenges that the IoT brings to future spectrum management. The rapid development of IoT is currently increasing the spectrum scarcity in the following aspects:

- In the sensor-actuator layer, more spectrum-dependent sensors and actuators have been equipped for various information discoveries and actuations.
- In the network layer, the spectrum demand of the data transmission from the sensor-actuator layer to the network layer is tremendous. And the wireless networks to ensure the interconnection of the devices and systems, such as WLAN, 3G, 4G, and satellite communication, are aggravating the spectrum scarcity.

- In the application layer, the number of multiple terminals to obtain the various services is many times that than from before.
- In layers for ubiquitous IoT, how to protect the coordinated and harmonized use of the spectrum among different regions, industries, and especially nations from various interferences is another huge problem.

Among the challenges introduced above, how to meet the spectrum demand of the tremendous number of sensors, actuators, and other spectrum-dependent devices is the basic problem. International and global spectrum coordination is an increasingly important issue, because electromagnetic energy has no international boundary and electromagnetic interference (EMI) is a common problem for the utilization of the spectrum in every nation, state, province, city, and village. Effective utilization of the spectrum in every nation will typically require high coordination with neighboring countries to mitigate the extent of harmful interference, especially nations that are gathered in intensive regions, such as Europe and Southeast Asia. However, international and global spectrum coordination has several difficulties to tackle to break the national boundary of spectrum management: the spectrum plan and allocation of every nation are quite different, the spectrum demands and spectrum utilization technologies are multiple and different, and the spectrum management development situation is different. So, international spectrum coordination will be a global task that requires every nation's cooperation.

### 11.3.2 Spectrum Management Scheme in IoT

While spectrum management in IoT is facing challenges of growing spectrum demands and requirements, a spectrum management scheme can enhance the flexible, dynamic, and coordinated spectrum access for unit and ubiquitous IoT (U2IoT) architecture. The unit IoT management and data center (M&DC) can be applied to address multiple spectrum awareness and dynamic spectrum allocation tasks, and it can also integrate spectrum knowledge and send it to ubiquitous M&DC. The multilayered form of ubiquitous IoT can help to integrate spectrum utilization and allocation information and to make optimal decisions and management according to local, industrial, and national spectrum utilization knowledge. In this section, the unit IoT spectrum management scheme and the national spectrum management scheme, which are representative of spectrum management in ubiquitous IoT, are presented.

*11.3.2.1 Spectrum Management in Unit IoT*    The main task of spectrum management in unit IoT is to ensure that every device has access to the spectrum and to protect spectrum utilization from mutual interference. The high-level architecture of spectrum management in unit IoT is shown in Figure 11.2, and the detailed components are described as follows:

- *Devices and networks.* This component represents the entities that use spectrum resources in the contested environment.
- *Contested spectrum environment.* This component refers to the spectrum environment that is contested due to the increasing spectrum demands and the finite spectrum resources.
- *Unit IoT spectrum management center.* This component receives the application from the spectrum users, and assigns a spectrum license to them according to the spectrum knowledge from the ubiquitous management center, and enables that the spectrum in the unit IoT is flexible and stable.

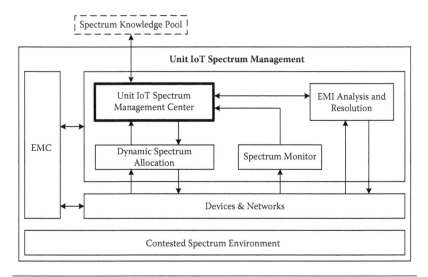

**Figure 11.2**    Spectrum management in unit IoT.

- *Dynamic spectrum allocation.* This component is the process where the unit IoT spectrum management center allocates certain available frequency bands to the spectrum-dependent devices for a certain period of time, which should also consider the spectrum allocation knowledge from the ubiquitous IoT.
- *Spectrum knowledge pool.* The spectrum knowledge pool for unit IoT spectrum management consists of two parts. One is information of the spectrum utilization in unit IoT, such as frequency, location, and use time, and this information is shared with the national IoT spectrum management center. The other refers to the requirement and assignment appointed by ubiquitous IoT.
- *EMI.* This component analyzes the data transmitted in IoT to address the EMI problem.
- *EMC.* This component works throughout spectrum management. The EMC analysis is to predict any possible EMI, and alleviates the EMI influence.
- *Spectrum monitor.* This component is used to offer spectrum monitoring information to the unit IoT spectrum management center to perform EMI analysis, EMI resolution, and EMC.

Spectrum management in unit IoT is to provide a flexible spectrum assessment for the electronic systems in the contested spectrum environment, and enable spectrum utilization in unit IoT that is flexible and stable. It should be under the management of national IoT to realize efficient national spectrum management.

*11.3.2.2 Spectrum Management in Ubiquitous IoT* Spectrum management in ubiquitous IoT consists of a set of aspects, including a local spectrum management center, industrial spectrum management center, national spectrum management center, and international spectrum coordinator. This kind of scheme can provide hierarchical spectrum management. Each element in this scheme has its typical functions for spectrum management in ubiquitous IoT:

- The local spectrum management center manages the spectrum in particular regions, and its main task is coordinating and managing the spectrum utilization of its unit IoTs. It establishes a regional spectrum harmonization and includes the provincial and civic spectrum monitoring and management organizations.

- The industrial spectrum management center manages the spectrum within a particular industry. It is an essential connection between the national spectrum management center and the unit IoT spectrum management center, which are important participants in the spectrum management of individual nations. The entity of the industrial spectrum management center includes the civil aviation administration, the port authority, the meteorological administration, and so on.
- The national spectrum management center is the elementary unit that manages the spectrum within an individual nation. The goal of the national spectrum management center is to provide flexible spectrum access for every unit IoT without any kind of interference by planning and coordinating the spectrum allocation of every local and industrial IoT.
- The international/national spectrum coordinator provides flexible and dynamic spectrum access for the electric devices and systems around the world without experiencing interference from different nations. Many organizations are playing the role of international spectrum coordinator, for example, the ITU, the World Trade Organization (WTO), and the Federal Communications Commission (FCC).

Among the four kinds of spectrum management centers, the national spectrum management center is key to spectrum management in ubiquitous IoT, because it is the only one that can issue laws and provisions to guide the spectrum management and make plans for the spectrum's use of every unit IoT, local IoT, and industrial IoT. Thus, national spectrum management is presented representatively to discuss spectrum management in ubiquitous IoT.

National spectrum management has similar aspects in unit IoT, and additional components are introduced, such as new technology to improve spectrum management, national spectrum planning, and association. The general system model is shown in Figure 11.3, and detailed descriptions follow:

- *Spectrum knowledge pool.* This component manages unit IoT spectrum utilization and allocation. It also communicates spectrum knowledge with the international spectrum coordinator to prevent local spectrum utilization from EMI that

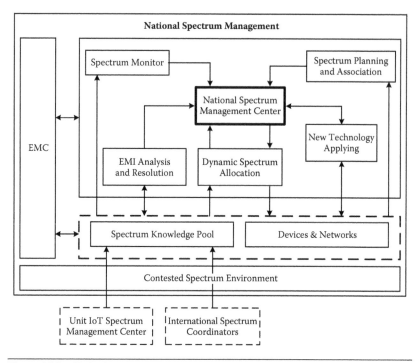

**Figure 11.3** National spectrum management in ubiquitous IoT.

comes from foreigners and supports the healthy spectrum utilization internationally.

- *International spectrum coordinators.* This component coordinates spectrum utilization on an international level, seeks a harmonious international and global spectrum environment, and reduces harmful interference between nations to improve use of the spectrum.

- *Spectrum planning and association.* This component is the basis of national spectrum management. It should consider the economical and technical elements of the spectrum together, and standardize the spectrum utilization. The planning should not only consider the general spectrum situation of the nation, but also refer to international spectrum coordinators.

- *New technology application.* This component benefits from emerging technologies such as cognitive radio, UWB, broadband, Wi-MAX, and 4G. New technologies can be used to increase the spectrum utilization rate by using frequency and broaden spectrum resources in a higher frequency.

National spectrum management is designed for national-scale spectrum management. Its main task is national spectrum planning and association, and spectrum knowledge management for unit IoT. The two schemes are proposed for spectrum management for U2IoT.

## 11.4 Conclusion

Spectrum is an essential and finite resource; the contested spectrum environment and the increasing spectrum demand in IoT bring severe difficulties and challenges to spectrum management. After a brief review of modern spectrum management, the vision and challenges of spectrum management in IoT are discussed. And the spectrum management scheme is presented for the U2IoT, to enable that the spectrum can be managed efficiently in such a hierarchical structure.

# References

1. National Telecommunications and Information Administration (NTIA). 2008. Department of Defense (DoD) strategic spectrum plan. http://www.ntia.doc.gov/files/ntia/publications/dod_strategic_spectrum_plan_nov2007.pdf (accessed August 18, 2012).
2. International Telecommunication Union (ITU). 2010. Guidance on the regulatory framework for national spectrum management. http://www.itu.int/dms_pub/itu-r/opb/rep/R-REP-SM.2093-1-2010-PDF-E.pdf (accessed August 18, 2012).
3. ICT Regulation Toolkit. 2012. Module 5. Radio spectrum management. http://www.ictregulationtoolkit.org/en/Section.1247.html (accessed August 18, 2012).
4. Luther, W. A. 2003. Spectrum management in the global village. In *IEEE International Symposium on Electromagnetic Compatibility*, 2: 701–704.
5. Chandra, A. 2009. Spectrum management for future generation wireless based technology. In *European Wireless Technology Conference*, 201–205.
6. Valetti, T. M. 2001. Spectrum trading. *Telecommunications Policy* 655–670.
7. Qing, Z., and B. M. Sadler. 2007. A survey of dynamic spectrum access. *IEEE Signal Processing Magazine* 24: 79–89.
8. Sridhara, K., A. Chandra, and P. S. M. Tripathi. 2008. Spectrum challenges and solutions by cognitive radio: An overview. *Wireless Personal Communications* 45: 281–291.
9. ISYAM: Communications & Spectrum Management Research Center. http://www.isyam.bilkent.edu.tr/about.html (accessed August 18, 2012).

10. ISYAM: Communications & Spectrum Management Research Center. 2009. National Frequency Management System. http://www.isyam. bilkent.edu.tr/nfms.html (accessed August 18, 2012).

11. Ofcom. 2007. Digital dividend review. http://stakeholders.ofcom.org.uk/ consultations/ddr/statement/ (accessed August 18, 2012).

12. Ofcom. Spectrum information system (SIS). http://spectruminfo.Ofcom. org.uk/spectrumInfo/ (accessed August 18, 2012).

13. Industry Canada. Spectrum management and telecommunications. http://strategis.gc.ca/spectrum (accessed August 18, 2012).

14. Rohde & Schwarz. ARGUS-IT spectrum monitoring and management system. http://www.rohde-schwarz.us/product/ARGUS-IT.html (accessed August 18, 2012).

15. Glowlink Communications Technology, Inc. Model 1000 satellite spectrum monitoring system. http://www.glowlink.com/products_ model1000.html (accessed August 18, 2012).

16. RT Logic Technology Company. Sentinel system. http://www.rtlogic. com/prodsignal.php (accessed August 18, 2012).

17. TCI International Company. Model 725 spectrum monitoring system. http://www.tcibr.com/?PageID=150 (accessed August 18, 2012).

18. Agilent Technologies. N6841A RF Sensor. http://www. home.agilent. com/agilent/product.jspx?cc = FR&lc = fre&ckey = 1414739&nid = -35189.804598.00&id = 1414739&cmpid = 21422 (accessed August 18, 2012).

# 12

# Nanotechnology

## 12.1 Introduction

Nanotechnology is an emerging technology of controlling matter on the scale of 1–100 nm [1]. It involves many disciplines and technologies, such as electric engineering, biology, chemistry, physics, and machinery. With the development of Internet of Things (IoT) and nanotechnology, the fusion of the two will make a great difference to society. Nanotechnology promises new solutions as well as injects new vitality to IoT. On the one hand, nanotechnology brings new solutions to the sensor-actuator layer, network layer, and application layer by creating new kinds of sensors and actuators, high-bandwidth and energy-efficient communication channels, and high-performance application platforms. On the other hand, nanotechnology opens up a new nanoscale territory for future IoT, and helps to realize the Internet of everything. The following is a discussion on how nanotechnology is propelling IoT development from three aspects: ubiquitous sensing and controlling, communication network, and high-performance computing (HPC).

## 12.2 Nanotechnology in Ubiquitous Sensing

### 12.2.1 Nanotechnology-Based New Sensors and Actuators

Nanotechnology is attractive in designing new sensors and actuators with improved performance (e.g., higher sensitivity and selectivity, shorter response time, and lower power consumption) and longer lifetime (e.g., in chemical sensing scenarios) than most non-nanotechnology-based sensors. Many nanomaterials (e.g., carbon nanotubes [2], graphene [3], gold nanoparticles [4], and nanowire [5]) have been used in sensors within a wide range of applications.

Among these nanomaterials, carbon nanotube (CNT)–based materials have been studied most extensively in designing new sensors, and are widely used in environmental monitoring, chemical sensing, and biomedical and health monitoring. CNT was first discovered in 1991 and has drawn great attention. There are two kinds of carbon nanotubes (i.e., single-wall carbon nanotubes and multiwall nanotubes) with different characteristics. Due to the special properties that the nanomaterial shows, such as surface-to-volume ratio, volumetric and surface diffusivity, optical reflection and absorption, and high thermal conductivity, the performance and energy efficiency of nanotechnology-based sensors will be much better than those of non-nanotechnology-based sensors.

### 12.2.2 Nanoscale Sensor Networks

Nanotechnology facilitates IoT development by sensing, manipulating, and connecting things in nanoscale. This new networking paradigm of nanoscale devices is referred to as the nanoscale sensor network. The nanoscale sensor network belongs to new content for the sensor-actuator layer and creates large numbers of new services and applications (e.g., cell-level health monitoring). Similar to the wireless sensor network (WSN), the wireless communication and cooperation among nanodevices will expand the potential applications of individual devices in terms of complexity and operation range. The major challenge of realizing nanoscale sensor networks is establishing communication channels between different nanonodes and nanodevices. Several candidates of communication channels for nanonodes have been proposed, including molecule communication, nanoelectromagnetic communication, and quantum communication.

- *Molecule communication.* Molucule communication is promising in short-range communication between nanodevices/nanomachines and sending/receiving carrier molecules, and it is attracting more and more attention because main communication technologies, such as wireless telecommunication and optical communication, are not suitable for nanodevices: complex system architecture and low energy efficiency. Molecule communication is enlightened by the cells' communication process, in which information is carried by particular molecules released by the "sender" cells and received by the "receiver" cells. The transmission channel of the carrier molecule is the molecular motor (e.g., molecules that transfer chemical energy into machinery energy) [6].

- *Nanoelectromagnetic waves.* Another choice for nanodevices communication is using electromagnetic waves as the information carrier. When it comes to the communication of nanodevices, the networking concept should be rebuilt carefully due to nanodevice properties. First, the operating frequency band of nanodevice communication reaches terahertz due to its small scale. Second, the information modulation and protocol designation of nanodevice networks should be reconsidered on the basis of the device resource situation and channel model [7].

- *Quantum communication.* Quantum communication is promising in establishing communication channels for nanoscale things, and quantum communication will be discussed further in Chapter 13.

## 12.3 Nanotechnology in Communication Networks

Future IoT enabling ubiquitous connectivity and pervasive intelligence will cause a faster increase of data traffic load in both wired and wireless communication networks. An important part of wired communication, optical communication is promising to offer high bandwidth with relative low energy consumption. However, there are breakthroughs that need to be made to promote the performance of optical communication in order to reach a satisfactory level. For example, in optical core networks, electronic processing–based core switching and routing devices have been the bottleneck of optical communications. Meanwhile, the high-bandwidth demands and low energy efficiency of wireless communication networks require new supporting technologies in radio frequency (RF) communication. Nanotechnology has been proven to be promising in improving performance in both wired and wireless communications. A discussion on how nanotechnology affects the IoT network layer is presented in terms of high-performance routing/switching devices and RF communication.

### 12.3.1 High-Performance Routing and Switching Devices

Switching/routing devices in core optical communication networks have been the obstacle that has prohibited further bandwidth promotion. In addition, the high energy consumption and low energy efficiency of these devices are obstacles for achieving "green IoT." The interconnections in electronic high routing and switching devices (such as copper-based interconnections and semiconductor-based interconnections) prohibit further data rate promotion, size miniaturization, and energy consumption reduction. Therefore, new materials-based interconnections with higher performance (e.g., data transfer, conductivity, and mechanical strength) are urgently needed. Nanotechnology-based interconnections such as nano-optical interconnections; plasmotics interconnections, nanotubes, graphene, and nanowire have been studied to replace the copper-based interconnections in high-performance routing and switching devices [8]. In order to satisfy the requirements brought by IoT, new switching and processing technologies (such as optical switching) should be adopted to overcome the limitation of electronic switching systems. In these terms, nanotechnology will play an important role in building the key component (e.g., optical storage component and optical logic component).

### 12.3.2 Radio Frequency (RF) Communication

Nanomaterials have shown great potential to change RF communication devices and improve their performance. As the current RF low-noise amplifier confronts limitations in terms of limited operation frequency, nonlinearity, and low energy efficiency, new amplifiers that are based on advanced materials and technology should be designed to overcome these limitations. Among the advanced materials and technologies, nanomaterials and nanotechnologies have shown great potential. For example, graphene, as a newly discovered nanomaterial, is proving to be competent for addressing some traditional challenges. Properties such as high electron-hole mobility, zero band gap, and unprecedented carrier confinement make it fascinating to build new-generation low-noise amplifiers, ambipolar nonlinear electronics, resonators, and switches [9].

## 12.4 Nanotechnology in High-Performance Computing

In IoT, high-performance computing devices build the platforms on which diversity applications run. Currently, high-performance computing devices are based on silicon semiconductor technology. However, with the miniaturization of computing devices, silicon-based complementary metal oxide semiconductor (CMOS) technology has reached its limit. What makes the situation worse is that with the increasing density of logics in integrated circuits (ICs), the thermal problem is getting unprecedentedly serious and becomes an obstacle for further performance promotion. In addition, another defect of CMOS computing devices is their low energy efficiency. Along with IoT development, energy consumption of computing devices will be a severe problem. Owing to this, new technologies that can handle the above problems should be developed to replace the silicon-based computing platforms. Fortunately, nanotechnology has proved to be effective in providing new solutions. In the following, some new nanomaterials that are promising in designing high computing systems are discussed.

- *Molecular electronic devices.* Molecular electronic devices, which utilize a few molecules or even a single molecule to perform the function of digital electronics [10], are promising to bring new opportunities for overcoming the challenges that traditional silicon-based semiconductors are facing. The silicon-based semiconductor, which is the basis of current high-performance computing devices, will get into trouble with the miniaturization process. This is for a few reasons. For example, when the size of an electronic component reaches the scales of an atom and molecule, quantum effects dominate the physical laws, and this causes trouble to the normal operation for components based on macro-physical laws. On the contrary, molecular electronics tries to make use of quantum effects to implement digital electronic functions.

- *Carbon-based nanomaterial.* Carbon-based nanomaterials (i.e., carbon nanotubes [CNTs] and graphene) have been expected to change future high-performance computing devices. For example, graphene is a candidate for building ultra-fast logic that is very important to high-performance computing. Though carbon-based nanomaterials are attractive in promoting future computing performance, currently, the synthesis process of these materials is not suitable for large-scale production.

- *Nanophysical computing.* Nanophysical computing is computing based on the physics of nanodevices, such as resonance [11]. It is suitable to build human brain-like processing devices due to the similarity between the computing unit (e.g., transistors with resonance characteristics) and human brain neurons. A large amount of the above computing units can be integrated into ICs with high processing and pattern recognizing performance. Human brain-like processing is a new processing paradigm that overturns traditional processing logic, and it has been used in specific scenarios, such as pattern recognition.
- *Memristors.* As an achievement of nanotechnology, memristors have been given high expectations to trigger a revolution in computing and information storage. Memristors not only have the feature to resist current flow through them, but also have the ability to memorize the last current they experienced. This characteristic makes memristors one of the most attractive candidates of next-generation computing and storage devices.
- *Quantum dots and spintronics.* Quantum effects such as spin characteristics and tunneling characteristics bring new opportunities to high-performance computing. Quantum dots and spintronics are two promising technologies for building next-generation computing logic circuits with higher speed and lower energy consumption—the details are discussed in Chapter 13.

Apart from the materials that can be used to build high-performance computing devices, other ways that nanotechnology can affect high-performance computing are listed as follows:

- *Promoting devices' production process.* Nanotechnology manipulates matter in nanoscale, which lays the foundation of new computing structures. For example, in molecular electronics, nanotechnology can be used to build molecules that satisfy special function requirements with the help of DNA. The sequence of DNA can be programmed by enzymatic and synthetic approaches.
- *Cooling.* The cooling problem is an obstacle of further miniaturization and integration of high-performance devices. Nanotechnology can bring new, efficient methods to transfer

the heat generated by silicon-based computing devices with ultra–high speed and capacity. For instance, micro-multi-wall CNT (MCNT)-based micro-channel cooling can provide high heat transfer efficiency due to the compact integration of MCNT with a CMOS component [12].

# References

1. Ermolov, V., M. Heino, A. Karkkainen, R. Lehtiniemi, N. Nefedov, P. Pasanen, Z. Radivojevic, M. Rouvala, T. Ryhanen, E. Seppala, and M.A. Uusitalo. 2007. Significance of nanotechnology for future wireless devices and communications. In *IEEE 18th International Symposium on Personal, Indoor and Mobile Radio Communications*, 1-5.
2. Bogue, R. W. 2004. Emerald article: Nanotechnology: What are the prospects for sensors? *Sensor Review* 24: 253–260.
3. Sorkin, V., and Y. Zhang. 2011. Graphene-based pressure nano-sensors. *Journal of Molecular Modeling* 17: 2825–2830.
4. Storhoff, J. J., A. A. Lazarides, R. C. Mucic, C. A. Mirkin, R. L. Letsinger, and G. C. Schatz. 2000. What controls the optical properties of DNA-linked gold nanoparticle assemblies? *Journal of the American Chemical Society* 122: 4640–4650.
5. Cui, Y., Q. Wei, and H. Park. 2001. Nanowire nanosensors for highly sensitive and selective detection of biological and chemical species. *Science* 293: 1289–1292.
6. Suda, T., M. Moore, T. Nakano, R. Egashira, and A. Enomoto. 2005. Exploratory research on molecular communication between nanomachines. In *Genetic and Evolutionary Computation Conference*, 1–5.
7. Akyildiz, I. F., and J. M. Jornet. 2010. The Internet of nano-things. *IEEE Wireless Communications* 17: 58–63.
8. Islam, M. S., and V. J. Logeeswaran. 2010. Nanoscale materials and devices for future communication networks. *IEEE Communications Magazine* 48: 112–120.
9. Palacios, T., A. Hsu, and H. Wang. 2010. Applications of graphene devices in RF communications. *IEEE Communications Magazine* 48: 122–128.
10. Joachim, C., J. K. Gimzewski, and A. Aiviram. 2000. Electronics using hybrid-molecular and mono-molecular devices. *Nature* 408: 541–548.
11. Shibata, T. 2009. Computing based on the physics of nano devices—A beyond-CMOS approach to human-like intelligent systems. *Solid-State Electronics* 53: 1227–1241.
12. Wang, T., M. Jönsson, E. Nyström, Z. Mo, E. E. B. Campbell, and J. Liu. 2006. Development and characterization of microcoolers using carbon nanotubes. In *1st Electronics System Integration Technology Conference*, 881–885.

# 13

# QUANTUM TECHNOLOGY

## 13.1 Introduction

Quantum mechanics is an advanced and fundamental physical theory that describes the interactions of energy and matter. The development of device fabrication and experimental control has witnessed how quantum mechanics will be used to establish a new technology. This is referred to as emerging quantum technology, which may be defined as the engineering of physical devices and systems that work on quantum principles [1]. Compared to conventional technologies governed by classical mechanics, there are two main imperatives driving the development of quantum technology [2]. The first is that the design of physical devices should be based on quantum principles when the devices are at length scales of nanometers and action scales and approaching Planck's constant. The second is that quantum principles appearing to offer the promise of excellent performance can hardly be obtained within a classical physical framework.

The key quantum principles that are closely relevant to technological tasks mainly include quantization (i.e., quantum size effect), uncertainty principle, quantum superposition, tunneling, entanglement, and decoherence. The objective of quantum technology is to explore useful devices and processes by using the above principles. Some examples of existing or emerging quantum technologies are listed and described briefly as follows:

- *Quantum dots*. Generally, quantum dots refer to nanofabricated physical systems that make use of the quantum size effect. The technology of quantum dots can essentially be regarded as the technology of artificial atoms. Due to the outstanding luminescent properties of quantum dots, they have already been used in many practical applications, such as biological labels, optical sensors, and opt-electrochemistry (e.g., light-emitting diodes [LEDs], lasers, or solar cells) [3].

- *Quantum communication.* Quantum communication is the art of transferring a quantum state from one place to another. The quantum information coded by quantum states allows tasks to be performed much more efficiently in contrast to using classical information [4]. Two well-known examples of quantum communication are quantum key distribution (QKD) and quantum teleportation. QKD is the most important aspect in quantum cryptography and quantum secure communication, and was acknowledged as one of the most promising technologies of the 21st century [5]. An application of quantum teleportation is to implement quantum logic gate, which is a basic quantum circuit unit for realizing a quantum computer.

- *Quantum computer.* This is a new kind of machine that will make use of the full complexity of a many-particle quantum wave function to solve a computational problem [6]. A quantum computer is expected to be able to complete certain tasks (e.g., Shor's quantum algorithm for factoring large numbers [7]) that are far beyond the capability of today's most powerful machines. The enormous increase in efficiency for a quantum computer lies in the quantum superposition principle.

From the perspective of Internet of Things (IoT) development, there are many challenges for future IoT. For example, sensors play a crucial role in IoT to better monitor the status of things. How to develop the sensors with high performance and compact size continues to be an ongoing challenge. Security and privacy issues, as well as massive data processing and searching, are other important open challenges. The quantum technology described above can and will be a good candidate to address these challenges in future IoT, and the details are discussed below.

## 13.2 Quantum Technology: Driving IoT Development

Quantum technology will drive the development of IoT, and this can be embodied in the following three aspects.

### 13.2.1 Making Sensor Networks More Powerful

To achieve a comprehensive perception of the whole physical world, various kinds of sensors with compact size and high performance are highly desired for IoT development. Quantum technology may provide a solution to that, which will make sensor networks more powerful.

A promising property of quantum dots is that they can be excited in a wide range of wavelengths, and have a narrow emission spectrum [8]. The emission wavelength can be adjusted by changing the size of the nanocrystals. In addition, quantum dots exhibit an exceptional photostability and have a 50% higher quantum yield than regular fluorescent dyes used for sensing applications. Based on such characteristics, it has been demonstrated that temperature probes can be realized [9].

It has also been demonstrated that quantum dots are especially suitable for developing new chemical sensors based on energy transfer phenomena [10]. This approach appears to be a general strategy to realize new quantum dots–based sensor systems for analyses unsuitable for direct analysis via interaction with quantum dot particles. Moreover, the popularity of quantum dots as photoluminescent probes for optical sensing, as well as bioactive fluorescent probes for imaging and labeling applications in biological science, is steadily increasing. In general, the development of sensing networks will benefit from the continuous advances taking place in the science of quantum dots.

### 13.2.2 Making Communication More Secure

Security is essential for developing IoT. Classic cryptology has provided a useful way to ensure the creditability of communication networks. However, it cannot guarantee that the security is optimal or perfect [11]. Fortunately, some drawbacks may be avoided by using quantum technology. Here, the simple but useful QKD is illustrated, which will make the communications of IoT securer.

QKD distributes random-number keys securely by exploiting the Heisenberg uncertainty principle—no one can copy a message without it being corrupted. These keys can further be used for secure communication, and QKD offers an unconditionally secure mechanism. Currently, the emphasis of this research is focused on pushing the limits of practical QKD systems in terms of distance and secure key rate, and some industry-grade quantum cryptographic devices have been successfully implemented [12]. It has been demonstrated that the performance of quantum cryptographs can be greatly improved by using single-photon detectors and phase-shift keying technology. For example, in 2007, Takesue et al. [13] reported that secure keys in the QKD experiment were distributed over a 42 dB channel loss and 200 km of optical fiber, and they reached an impressive 17 kbit/s secure key rate over a distance of 105 km. Moreover, the integration of this QKD system into classical networking schemes can be significantly simplified due to the adopted differential phase-shift keying protocol.

It has also been found that many quantum information protocols, such as deterministic teleportation protocols and high-bandwidth QKD systems, could be achieved based on continuous-variable entangled states [14]. An advantage of working with continuous variables in optics is that a large number of highly developed and precise techniques are available for manipulating and measuring the quadrature amplitudes, and making the practical applications of quantum protocols more feasible. This is good news for IoT development.

### 13.2.3 Making Massive Data Processing More Efficient

Due to the high complexity and heterogeneity of IoT, the vast quantity and different types of data should be generated, including positional and environmental data, historical data, sensor data, command data, and so on [15]. With the quickly increased objects ranging from sensor inputs to actuators in IoT, there will be a rapid growth of these data, and how to store and process these massive data is a big issue for IoT. When more and more sensors are adopted as IoT goes further, efficient searching is another problem [16]. Along with cloud computing technology to solve the above issues, a more efficient way should also be developed.

The quantum computer is engineered to control coherent quantum mechanical waves and enable new algorithms that can efficiently solve computational problems that are impossible for a classical computer due to the required astronomical resources. An advantage of quantum computing is its inherent parallelism, and the Deutsch-Jozsa algorithm is a good example to illustrate that [7]. Furthermore, there is a class of algorithms based on Grover's algorithm for performing quantum searching that can provide remarkable quadratic speedup over the best possible classical algorithms. These characteristics make quantum technology a good candidate for efficient massive data processing and searching in IoT.

It is worth pointing out that the experimental implementation of quantum computation remains a challenge, and a fully operational quantum computer for practical applications is still a distant goal. However, remarkable progress toward quantum computing has been achieved, such as using natural and artificial atoms as qubits [17]. It is believed that such as first-generation quantum computer may be available in the near future, and that will make massive data processing more efficient.

## References

1. Miburn, G. J. 2005. Foundations of quantum technology. *Journal of Computational and Theoretical Nanoscience* 2: 161–179.
2. Dowling, P. J., and G. J. Miburn. 2003. Quantum technology: The second quantum revolution. *Philosophical Transactions of the Royal Society A* 361: 1655–1674.
3. Bastida, G., F. J. Arregui, J. Goicoechea, and I. R. Matias. 2006. Quantum dots-based optical fiber temperature sensors fabricated by layer-by-layer. *IEEE Sensors Journal* 6: 1378–1379.
4. Gisin, N., and R. Thew. 2007. Quantum communication. *Nature Photonics* 1: 165–171.
5. MIT. 2003. Technology review. http://www.technologyreview.com/Infotech/13060/.
6. Ladd, T. D., F. Jelezko, R. Laflamme, Y. Nakamura, C. Monroe, and J. L. O'Brien. 2010. Quantum computers. *Nature* 464: 45–53.
7. Nielsen, M. A., and I. L. Chuang. 2000. *Quantum computation and quantum information*. Cambridge: Cambridge University Press.
8. Atzori, L., A. Iera, and G. Morabito. 2010. The Internet of Things: A survey. *Elsevier Computer Networks* 54: 2787–2805.
9. Walker, G. W., V. C. Sundar, C. M. Rudzinski, A. W. Wun, M. G. Bawendi, and D. G. Nocera. 2003. Quantum-dot optical temperature probes. *Applied Physics Letters* 83: 3555–3557.
10. Zora, A., G. P. Triberis, and C. Simserides. 2011. Near-field optical properties of quantum dots, applications and perspectives. *Recent Patents on Nanotechnology* 5: 188–224.
11. Zeng, G. 2010. *Quantum private communication*. Beijing: Higher Education Press.

12. Trifonov, A. 2007. Quantum communication: Pushing the limits. *Nature Photonics* 1: 314–315.
13. Takesue, H., S. W. Nam, Q. Zhang, R. H. Hadfield, T. Honjo, K. Tamaki, and Y. Yamamoto. 2007. Quantum key distribution over 40 dB channel loss using superconducting single photon detectors. *Nature Photonics* 1: 343–348.
14. Ralph, T. C., and P. K. Lam. 2009. A bright future for quantum communications. *Nature Photonics* 3: 671–673.
15. Cooper, J., and A. James. 2009. Challenges for database management in the Internet of Things. *IETE Technical Review* 26: 320–329.
16. Zhang, D., L. T. Yang, and H. Huang. 2011. Searching in Internet of Things: Vision and challenges. In *9th IEEE International Symposium on Parallel and Distributed Processing with Applications*, 201–206.
17. Buluta, I., S. Ashhab, and F. Nori. 2011. Natural and artificial atoms for quantum computation. *Reports on Progress in Physics* 74: 104401.

# 14
# BIG DATA

## 14.1 Introduction

The amount of data is exploding due to the development of information technology. In addition, the types of available data are also increasing, such as sensing data and mobile multimedia [1], and they may be organized in structured, semistructured, and unstructured modes. This indicates that the era of big data is coming.

Big data is a data set far beyond most on-hand tools' ability to capture, manage, and process. IBM indicated that big data mainly includes four dimensions: volume, variety, value, and velocity [2].

Internet of Things (IoT) and big data are interdependent. On the one hand, more things are connected into the networks. Thus, it will bring a large amount of data that is an important source of big data, and IoT is promoting the development of big data. On the other hand, making better use of big data can improve the efficiency of data that are captured, stored, and computed in IoT.

Big data has become a contact bond of the cyber world, physical world, and social world. The data captured by ubiquitous sensors in the physical world are transmitted to the cyber world. And the data can reveal the social attributes in both the physical world and the cyber world. Data can reflect interrelationships and intrarelationships among ubiquitous networks, and represent the social relationships in human society [3].

Big data brings changes to data users in two aspects: (1) something can be realized with enough data since more information can be available, and (2) it is difficult to exact useful data from big data when lacking efficient tools.

Big data is applied in many applications, such as business intelligence, bioresearch, public service, and environmental monitoring.

It is noteworthy to study big data to explore its further value. For instance, big data can be applied in business for intelligent decision supports, and big data is widely used in bioresearch to analyze disease for therapeutic schedules and genomes. Currently, genomics study brings new changes and challenges due to increasing data size and positive response from the broader scientific community [4].

In the following, Section 14.2 introduces the related technologies and representative platforms and solutions and Section 14.3 provides a conclusion.

## 14.2 Technology and Application

Compared to traditional data, processing measures for big data have some new characteristics, such as large storage ability, high efficient computing ability, and strong data analysis ability. Some new technologies have emerged, including Hadoop, Greenplum, and ASTERIX. Meanwhile, some companies have proposed representative big data platforms, considerating the attractive commercial value and development opportunities.

Furthermore, cloud computing is important to big data, and is an efficient computing mode that is dynamically scalable and often virtualizes resources as a service over the network. It brings a revolution of computing power. Cloud computing makes it easier to manage big data, and such technology may propel big data development and business value mining.

### 14.2.1 Some Typical Technologies for Big Data

The commercial tools for big data are in their infancy, and several open-source frameworks have been established. Here, some typical programs for big data, Hadoop, MapReduce, Greenplum, and ASTERIX, are introduced as follows.

Hadoop is a framework that realizes reliable, scalable, distributed computing for big data. It is developed by Apache Software Foundation and enlightened by MapReduce and Google Files System, and works in a parallel type to improve performance. Currently, Hadoop is widely used in keyword searches on the Internet. According to users' information and questions, customized analyses can help to process complex data [5]. Hadoop consists of subprojects, such as Hadoop

Common and the Hadoop Distributed File System (HDFS). HDFS is a scalable and distributed file system that provides high-throughput access to application data [6].

MapReduce is a programming model for processing and generating large data sets. It is typically used for distributed computing [7]. The original idea of MapReduce is from map and reduce functions. Map means that users generate a key-value pair to a set of intermediate key-value pairs. Reduce refers to merging all intermediate values with the same intermediate key.

ASTERIX is a project that develops new technologies for ingesting, storing, managing, indexing, querying, analyzing, and subscribing to vast quantities of semistructured information [8]. It aims at creating an open-source software platform that can combine semistructured data, parallel databases, and data-intensive computing. The ASTERIX Data Model (ADM) is proposed to deal with data storage and query processing. In addition, ASTERIX Query Language (AQL) matches and handles the data constructed by ADM [9]. Currently, a typical application of ASTERIX is to try and build an event warehouse to combine all the traditional data.

Greenplum Database is proposed by Greenplum to support big data analysis, and it manages, stores, and analyzes data from terabytes to petabytes [10]. It can utilize a shared-nothing, massively parallel processing (MPP) architecture to process big data.

Additionally, based on MapReduce, Walmart has built the MapUpdate scheme to make future purchase predictions. MapUpdate can rapidly map a huge amount of data for tracking things bought by social media [10]. In addition, not only Structured Query Language (NoSQL) can be introduced in big data [11].

### 14.2.2 Application Platform and Solution

Big data has large commercial value in making business strategies and decisions, and some companies (e.g., IBM, EMC, and Oracle) have established several application platforms and solutions for big data.

- IBM has developed a platform, including visualization and discovery, Hadoop-based analytics, stream computing, data warehousing, and text analytics. The platform supports services such as accelerators, application development, information integration and governance, and systems management [12]. It can integrate and manage all kinds of data, and apply advanced analysis to information in its original form.

- EMC has proposed EMC big data solutions to transform the current business models. The solutions mainly include three phases: data infrastructure, agile analytics, and actionable insight [13]. Data storage and analysis are first performed as preprocessing operations. Thereafter, the data are analyzed to provide advanced intelligent decisions for clients, and they will be further analyzed to help clients with sensitive insights and competitive advantages [14].

- Oracle is also planning to offer a complete and integrated solution for enterprise big data requirements. It can propel the clients' current enterprise data architecture to incorporate big data and clients' value. It integrates the suitable software and hardware into an engineered system to deal with big data [15].

In addition, there are some other big data solutions, such as Amazon Web Service proposed by Amazon [16], and a Hadoop-based data platform proposed by Microsoft [17].

### 14.3 Conclusion

In this chapter, big data and the related application platforms and solutions are discussed. In addition, big data development also confronts some challenges, including quality of service (QoS) and secure data storage.

## References

1. Jain, A. K. 2010. *Data clustering: 50 years beyond K-means*, 651–666. Amsterdam: Elsevier.
2. IBM. 2012. What is big data? http://www-01.ibm.com/software/data/ bigdata/enterprise.html (accessed September 5, 2012).
3. Gan, X. 2012. Academician Li Guojie: Big data will become the new concern of information technology. *Science in China* 5557: 1. http://news. sciencenet.cn/dz/dznews_photo.aspx?id=14798.
4. Kahn, S. D. 2011. On the future of genomic data. *Science* 331: 728–729.

5. Network Science and Technology Key Laboratory, Chinese Academy of Sciences Institute of Computing Technology. 2012. Hadoop in China. http://www.hadooper.cn/dct/page/1 (accessed September 6, 2012).

6. Apache Software Foundation. 2012. Hadoop. http://hadoop.apache.org/index.html (accessed September 6, 2012).

7. Apache. 2011. MapReduce. http://wiki.apache.org/hadoop/MapReduce (accessed September 6, 2012).

8. ASTERIX. 2012. ASTERIX: A highly scalable parallel platform for semi-structured data management and analysis. http://asterix.ics.uci.edu/ (accessed September 17, 2012).

9. Behm, A., V. R. Borkar, M. J. Carey, R. Grover, C. Li, N. Onose, and R. Vernica. 2011. ASTERIX: Towards a scalable, semi-structured data platform for evolving-world models. *Distribute Parallel Databases* 29: 185–216.

10. EMC². 2012. Greenplum. http://www.greenplum.com/products/greenplum-database (accessed September 6, 2012).

11. Bakshi, K. 2012. Considerations for big data: Architecture and approach. In *2012 IEEE Aerospace Conference*, 1–7.

12. IBM. 2012. Big data platform. http://www-01.ibm.com/software/data/bigdata/enterprise.html (accessed September 5, 2012).

13. EMC. 2012. Big data transforms business: The EMC big data solution. http://www.emc.com/collateral/brochure/h10769-big-data-cta-brochure.pdf.

14. EMC. 2012. Navigating big data: Transforming the world. http://www.emc.com/microsites/bigdata/why-big-data-overview.htm (accessed September 5, 2012).

15. Oracle. 2012. Oracle: Big data for the enterprise. http://www.oracle.com/us/products/database/big-data-for-enterprise-519135.pdf.

16. Amazon. 2012. Big data. http://aws.amazon.com/big-data/ (accessed September 5, 2012).

17. Microsoft. 2012. Big data solution. http://www.microsoft.com/sqlserver/en/us/solutions-technologies/business-intelligence/big-data-solution.aspx (accessed September 5, 2012).

# Index